Essential Study Skills

Community College of Allegheny County

College Academic Strategies

Custom Eighth Edition

Linda Wong

CENGAGE Learning®

Australia • Brazil • Japan • Korea • Mexico • Singapore • Spain • United Kingdom • United States

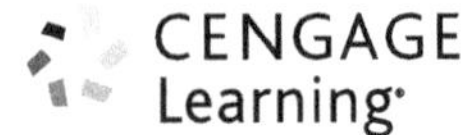

Essential Study Skills: Community College of Allegheny County;College Academic Strategies; Custom Eighth Edition

Senior Manager, Student Engagement:

Linda deStefano

Janey Moeller

Manager, Student Engagement:

Julie Dierig

Marketing Manager:

Rachael Kloos

Manager, Production Editorial:

Kim Fry

Manager, Intellectual Property Project Manager:

Brian Methe

Senior Manager, Production and Manufacturing:

Donna M. Brown

Manager, Production:

Terri Daley

Printed in the United States of America

ISBN-13: 978-1-305-30339-3

ISBN-10: 1-305-30339-3

WCN: 01-100-101

Cengage Learning

5191 Natorp Boulevard
Mason, Ohio 45040
USA

Cengage Learning is a leading provider of customized learning solutions with office locations around the globe, including Singapore, the United Kingdom, Australia, Mexico, Brazil, and Japan. Locate your local office at: **international.cengage.com/region.**

Cengage Learning products are represented in Canada by Nelson Education, Ltd.
For your lifelong learning solutions, visit **www.cengage.com/custom.**
Visit our corporate website at **www.cengage.com.**

Brief Contents

Preface

Welcome to the new edition of ***Essential Study Skills***. As in the Seventh Edition, the Eighth Edition empowers students to excel by using a metacognitive, multisensory approach throughout the textbook to provide them with essential study skills to increase their academic performance. Changing behaviors occurs most successfully when students understand *how* they learn, *what* skills they need to learn to use to perform specific tasks, and *which* strategies work most effectively to achieve desired outcomes. In the new world of ever-increasing technological distractions, the Eighth Edition of ***Essential Study Skills*** specifically shows students how to refocus on student-oriented strategies that work and how to consider ways to use technology to their advantage when studying. The textbook is designed to encourage all students—freshmen, nontraditional, and returning—to take greater responsibility for their learning, increase their self-confidence and motivation, discover strategies that work for them as individuals, and implement plans of action to achieve their academic and personal goals. The majority of students *want* to learn! This Eighth Edition provides students with exciting tools to turn *wants* and *desires* into reality and academic success.

Helping Students Study and Learn

Essential Study Skills, Eighth Edition, is a student-friendly textbook that builds a strong foundation of essential study skills strategies designed to boost memory, integrate skills and concepts, and excel in the classroom. The following chart highlights the book features in the Eighth Edition that make this edition unique, engaging, appealing—and most important of all—highly effective.

Book Features to Help Students

Features to Help Students Grasp Key Concepts and Main Ideas in Chapters	• Clear chapter Learning Objectives • Chapter Outline • Chapter Visual Mapping to expand with details of topics • Concise Learning Objectives Review
A Wealth of Step-by-Step Approaches	• Direct, easy-to-read and learn strategies • Clear steps for using memory tools • Concise bulleted points to clarify important concepts • Clear examples to explain new concepts
Features to Enhance Learning	• List of chapter terminology to learn • Marginal notes with definitions of terms to know • Visually appealing charts that summarize strategies • Multicolor format showing levels of information • Exercises that reinforce learning strategies

(continued)

Book Features to Help Students *(continued)*

Self-Assessment Tools	• Chapter Profiles to examine attitudes and behaviors • Checklists in the textbook to assess skills and progress • Concept Checks to strengthen comprehension • Self-correcting Check Points to verify understanding • End-of-the-chapter Review Questions
Activities to Engage Students	• Textbook exercises • Textbook Case Studies • Group Processing activities • Reflective Writing assignments • Critical Thinking activities
Appendix A	A comprehensive Essential Test-Taking Skills guide with fifty-two test-taking strategies and tips to apply to all kinds of test questions and test-taking situations
Appendix B	Answer keys for Chapter Profiles, Check Point quizzes, and Chapter Review Questions
Appendix C	Inventories and checklists to self-assess performance and skill levels
Appendix D	Textbook excerpts from a variety of content areas to reinforce skills used throughout the textbook

Online Features to Help Students

The Eighth Edition recognizes that technology motivates many students and provides them with multisensory approaches for working with course materials and skills. Many online materials and options are available for students to use to enhance the learning process. Students will be delighted to see the following online materials available for the ***Essential Study Skills,*** Eighth Edition textbook:

- The **online textbook** in the student College Success CourseMate
- Self-correcting **Chapter Profile** questions
- Printable **Chapter Visual Mapping** to expand with details
- An **expanded Chapter Outline** to use for studying and reciting
- Complete **list of Concept Check questions** to use for self-quizzing
- **Textbook Case Studies** and **Reflective Writing assignments**
- **Topics In-Depth** that present information that is only available online
- **Practice Quizzes** available only online for each chapter Check Point
- **Enhanced Quizzes** that link to sections of the online textbook
- **Flashcards** and an **online glossary** of terminology
- New **Chapter Study Guides** for each chapter

Helping Instructors Teach with Resources

Essential Study Skills, Eighth Edition, is an instructor-friendly textbook that provides the pedagogy and resources to help students build a strong foundation of essential study skills strategies, heighten their understanding of the learning process, and increase their performance and excellence in the classroom. The Eighth Edition recognizes instructors' needs to have a wealth of resources available at their fingertips to use to create a dynamic, engaging, and highly effective study skills course. The following chart highlights the book features in the Eighth Edition that make this edition ideal for instructors who want a textbook packed with resources and instructional options oriented to active learning.

Book Features to Help Instructors

Chapter Sequencing	• Flexible format allows you to select the most effective order of chapters to teach • Instructor options for best time to teach Appendix A, Essential Test-Taking Skills
Structured Chapters	• Color-coded headings related to the chapter Learning Objectives • Clear subheadings to identify specific topics • Bulleted points to identify important details and steps • Consistent chapter format with Concept Checks, Check Points, definitions in margins, and types of chapter exercises
Ready-to-Use Classroom Activities	• A variety of exercises in the textbook that you can use for class activities for which only you have the answer keys • Concept Check questions in margins for small group or class activities, writing assignments, or short pop quizzes • List of Terms to Know for partner vocabulary drills and quizzing • Group Processing activities designed to use with small groups • Critical Thinking activities for homework assignments, small group activities, or whole class discussions
Ready-to-Use Self-Assessment Tools	• Checklists within chapters for students to engage in the topics • Self-scoring Checklists in Appendix C for students to complete, reflect on, and discuss in class • Inventories for students to analyze their behaviors and skills
Instructor Resource Manual (IRM)	• A printed version and an online version available • Suggestions for organizing your course and grading system • Step-by-step teaching tips • Answer keys for chapter exercises • Reduced images of PowerPoint slides • Reduced images of transparency masters that you can use in class or as handouts

(continued)

Book Features to Help Instructors *(continued)*

Excerpts in Appendix D to Use for Instructional Purposes	Use the following excerpts to practice reading, annotating, notetaking, and test-taking skills: • Excerpt 1: Understanding Stress and Stressors • Excerpt 2: Practice Visualization • Excerpt 3: Adopting a Healthy Lifestyle • Excerpt 4: Semantic Networks • Excerpt 5: Building Blocks of Medical Language • Excerpt 6: Professional Leadership • Excerpt 7: The Scientific Method • Excerpt 8: How to Listen Critically
Self-Scoring Activities	• Students have answer keys to score Chapter Profiles • Students have answer keys to score Check Point quizzes • Students have answer keys to score chapter Review Questions

Online Features to Help Instructors

The **Instructor Website** is a comprehensive website that puts teaching tools and resources at your fingertips. By logging in at *CengageBrain.com*, you will find the following valuable instructor resources:

- The complete **Instructor Resource Manual** online, which includes teaching tips, answer keys to chapter exercises, and ready-to-use tests. (A printed version is also available upon request.)
- The **transition guide** that helps you move from the Seventh Edition to the Eighth Edition
- **Expanded Chapter Outlines** and **Lists of Concept Checks**
- **Ready-to-use tests** and **answer keys** for each chapter
- **Grading rubrics** to use for inventories, writing assignments, and homework exercises
- Full-size **transparency masters and PowerPoint slides** to download for classroom lectures, presentations, and handouts for each chapter
- The twelve new **Chapter Study Guides** to print for students, make available on your class website, or request students to download and print from the College Success CourseMate
- **Answer Keys for the new Chapter Study Guides**
- The **Cognero Online Testing Program** is the flexible online testing system that allows you to author, edit, and manage test bank content. You can create multiple test versions instantly and deliver them through your Learning Management System from your classroom, or wherever you may be, with no special installs or downloads required.

What's New in the Eighth Edition of *Essential Study Skills*

The Eighth Edition has a new chapter on technology (Chapter 12); a revised chapter organization that puts earlier emphasis on self-management or self-regulatory skills; new pairings and integration of related topics; new topics in chapters; and more comprehensive coverage of high-demand topics.

Reorganized Chapters

As you examine the full table of contents for the Eighth Edition, you will discover the new lineup of chapters, topics, and study strategies:

- **Chapters 1 through 4 Focus on Personal Preferences and Self-Management Skills**
  - Working with learning style and personality preferences and multiple intelligences
  - Developing a powerful mindset that includes attitudes and beliefs
  - Strengthening critical thinking skills
  - Managing time and increasing concentration
  - Achieving goals and increasing motivation
  - Reducing stress and procrastination
- **Chapters 5 and 6 Focus on Strengthening Memory**
  - Exploring how memory works in the Information Processing Model
  - Learning how to use new memory processes and strategies
  - Understanding ways to combat six kinds of forgetting
  - Applying the Twelve Principles of Memory
  - Using mnemonics effectively
- **Chapter 7 Focuses on Preparing for Tests**
  - Organizing materials and time to prepare for upcoming tests
  - Understanding different kinds of test questions
  - Using Appendix A, the Essential Test-Taking Skills pull-out guide
  - Managing test anxiety
- **Chapters 8 through 11 Focus on Reading, Notetaking, and Listening Skills**
  - Improving textbook reading skills by understanding the reading process
  - Using different reading systems for different kinds of textbooks
  - Learning skills for reading online (digital) e-textbooks
  - Working with paragraph-levels skills, such as vocabulary and organizational patterns
  - Annotating (highlighting, marking, and making marginal notes) in textbooks
  - Using a variety of notetaking systems to take textbook and lecture notes
  - Adjusting reading strategies for reading in a variety of content areas
  - Creating and using visual notes to learn course content
  - Strengthening listening skills and developing effective lecture notes
- **NEW: Chapter 12 Focuses on Using Technology**
  - Understanding basic computer concepts and computer literacy skills
  - Learning about the structure, requirements, bulletin boards, and etiquette for online courses

- Exploring the Internet and websites; using online resources and research skills
- Evaluating online materials
- Avoiding intentional and unintentional plagiarism
- Exploring new digital devices and apps (applications) for tablets, iPads, and smartphones

New Topics in the Eighth Edition

The following topics are new for the Eighth Edition, so taking time to familiarize yourself with the topics is recommended.

- **Eight Personality Types:** Chapter 1 now includes descriptions and checklists to estimate individual personality preferences that result in eight possible personality types based on the Myers-Briggs Type Indicator® assessment. A personality preference refers to a way of doing or responding that feels more natural, automatic, or comfortable, and which produces better results in the following four categories: (1) where you focus your attention, (2) how you take in information, (3) how you make decisions, and (4) how you approach or structure your life. Understanding the basic characteristics of the following eight personality preferences provides insight about oneself, friends, and classmates: Extraversion–Introversion, Sensing–Intuition, Thinking–Feeling, and Judging–Perceiving.

- **Time Management and Personality Preferences:** Chapter 2 discusses ways the personality preference styles of Sensing, Intuition, Judging, and Perceiving affect the way students perceive and use time-management strategies.

- **GPS Strategy for Setting Goals:** Chapter 4 introduces a new, simplified strategy for setting goals or creating plans of action. This strategy consists of three steps:

  1. G = Goal — Set a specific, realistic goal with target dates and times.
  2. P = Purpose — Identify the purpose, intention, or significance of the goal.
  3. S = Steps — Identify specific steps to achieve the goal.

- **Twelve Memory Processes:** Chapter 5 identifies twelve specific memory processes that play an active role in developing memory. The twelve processes summarize important information, but do not need to be memorized or learned as a set of twelve processes. These processes include: selective attention, deeper levels of encoding, immediately working with stimuli, Magic 7 ± 2 Theory, schemas, factual and procedural information, elaborative rehearsal, multisensory strategies, selectivity, feedback, associations and retrieval cues, and not rushing the learning process.

- **Six Forgetting Theories:** Chapter 6 includes information that explains why forgetting sometimes occurs in our information processing system and memory. The seventh edition had one excerpt in Appendix D that discussed five forgetting theories; for the Eighth Edition, the Emotional Blocks Theory has been added to explain why some learned information cannot be accessed or located in long-term memory.

- **Outline Reading System:** In Chapter 8, students learn to use an outline reading system by creating informal outline notes during the reading process. These notes become excellent guides for reciting information, writing summaries, and using as review tools.
- **Organizational Patterns and Graphic Materials:** Chapter 10 uses an integrative skills approach with the organizational patterns. After reading the new paragraph examples, students annotate and create diagrams to show the details. In the graphic materials section, new graphics to analyze are followed by comprehension and discussion questions.
- **An Effective Listening Plan:** Chapter 11 introduces students to a listening plan that helps increase the quality of listening experiences. The steps include: (1) attitude, (2) purpose, (3) image, (4) depth, (5) notes, (6) refocus, (7) feedback, and (8) open-ended, closed, probing, and leading questions.
- **Top Twenty Technology Picks:** Lucy MacDonald, an expert in online education and digital materials, offers her top twenty technology picks for students to explore. This resource in Chapter 12 provides students with a variety of applications, videos, and comprehensive websites to enhance the use of technology.
- **Online Chapter Study Guides:** Comprehensive Chapter Study Guides (available only online) require students to return to the chapter to use the "cloze reading technique" that requires students to locate specific words to complete statements. The Study Guides also include closed and open-ended questions for topics throughout the chapter. These study guides provide a thorough review of chapters.

What's Revised in the Eighth Edition of *Essential Study Skills*

Examples, exercises, and excerpts are updated with more current topics to engage students in the study skills processes and to better prepare them for a broader range of academic challenges that they will encounter in their classes. More details about revisions are available on the **Instructor Website, Transitioning to the Eighth Edition**. The following chart summarizes major revisions.

Revisions to the Eighth Edition

Early Introduction of Critical Thinking Skills and New Activities	*Teaching students to think on higher levels, to interpret, to evaluate, and to apply what they are learning to other content areas as well as to their personal lives is emphasized in each chapter.* • Critical thinking now introduced in Chapter 2 • New Critical Thinking activities for each chapter

Transfer These Skills Activities	*Teaching students to transfer skills to other courses is valuable and essential for meaningful, long-term learning. New exercises to transfer skills include:* • Chapter 1: Using the See-Say-Do Strategy • Chapter 2: Personalizing the Self-Efficacy Cycles • Chapter 3: Prioritizing and Creating a Task Schedule • Chapter 4: Planning a Term-Long Project • Chapter 5: Drawing Semantic Networks and Schemas • Chapter 6: Using The Loci Method • Chapter 7: Developing Summary Notes and a 5-Day Study Plan • Chapter 8: Surveying a Chapter and Applying SQ4R • Chapter 9: Applying Vocabulary Skills • Chapter 10: Creating a Visual Mapping • Chapter 11: Developing Two-Column Notes and PowerPoint Notes • Chapter 12: Conducting Internet Searches
Appendix A: Essential Test-Taking Skills	*Being prepared for tests and knowing how to perform well on tests are valuable skills for all college students.* • Appendix A has been condensed to fifty-two strategies. • The strategies in Appendix A are reinforced throughout the textbook. Each Check Point quiz and Chapter Review quiz refers students to specific strategies in Appendix A for responding to the type of question posed in the quiz.
The Information Processing Model	*Metacognition involves understanding the basic processes involved in learning and developing memory.* • The memory model has been condensed and is now presented in a more direct, easy-to-understand model. • Twelve memory processes reinforce the processes used in the Information Processing Model and working memory.
Bloom's Taxonomy	*Understanding and using the six cognitive levels in Bloom's Taxonomy is a foundation for critical thinking skills.* • Emphasis in Chapter 2 is on the six revised levels in Bloom's Taxonomy: Remembering, Understanding, Applying, Analyzing, Evaluating, and Creating. • A website appears in the Twenty Top Technology Picks for students to explore descriptions and prompt words for questions.

Revised Critical Thinking Activities

Each chapter ends with a Critical Thinking activity that you can use for class or small group discussions or for homework writing assignments. These activities are open-ended and engage students in the process of paying closer attention to the integration of concepts, to relationships beyond those stated in the textbook, and to analysis of information they are studying.

- **Chapter 1 Critical Thinking:** Examine the fairness of employers using personality tests to find applicants who fit specific jobs. A new excerpt, "Personality Tests Help Employers Find Applicants Who Fit," is included.
- **Chapter 2 Critical Thinking:** Discuss relationships among cognitive learning styles, multiple intelligences, and personality types described in Chapter 1.
- **Chapter 3 Critical Thinking:** After reading a new excerpt, "The Power of Chunking," define the term and compare and contrast the processes of *chunking up* and *chunking down.*
- **Chapter 4 Critical Thinking:** Use Excerpt 3 in Appendix D, "Adopting a Healthy Lifestyle," for writing long-term, intermediary, short-term, and immediate goals applicable to the content of the excerpt.
- **Chapter 5 Critical Thinking:** Select one of several multisensory options to *create* a product that shows understanding of the Twelve Principles of Memory.
- **Chapter 6 Critical Thinking:** Identify relationships between the Twelve Principles of Memory and the three memory centers introduced in Chapter 5; identify ways each principle of memory activates other principles of memory.
- **Chapter 7 Critical Thinking:** Write practice test questions using all six levels in Bloom's Taxonomy. Questions may be discussed in class, presented as a review activity, or used on an upcoming test.
- **Chapter 8 Critical Thinking:** Locate an online news article. Use the criterion provided to evaluate the article in terms of reliability, quality, and usefulness.
- **Chapter 9 Critical Thinking:** Apply and create a set of two-column notes for their choice of subject matter.
- **Chapter 10 Critical Thinking:** Apply different forms of test-taking questions to the information in Excerpt 7 in Appendix D, "The Scientific Method."
- **Chapter 11 Critical Thinking:** Read Excerpt 8 in Appendix D, "How to Listen Critically" and the table "Guidelines for Critical Listening," and then compile key words and key actions used in critical reading, critical listening, and critical thinking processes.
- **Chapter 12 Critical Thinking:** Optional activities are designed by the instructor to interact with online discussion boards, Internet research, forums, wikis, blogs, tweets, and mobile device applications.

Features Retained from the Seventh Edition

Instructors who have used previous editions of ***Essential Study Skills*** will find many familiar features that continue to be an essential part of this student-oriented textbook:

- **Chapter Learning Objectives and Chapter Outlines** provide students with the "big picture" of a chapter before they begin more in-depth reading.
- **Your Chapter Mapping** is a study tool that students expand by adding important details for each heading of the chapter that appears on the visual mapping.
- **Chapter Profiles** provide students with a self-correcting series of ten questions to assess their current attitudes and behaviors at the beginning and at the end of the term.
- **Essential Strategies Charts** that appear throughout each chapter highlight and summarize essential strategies presented in the chapter.

- **Concept Checks** in the margins provide students with questions to assess their understanding of concepts discussed in the adjacent paragraphs.
- **Definitions in the Margins** provide students with course-specific definitions for all the key terms that appear in bold colored print.
- **Case Studies** in every chapter present students with real-life student situations to analyze and then suggest strategies to address the problems posed in the case studies.
- **Reflective Writing assignments** provide students with opportunities to personalize the chapter content, discuss their current skills and attitudes, and integrate the chapter's skills with other study skills and personal experiences.
- **Group Processing: A Collaborative Learning Activity** in each chapter provides a small-group activity that enhances student interest and creates a forum for student interaction, brainstorming, discussion, problem-solving, critical thinking, and cooperative work.
- **Student exercises** reinforce skills that appear throughout each chapter. Instructors may select appropriate exercises to use for homework assignments, class discussions, or for small-group activities in the classroom. Answer keys appear in the Instructor Resource Manual; students do not have access to answer keys for exercises.
- **Check Points at the end of each main heading** provide students with several questions to assess how well they comprehended the textbook information. Students can refer to Appendix A if they need help answering specific kinds of questions. Students self-correct by using the answer keys in Appendix B.
- **Practice and Enhanced Quizzes in the College Success CourseMate** provide students with additional practice working with course content and test-taking skills. Quizzes are scored online and can be repeated multiple times.
- **Learning Objectives Review** at the end of each chapter uses bulleted points to summarize the most important points for each of the chapter's objectives.
- **Terms to Know** identify the key terms in the chapter that students need to be able to define.
- **Chapter Review Questions** provide students with a tool to assess their understanding and recall of essential concepts, skills, and strategies discussed in the chapter. Answer keys appear in Appendix B.
- **Appendix A** provides students with a comprehensive resource for developing test-taking skills. The direct, step-by-step approach for true-false, multiple-choice, matching, fill-in-the-blanks, listing, definition, short answer, math, and essay test questions is easy to use.
- **Appendix B** provides students with answers to their Profile Charts, a Master Profile Chart to record their results, and answer keys for Check Point quizzes and Chapter Review questions.
- **Appendix C** provides students with an array of exercises and self-assessment inventories or checklists to use to assess their strengths and weaknesses and adjust their strategies.
- **Appendix D** gives students the opportunity to apply critical thinking and study skills to materials that originated in a variety of textbooks from across the curriculum.

Dedication

I dedicate this new edition to the thousands of educators who demonstrate an endless commitment to providing high-quality, valuable educational experiences for their students, and to all students who strive to excel and benefit from their educational opportunities.

Acknowledgments

My appreciation is extended to the following reviewers who dedicated their time and expertise to contribute ideas to enrich this textbook and further strengthen the effectiveness of this instructor-friendly and student-friendly textbook. Thank you all for your contributions: Melanie Abst, Cynthia Avery, Judith Colson, Valerie Cunningham, Karen Fenske, SusAnn Key, Lucy MacDonald, Pamela Moss, Janet Moynihan, Amanda Nimetz, Brenda Wallace, and Alice Warner.

I extend my sincere appreciation for the outstanding editorial and production staff that has worked diligently with me through all the phases of creating the Eighth Edition of *Essential Study Skills*. Most readers of this textbook are unaware of the high degree of coordination, teamwork, time commitment, and resources required to produce a new edition of a textbook and all its companion resources. The process is extensive and requires the utmost attention to details. I acknowledge your level of dedication and your utmost commitment to the development of this Eighth Edition. I appreciate and value you for your contributions. Thank you!

To the Student

Essential Study Skills, Eighth Edition is a valuable resource designed to provide you with an array of study skills strategies that will unlock your learning potential and empower you to improve your academic performance. Reading the following section carefully will provide you with important information that explains how to get the most out of ***Essential Study Skills,*** Eighth Edition.

Quick Start Checklist

Go to the College Success CourseMate for a Quick Start Checklist to use to prepare for an upcoming term. Look for the Quick Start Checklist link on the left side of the home page screen. Click on it to learn about the following topics:

- Creating class schedules
- Familiarizing yourself with your campus
- Organizing your notebooks
- Selecting a system to record homework assignments
- Getting off to a good start on the first day of class
- Planning sufficient study time for your classes
- Other suggestions and tips for getting off to a good start

Steps to Access the College Success CourseMate
Go to *CengageBrain.com* to access these resources, and look for this icon to find resources related to your textbook in College Success CourseMate. You will be prompted to enter the required CourseMate access code. If you do not have an access code, you will be able to purchase one at *CengageBrain.com*.

Starting the Term: Getting an Overview

As soon as you purchase this book, begin familiarizing yourself with the textbook. Read through the **Preface** and this introductory **To the Student** section carefully, examine the **Table of Contents**, and familiarize yourself with the end matter that follows Chapter 12: **Appendix A:** Essential Test-Taking Skills; **Appendix B:** Master Profile Chart and Answer Keys; **Appendix C:** Exercises, Inventories, and Checklists; **Appendix D:** Excerpts; and the textbook **index**.

Essential Study Skills, Eighth Edition, has a College Success CourseMate to enhance your learning experience and strengthen your understanding of course materials. Each time you see this icon in your textbook, visit the College Success CourseMate for interactive quizzes and online materials. Your instructor may assign these activities, or you may complete the activities independently to strengthen your comprehension and learn content more thoroughly. Take time now to familiarize yourself with the wealth of online resources available to assist you throughout the term. As you click on the main menu for each chapter, you will see the following categories of your online materials:

- Chapter E-Book
- Chapter Profile
- Chapter Visual Mapping
- Expanded Chapter Outline

- Chapter Concept Checks
- Reflective Writing Assignments
- Textbook Case Studies
- Topics In-Depth
- Practice and Enhanced Quizzes
- Chapter Study Guide
- Glossary
- Flashcards

Essential Study Skills E-Book

The College Success CourseMate for ***Essential Study Skills,*** Eighth Edition, has an interactive e-book for you to use with this textbook. If you have not yet experienced using an e-book, you are in for an exciting new learning experience! You can go to Chapter 8, pages 255–258 to learn about reading e-books and the Chapter 8 online Topics In-Depth to learn more about this book's e-textbook and the online features associated with it.

Starting Each Chapter

Surveying is an effective study strategy that provides you with an overview of a chapter before you begin the process of careful reading. Surveying familiarizes you with the topic, creates a mindset for studying, and prepares your memory to receive new information. Use the following steps for surveying a new chapter:

1. Read the ***Chapter Objectives*** that list learning goals or objectives for the chapter. The chapter objectives clearly indicate the skills you will learn and will be able to demonstrate when you finish studying the chapter. The color-coding used for the chapter objectives correlates with the color-coded headings throughout the chapter.
2. Read through the ***Chapter Outline*** for an overview of the organization and content of the chapter. You will find an expanded chapter outline on CourseMate.
3. Glance at the main topics in the ***Your Chapter Mapping*** to get a clear, visual image of the main headings in the chapter. After reading the chapter information under a heading, return to your visual mapping. Attach key words to show subheadings and important details for each heading on the visual mapping.
4. Complete the ***Chapter Profile*** before continuing to survey the chapter. This is not a graded assignment; answer the questions honestly. The profiles are designed to examine your current attitude and habits in specific skill areas. These scores will be compared to end-of-the-term scores to show your progress and growth. You can complete the profile in the textbook, or you can complete it online in the College Success CourseMate.
5. Survey or skim through the chapter by examining the following items and features:
   - All of the bold ***headings*** and ***subheadings***
   - The ***information in the margins,*** which includes Concept Check questions and definitions of terminology

- ***Terminology*** that appears in bold colored print in paragraphs
- ***Graphic materials,*** which include figures and charts
- ***Check Point questions*** at the end of information under each main heading

6. Read the ***Learning Objectives Review*** at the end of the chapter. Key points for each of the objectives provide you with additional insights about the content of the chapter.
7. Read through the ***Terms to Know*** that lists the course-specific terminology. The definitions for these terms appear in the margins of the chapter.
8. Read through, but do not answer, the ***Chapter Review Questions***. Plan to answer these questions after you have read the chapter carefully. For immediate feedback, you will be able to check your answers with the answer keys in Appendix B.

Using Chapter Features

The following chapter features are designed to increase your comprehension and reinforce key concepts and skills in each chapter. Using these features consistently facilitates the process of mastering the concepts and skills in the chapter.

Your Chapter Mapping shows you the basic skeleton or topic and the main headings used in the chapter. To create a visual study tool, expand the chapter visual mapping by connecting key words to show important details for each of the main headings. Chapter visual mappings also appear in the College Success CourseMate.

Definitions in the margins provide a quick view of key terminology and definitions to learn. Review these definitions when you study for tests. Practice reciting the full definition without looking at the textbook, and then check the accuracy of your definition.

Concept Checks in the margins provide you with study questions to assess your comprehension and promote critical thinking skills. For each Concept Check, answer the questions on paper, mentally, or out loud to yourself. At times, your instructor may ask you to write responses, or these questions may be used for short pop quizzes or on chapter tests. Return to these questions when you prepare for tests.

Check Points in each chapter provide you with short assessment tools to check your comprehension of information presented under each main heading in the chapter. Refer to the Appendix A strategies to review answering specific kinds of questions. Answer keys in Appendix B provide you with immediate feedback.

Exercises appear throughout each chapter. Your instructor will assign some, but usually not all, of the exercises in the chapter. Notice that some exercises appear in the chapter, and other longer exercises appear in Appendix C. For practice and enrichment, you may complete any of the exercises that your instructor does not assign you to complete.

Case Studies are exercises that describe student situations or problems. After reading a case study, identify the key issues or problems that appear in the case study. Answer the question at the end of each case study by providing specific answers or suggestions that deal with the problem. Use specific strategies and terminology from the chapter in your answers. Case studies use open-ended questions, meaning there are many possible answers. They can be completed on paper or in your College Success CourseMate.

Practice Quizzes in the College Success CourseMate consist of self-correcting quizzes that provide you with additional practice and reinforcement of the skills in the chapter. You can complete these quizzes as many times as you wish. You will receive feedback and brief explanations with each answer.

Essential Strategy Charts highlight key strategies to use to improve the way you study, process information, and master course content. Applying the essential strategies in these charts will increase your performance and academic success. Refer to these charts when you want to brush up on essential study skills or review for tests.

Terms to Know list the course-specific vocabulary terms that you should know how to define. Practice defining these terms. You can go to the College Success CourseMate to practice flashcards and to review the online glossary.

Chapter Review Questions provide you with practice test questions to assess your memory or recall of chapter concepts and key terms. Refer to the Appendix A strategies to review answering specific kinds of questions. Complete the Chapter Review Questions without referring to your textbook pages or your notes. Check your answers with the answer keys in Appendix B.

Enhanced Quizzes in the College Success CourseMate provide you with additional practice answering objective test questions and assessing your level of comprehension of chapter skills and concepts. The Enhanced Quizzes link you to the heading in the e-textbook that covers the content of the quiz question.

Chapter Study Guides in the College Success CourseMate provide you with a detailed study guide to complete for a thorough review of each chapter.

Appendix A: Essential Test-Taking Skills

Many college students feel overwhelmed and underprepared for the variety of test-taking situations and test questions that they encounter in their courses. Do you experience any of the following test-taking issues or concerns?

- *Do you sometimes struggle with taking tests because you have never really learned how to take tests?* Appendix A provides you with a direct, step-by-step approach as well as clear explanations and examples for learning fifty-two essential test-taking strategies.
- *Do you sometimes have difficulty answering certain kinds of test questions?* Easy-to-use strategies provide you with the skills to answer true-false, multiple-choice, matching, fill-in-the-blanks, listing, definition, short-answer, math, and essay test questions.
- *Do you sometimes have difficulty understanding or interpreting questions?* Through easy-to-read bulleted points, Appendix A teaches you strategies for reading, understanding, and interpreting objective, recall, math, and essay test questions.

- *Do you sometimes get confused and waste valuable test-taking time trying to figure out how to move through a test?* In Appendix A, you will learn the value of using systematic approaches for answering questions. These approaches increase your accuracy rates and lead to higher grades on tests.

Appendix A, the Essential Test-Taking Skills guide, is a valuable resource that provides a flexible format for acquiring essential test-taking skills whenever the need arises. You can use this pull-out guide for independent study at any time during the present or future terms to prepare for upcoming tests. You may go directly to a specific section in Appendix A to prepare for a specific kind of test or to answer questions in the textbook's **Check Points** and **Chapter Review Questions.**

Your instructor will provide you with additional information about using Appendix A. Your instructor may choose to discuss Appendix A in conjunction with Chapter 7, "Preparing for Upcoming Tests," or your instructor may choose to discuss Appendix A at a different time during the term. Refer to your course syllabus or list of chapters and topics for the term.

Appendix B: Answer Keys

Use **Appendix B** to score and chart your **Chapter Profile** questions, and use the chapter answer keys for all **Check Points** and **Chapter Review Questions.**

Appendix C: Exercises, Inventories, and Checklists

For some exercises in the textbook chapters, you will be directed to **Appendix C.** Follow the directions for completing the exercises, inventories, and checklists. Use these self-assessment tools to strengthen your study skills strategies and improve your approaches to learning.

Appendix D: Excerpts

For some exercises, you will be directed to **Appendix D** to use excerpts from a variety of content areas to practice reading, annotating, notetaking skills, and other textbook study skills.

A Note to You from the Author

Your goal is not to learn *about* study skills, but to learn to *use* powerful study skills to consistently achieve your goals and experience success. Learning is a lifelong process. Each time you are faced with a new learning situation—whether at school, at home, or at work—you can draw upon the skills you have learned in this textbook. By applying the skills of time management, goal setting, concentration, processing information, strengthening memory, test taking, reading comprehension, and an array of additional strategies in this textbook, you will be prepared to experience the rewards of success ... again and again and again. May my commitment to you, belief in you, and support of you in the learning process be reflected in the pages of this textbook.

—Linda Wong

1 Discovering Your Learning Styles and Preferences

© Digital Vision/Getty Images

Do you know your learning style preference, your strongest intelligences, and your personality type? In this chapter, you will gain insights about yourself as a learner. You will learn skills that empower you and utilize your personal preferences so learning feels more natural and effective. By identifying your learning style preference, you are able to select powerful multisensory strategies to increase academic performance. As you explore multiple intelligences, you will realize that you already have skills and abilities in all eight intelligences. Finally, as you explore your personality type, you will gain insights about where you focus your attention and how you take in information, make decisions, and structure your life. After completing this chapter, you will understand more about yourself and about people you encounter at school, at work, and in your personal life.

CHAPTER OUTLINE

1 **THREE COGNITIVE LEARNING STYLES**
Learning Style Preferences
Characteristics and Essential Strategies
Multisensory Learning Strategies

2 **MULTIPLE INTELLIGENCES**
Subintelligences
Linguistic Intelligence
Logical-Mathematical Intelligence
Musical Intelligence
Bodily-Kinesthetic Intelligence
Spatial Intelligence
Interpersonal Intelligence
Intrapersonal Intelligence
Naturalist Intelligence

3 **PERSONALITY TYPES**
Eight Personality Preferences of MBTI Personality Types
Four Core Building Blocks of MBTI Personality Types
Sixteen Personality Types
Extraversion and Introversion
Sensing and Intuition
Thinking and Feeling
Judging and Perceiving
Understanding Yourself and Others

Access Chapter 1 Expanded Chapter Outline in your College Success CourseMate, accessed through *CengageBrain.com*.

YOUR CHAPTER MAPPING

After reading information under each heading, return to the chapter visual mapping below. Add key words to show subheadings and important details related to each heading.

Access Chapter 1 Visual Mapping in your College Success CourseMate, accessed through *CengageBrain.com*.

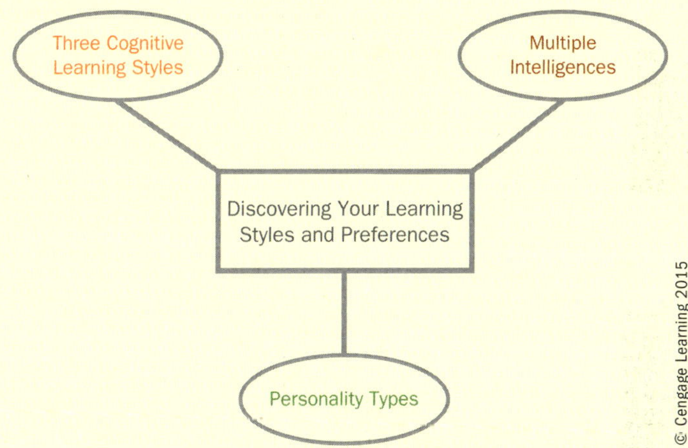

LEARNING OBJECTIVES

1 *Identify your preferred cognitive learning style and describe learning strategies you can use to utilize your preferred learning style and strengthen your other modalities.*

2 *Define the term* intelligences *and describe the common characteristics of each of Howard Gardner's eight intelligences.*

3 *Identify the eight personality preferences defined by Myers and Briggs and discuss the use of opposite preferences in their theory.*

CHAPTER 1 PROFILE

Discovering Your Learning Styles and Preferences

Access Chapter 1 Profile in your College Success CourseMate, accessed through *CengageBrain.com*.

ANSWER each profile question honestly. Your answers should reflect what you do, not what you wish to do. Check YES if you do the statement always or most of the time. Check NO if you do the statement seldom or never.

SCORE the profile. To get your score, give yourself one point for every answer that matches the answer key on page B2 in the back of your book. If you complete the profile online, the profile will be scored for you.

RECORD your score on the Master Profile Chart on page B1 in the column that shows the chapter number.

ONLINE: You can complete the profile and get your score online in this textbook's College Success CourseMate.

	YES	NO
1. I am aware of my learning style preference as a visual, auditory, or kinesthetic learner.	______	______
2. I can describe the modality involved in four or more learning strategies that I use on a regular basis.	______	______
3. Instead of using a multisensory learning strategy such as the See-Say-Do Strategy, I select one learning activity or process and use that to study material in all of my courses.	______	______
4. I usually study new information in a straightforward manner without spending time making creative study or review tools.	______	______
5. I recognize which of Howard Gardner's eight intelligences are my strongest.	______	______
6. I have the potential to acquire new skills that will increase my abilities in the eight intelligences.	______	______
7. I understand the differences between Extraversion and Introversion personality preferences, and I know which preference is mine.	______	______
8. I understand how my "Thinking" personality preference or my "Feeling" personality preference affects the way I make decisions.	______	______
9. I understand basic ways in which different personality preferences can affect people's attitudes, behaviors, and decision-making processes.	______	______
10. I am confident that I can adjust my learning strategies to meet the demands of new learning situations or tasks.	______	______

QUESTIONS LINKED TO THE CHAPTER LEARNING OBJECTIVES:

Questions 1–4: objective 1

Questions 5–6: objective 2

Questions 7–9: objective 3

Question 10: all objectives

Three Cognitive Learning Styles

Identify your preferred cognitive learning style and describe learning strategies you can use to utilize your preferred learning style and strengthen your other modalities.

Learning is an individualized process; different educational and background experiences, personality traits, levels of motivation, and numerous other variables affect the way you learn. The term *cognitive* refers to thinking and reasoning processes, so ***cognitive learning styles*** refers to the general ways people *prefer* to have information presented in order to problem solve, process, learn, and remember new information. Three commonly recognized cognitive learning styles, or ***learning modalities***, are *visual, auditory,* and *kinesthetic.* **Figure 1.1** shows these three main cognitive learning styles.

Cognitive learning styles refers to the general ways people *prefer* to have information presented in order to problem solve, process, learn, and remember new information.

Learning modalities refers to cognitive learning styles such as visual, auditory, and kinesthetic.

Learning Style Preferences

Most people have a ***learning style preference***, which is a tendency to use a visual, auditory, or kinesthetic modality when there is a choice of ways to learn and process new information. For example, a *visual learner* may prefer to read a manual or a textbook or learn from pictures, charts, or graphs. An *auditory learner* may prefer to be told how a new process or piece of equipment works. A *kinesthetic learner* may prefer to be given an opportunity to perform each step as he or she learns a new process or operation of equipment.

Learning style preference indicates a tendency to use a visual, auditory, or kinesthetic modality when there is a choice of ways to learn and process new information.

Your learning style preference started in your childhood. As you matured, entered into the educational system, and were exposed to new learning situations, you learned to use, strengthen, and integrate all of your modalities. The childhood modality preference may still be dominant, but as an adult with broadened skills, in most situations, you are able to learn even when information is presented in a form that is not based on your preferred method of learning. Your learning style preference is just that—a preference—and not a limitation as to your ability to process information.

Understanding your cognitive learning style preference can guide your selection of effective learning strategies that capitalize on your strengths, boost your memory, and strengthen your ability to recall information. As you take in and process information, your brain uses visual, auditory, and kinesthetic (motor) codes to accept

CONCEPT CHECK 1.1

In general terms, how do you go about learning something new? What study or learning techniques generally work best for you?

FIGURE 1.1 Cognitive Learning Styles

1. **Visual learners** learn and remember best by *seeing* and *visualizing* information.
2. **Auditory learners** learn and remember best by *hearing* and *discussing* information.
3. **Kinesthetic learners** learn and remember best by using large and small body *movements* and *hands-on experiences*.

and move the information into different locations in your memory system. The following points are important to understand:

- When you use your strongest modality or your preferred learning style to take in and process information, learning can occur more efficiently and recalling information at a later time may occur more smoothly.
- Many learning strategies involve the use of more than one modality. In other words, more than one kind of coding into memory occurs. Multisensory strategies, such as the *See-Say-Do Strategy* (page 13), utilize all three modalities to process information into memory.
- When you use more than one sensory channel to process information, you create a stronger imprint or impression of the information in your memory, so recalling information often occurs more rapidly and accurately.
- Situations that require you to learn information using one of your less developed learning modalities may be more difficult than anticipated and may require you to activate a modality that does not use your preferred learning style.

EXERCISE 1.1

Learning Styles Inventory

DIRECTIONS: Go to the Learning Styles Inventory in Appendix C, pages C1–C3, to identify your learning style preference and strength of your modalities. After reading each statement carefully, you will select a YES or a NO answer. Directions for scoring your inventory are included. **Return to this page to write your scores on the following lines:**

_____ VISUAL _____ AUDITORY _____ KINESTHETIC

ANALYZING YOUR SCORES:

Highest Score = Preferred modality and way to process new information

Lowest Score = Weakest or least frequently used modality

Scores > 10 = Frequently used modality

Scores < 10 = Less frequently used modality

- If your two highest scores are the same, you use both modalities equally well.
- Your weakest modality and any modalities with scores lower than 10 may be the result of limited experiences that utilize this modality.
- Your weakest modality and any modalities with scores lower than 10 may be due to physical or neurological impairments, which may include learning disabilities.

Characteristics and Essential Strategies

As you read through the following common characteristics for each of the three types of learners or learning style preferences, relate this information to what you learned about yourself in the Learning Styles Inventory (**Exercise 1.1**). Do you have the same or similar characteristics? Note that a person does not necessarily possess abilities or strengths in all of the characteristics but may instead demonstrate strengths in specific characteristics. Your strengths may reflect your educational or personal background. For example, an auditory learner may be strong in the area of language skills but may not have had the experience or the opportunity to develop skills with a foreign language or music. Finally, pay close attention to the variety of essential learning strategies that you can incorporate into your approach to learning. **Figure 1.2** summarizes essential strategies for each modality.

Visual Learners

Visual learners are learners who prefer to process and learn information in visual forms such as pictures, charts, lists, paragraphs, or other printed formats. They learn and remember best by *seeing* and *visualizing* information. The following are additional characteristics of visual learners:

Visual learners are learners who prefer to process and learn information in visual forms such as pictures, charts, lists, paragraphs, or other printed formats.

- Can easily recall information in the form of numbers, words, phrases, or sentences
- Can easily understand and recall information presented in pictures, charts, or diagrams

FIGURE 1.2 Essential Strategies for Visual, Auditory, and Kinesthetic Learners

VISUAL	Highlight textbooks and notes. Write notes in textbooks. Create movies in your mind. Create visual study tools. Use color coding. Visualize information. Add pictures. Write to remember. Make writing a habit. Be observant.
AUDITORY	Participate in discussions. Paraphrase and summarize. Ask questions. Verbalize. Recite frequently. Tape lectures. Create study tapes or recordings. Create rhymes, jingles, or songs. Use technology.
KINESTHETIC	Use hands-on learning. Create hands-on study tools. Get out of the chair. Work standing up. Use action-based activities. Create action-oriented games. Use creative movement. Use a computer or electronic devices.

- Have strong visualization or visual memory skills and can look up (often up to the left) and "see" information
- Make "movies in their minds" of information they are reading
- Have strong visual-spatial skills that involve sizes, shapes, textures, angles, and dimensions
- Have a good eye for colors, design, visual balance, and visual appeal
- Pay close attention and learn to interpret body language (facial expressions, eyes, stance)
- Have a keen awareness of aesthetics, the beauty of the physical environment, and visual media

CONCEPT CHECK 1.2

Visual learners can easily recall which kinds of visual information? What other abilities do visual learners exhibit?

Visual learners often favor creating and using visual strategies when they study. Having something that they can *see*, examine for details, and memorize as a mental image is important and effective for visual learners. The following essential strategies for visual learners strengthen and utilize visual skills. Check YES if you already use the strategy. Check TRY if you are willing to try using this strategy. Check NO if the strategy does not interest you. **Check a response for each bulleted point.**

	YES	TRY	NO
• **Highlight textbooks and notes.** Use colored highlighter pens to create a stronger visual impression of important facts, definitions, formulas, and steps.	____	____	____
• **Write notes in textbooks.** Write questions in the margins, highlight the answers, and then picture the answers as you review the questions.	____	____	____
• **Create movies in your mind.** Use your visual memory as a television screen with the information that you read (and hear) moving across the screen as a "movie with the cameras rolling." Practice reviewing or replaying the movie in your mind.	____	____	____
• **Create visual study tools.** Create visual mappings, hierarchies, and comparison charts to show levels of detail. Practice visualizing and recalling the images of the study tools.	____	____	____
• **Use color coding.** Color-code different levels of information in your visual tools, your textbook highlighting, your time management schedules, and your notes. Using different colors facilitates the process of memorizing and recalling visual images.	____	____	____
• **Visualize information.** Visually memorize pictures, graphs, study tools, or small sections of printed information. Practice looking away, visualizing, and then checking the accuracy and details of your visual images.	____	____	____

	YES	TRY	NO
• **Add pictures.** As you expand chapter visual mappings, hierarchies, and other visual study tools or as you review your notes and study tools, add pictures that depict the information. The pictures become association cues to assist recall of the information stored in memory.	_____	_____	_____
• **Write to remember.** Copy textbook information into notes because information written in your own handwriting often is easier to visualize and recall than printed text.	_____	_____	_____
• **Make writing a habit.** Create the habit of writing directions and other important information in notebooks, on small note pads, or in electronic devices as words you write frequently are easier to visually memorize and recall.	_____	_____	_____
• **Be observant.** Pay attention to details of objects and people. Observe nonverbal clues for body language that signal attitudes, feelings, or important points.	_____	_____	_____

Auditory Learners

Auditory learners are learners who prefer to process and learn by hearing and discussing information. They prefer to have information presented to them verbally instead of, or in addition to, in writing. They learn by listening to others explain, debate, summarize, or discuss information about topics they are studying. Auditory learners, however, are not passive. Auditory learners like to *talk* and *listen* as they learn. The following are additional characteristics of auditory learners:

Auditory learners are learners who prefer to process and learn by hearing and discussing information.

- Often engage in discussions and enjoy the process of communication
- Learn by explaining information in their own words, expressing their understanding or opinions, and providing comments and feedback to other speakers
- Can accurately remember details or specific information heard in conversations, lectures, movies, or music
- Have strong language and vocabulary skills and an appreciation of words, their meanings, and their etymology (word history)
- Have strong oral and expressive communication skills and are articulate
- Have "finely tuned ears" and may find learning a foreign language relatively easy
- Have above average ability to hear tones, rhythms, and notes of music, and often excel in areas of music
- Have keen auditory memories

Auditory learners often select learning strategies that code or process information through their auditory channel into memory. The following essential strategies for auditory learners strengthen and utilize auditory skills. Check YES if you already use this strategy. Check TRY if you are willing to try using this strategy. Check NO if the strategy does not interest you. **Check a response for each bulleted point.**

	YES	TRY	NO
• **Participate in discussions.** Actively engage in group activities, discussions, study groups, and in tutoring sessions.	____	____	____
• **Paraphrase and summarize.** Express your ideas to others, paraphrase speakers, and summarize what you learn from lectures, conversations, and discussions.	____	____	____
• **Ask questions.** Show your interest and clarify information by asking questions. Practice recalling information and answers that you hear.	____	____	____
• **Verbalize.** Read out loud to activate your auditory channel or auditory processes. For difficult materials, read with exaggerated expression as the natural rhythm and patterns of language tend to group words into units of meaning when spoken.	____	____	____
• **Recite frequently.** Reciting involves stating information out loud, in your own words, in complete sentences, and without referring to printed information. Reciting provides you with feedback to gauge how well you remember and understand information.	____	____	____
• **Tape lectures.** In difficult classes, request permission to tape lectures. Use the tapes to review and complete your notes after class.	____	____	____
• **Create study tapes or recordings.** Tape yourself reading or reciting main ideas, facts, details, or lists. Use your study tapes or recordings to review information and prepare for tests. Your ability to recall information from tapes that have your own voice may strengthen your auditory memory and recall abilities.	____	____	____
• **Create rhymes, jingles, or songs.** Short, catchy sayings or tunes that contain information you need to remember are effective study tools for recalling information. Original rhymes, jingles, or songs work as mnemonics or memory tools and associations to recall information. To increase accuracy, practice the rhymes, jingles, or songs multiple times.	____	____	____
• **Use technology.** Check with your learning labs, library, Internet resources, and electronic applications for audio materials and products to use to reinforce learning.	____	____	____

Kinesthetic Learners

Kinesthetic learners are learners who prefer to process and learn information through large and small muscle movements and hands-on experiences. Large and small muscles hold memory, so involving movement in the learning process creates muscle memory. The following are additional characteristics of kinesthetic learners:

- Learn best by working with physical objects and engaging in hands-on learning that involves feeling, handling, using, manipulating, sorting, assembling, and experimenting with concrete objects
- Can recall information by duplicating the movement or hand motions involved in the learning process
- Learn well by using large muscle or full body movements, such as movements used when working at large charts, working at a chalkboard or white board, role-playing, dancing, or performing
- Work well with their hands in areas such as repair work, sculpting, and art
- Are well coordinated, with a strong sense of timing and body movements
- Have a strong awareness of their need or interest to add movement to study and work situations
- Are able to focus better when they can engage in movement, which may include wiggling, tapping hands or feet, or moving legs when sitting

Kinesthetic learners are learners who prefer to process and learn information through large and small muscle movements and hands-on experiences.

Kinesthetic learners often prefer to use strategies that engage their small and large muscles in the learning process. The following essential strategies for kinesthetic learners strengthen and utilize kinesthetic skills. Check YES if you already use this strategy. Check TRY if you are willing to try using this strategy. Check NO if the strategy does not interest you. **Check a response for each bulleted point.**

	YES	TRY	NO
• **Use hands-on learning.** Handle objects, tools, or machinery that you are studying. For processes such as computer applications, repeat the hands-on learning applications several times to create muscle memory.	_____	_____	_____
• **Create hands-on study tools.** Create flash-cards that you can shuffle, spread out, sort, categorize, and review. Copy charts, diagrams, visual mappings, or hierarchies; cut them apart and practice reassembling the pieces.	_____	_____	_____
• **Get out of the chair.** When you study, engage large muscles by using exaggerated hand expressions or body movements. Pace or walk with study materials in hand.	_____	_____	_____
• **Work standing up.** Work at a chalkboard, white board, or flip chart to list, draw, practice, or rework problems. Use poster paper to create study tools, such as large visual mappings, charts, or timelines.	_____	_____	_____

	YES	TRY	NO
• **Use action-based activities.** Create ways to add action to the learning process; for example, if you are studying perimeters, tape off an area and walk the perimeter.	____	____	____
• **Create action-oriented games.** Convert information you are studying into a game such as Twenty-One Questions, Jeopardy, or Concentration. Review the information by playing the game with another student or group.	____	____	____
• **Use creative movement.** When feasible, incorporate drama, dance, pantomime, or role-playing into your study sessions.	____	____	____
• **Use a computer or electronic devices.** Type information and create notes, tables, and charts on the computer. Enter or access information on electronic devices. Keyboard strokes help create muscle memory that you can use to simulate the actions and recall information.	____	____	____

CONCEPT CHECK **1.3**

Define the terms visual learner, auditory learner, *and* kinesthetic learner. *Describe the characteristics of each type of learner.*

GROUP PROCESSING

A Collaborative Learning Activity

DIRECTIONS:

Form groups of three or four students. Then complete the following directions. Create a chart with three columns. Label the columns *Visual, Auditory,* and *Kinesthetic.* As a group, brainstorm different learning strategies or "things you can do when you study" that capitalize on each of the learning modalities. Use your own experiences and ideas for study strategies as well as ideas presented in this textbook. You may use the following examples to begin your chart.

Visual	Auditory	Kinesthetic
Use colored pens to highlight.	*Talk out loud to study.*	*Make wall charts to review.*

Multisensory Learning Strategies

Multisensory strategies are learning strategies that combine two or more modalities.

Now that you are aware of your learning style and learning preference, you can begin the process of exploring new learning strategies; select some that utilize your strengths and some that help you "stretch" and strengthen your other modalities. As you experiment with the various essential learning strategies, strive to design ***multisensory strategies***, strategies that combine two or more modalities. The incorporation of multisensory strategies benefits you in the following ways:

- You boost your memory by coding information in more than one way or with more than one sensory channel.
- You create stronger sensory paths into long-term memory so information is more clearly imprinted in your long-term memory.
- You create multiple ways to access and recall information at later times. If one recall process does not produce results, you have another process to use to search for information in memory.
- You add motivation and interest to the learning process, and you remind yourself on a regular basis that there is always more than one way to process information.

When you strive to design multisensory learning strategies, frequently you will use the following four common sensory-related processes:

1. ***Visualizing*** is the process of creating mental images of pictures and colors. Once you memorize or place the images in memory, you must then take time to recall, practice, and rehearse the images.
2. ***Verbalizing*** is the process of speaking or reading out loud to activate the auditory channel and build auditory memory. Verbalizing involves vocalizing information that you are looking at or reading. Verbalizing is less demanding on memory than reciting.
3. ***Reciting*** is the process of explaining information out loud, in complete sentences, and in your own words without looking at printed information. Reciting provides immediate feedback as to how well you do or do not understand and remember information. When you are not able to explain information out loud and in your own words, restudy the printed material before repeating the process of reciting.
4. ***Developing muscle memory*** is a kinesthetic process that involves performing multiple repetitions of steps or actions until the actions become automatic. Copying, assembling, constructing, or performing problem-solving steps are hands-on processes that create automatic muscle memory when practiced repeatedly.

Visualizing is the process of creating mental images of pictures and colors.

Verbalizing is the process of speaking or reading out loud to activate the auditory channel and build auditory memory.

Reciting is the process of explaining information out loud, in complete sentences, and in your own words without looking at printed information.

Developing muscle memory is a kinesthetic process that involves performing multiple repetitions of steps or actions until the actions become automatic.

The See-Say-Do Strategy

The ***See-Say-Do Strategy*** is a multisensory learning strategy that involves visual, auditory, and kinesthetic actions or processes. Using this strategy involves making a conscious effort to create learning combinations that help you *see* the information in new ways, *say* the information you are learning, and *do* some type of movement or hands-on activity. The following example shows how easily you can encode information into memory using three sensory channels.

To learn a process to solve a difficult math problem:

- **See:** Read the math problem and examine the significant details.
- **Say:** Verbalize the steps for a solution.
- **Do:** Copy the steps into your notes.
- **See:** Color-code each step.
- **Say:** Recite the problem-solving steps for the problem.
- **Do:** Rework the problem multiple times. Check your accuracy.

See-Say-Do Strategy is a multisensory learning strategy that involves visual, auditory, and kinesthetic actions or processes.

CONCEPT CHECK 1.4

Why are multisensory strategies so effective? Give an example of using a See-Say-Do approach for a specific learning task.

EXERCISE 1.2

Transfer These Skills: Using the See-Say-Do Strategy

DIRECTIONS:

1. Look at the following examples of students using the See-Say-Do Strategy.

   Mark reviews a section of a chapter by:

   Visual: looking at the ceiling to mentally recall textbook pictures and graphs

   Auditory: reciting information about each visual image

   Kinesthetic: redrawing diagrams from memory and checking his accuracy

   Lisa uses the following strategies to write reports and essays:

   Visual: creates an outline or organizational chart for her writing assignment

   Auditory: reads her work out loud or asks someone to read it to her

   Kinesthetic: types her papers

2. **Transfer These Skills:** On separate paper, describe a learning process or activity that you have to do for one of your classes. Then identify how you can use the See-Say-Do Strategy. What can you do that is visual? Auditory? Kinesthetic? Describe your process.

3. **BONUS CHALLENGE:** Solve the following problem. Pay attention to the approach you use to find the answer.

   A parent and a child are standing together on the sidewalk. They both start walking at the same time. Each person begins the first step with the right foot. The child must take three steps for every two steps the parent takes. How many steps must the child take until they both land again on the same foot?

   - How many steps did the child need to take?
   - Did they both land on the right foot or the left foot?
   - How did you solve this problem?

Diverse Learners in the Classroom

In every one of your classrooms, you can be assured that you are a member of a diverse group of learners. Students with visual, auditory, and kinesthetic learning style preferences sit side by side, taking in and processing information differently. Different learning styles and learning preferences partially explain why some students seem to grasp information more readily while other students struggle with making sense of new information.

Instructors' teaching styles often reflect their own individual learning styles and preferences. Historically, the American approach to education favored visual learners. As instructors learned new teaching methods and perhaps even modified their learning style preferences, many instructional approaches became more multisensory and better suited to meeting the needs of those with different learning styles. However, at some point, you will find yourself in a classroom with an instructor whose teaching style differs from your learning style preferences. To do well in such classes, you will need to vary your learning strategies to adjust to the instructor, the classroom approach, and the materials. Your goal as an adult learner is to increase your ability to perform well in a wide range of learning situations.

When you have the option, consider the following suggestions for identifying courses and instructors that are compatible with your learning style preferences:

1. Before enrolling in a course that offers several sections with different instructors, talk to other students, instructors, and counselors to learn more about the teaching and classroom styles of each instructor. *If you have a choice,* enroll in the section with the instructor who seems most compatible with your learning styles and preferences.
2. Find out what support services are available for the course. Are there study guides, study groups, supplemental computer instruction, videos, or tutors available? If so, use them.
3. Find out what forms of assessment are used in the course. Are grades based solely on tests or do grades include group or individual projects, assignments, or portfolios?

CHECK POINT 1.1

Answers appear on page B2.

True or False? See Test-Taking Strategies 1–9 in Appendix A.

_____ 1. The term *cognitive* refers to people's awareness of their surroundings.

_____ 2. To be considered a "visual learner," one must possess all the characteristics of a visual learner, have strong visualization skills, and make movies in his or her mind during the reading process.

_____ 3. To some degree, a person's learning style preference reflects his or her personal background and educational experiences.

_____ 4. Having a learning style preference means that a person is strong in only one of the three cognitive learning styles.

_____ 5. Multisensory learning strategies include some form of learning that involves two or all three learning modalities.

_____ 6. The three cognitive learning styles are hands-on, visual, and kinesthetic.

_____ 7. The See-Say-Do Strategy is a multisensory approach that seldom incorporates more than two cognitive learning styles or modalities.

_____ 8. *Reciting* and *verbalizing* are two terms used for the same process that basically means a person talks out loud.

Access Chapter 1 Practice Quiz 1 in your College Success CourseMate, accessed through *CengageBrain.com.*

EXERCISE 1.3

Textbook Case Studies

DIRECTIONS:

1. Read each case study carefully. Respond to the question at the end of each case study by using *specific* strategies discussed in this chapter. Answer in complete sentences.
2. Write your responses on paper or online in this textbook's College Success CourseMate, Textbook Case Studies. You will be able to print your online response or e-mail it to your instructor.

CASE STUDY 1: Elaine is an outgoing person who does not know anyone on campus. Consequently, she usually studies alone in the library. She knows that she is an auditory learner. Her midterm grades confirmed that she is having difficulty retaining information. Her motivation and interest in her classes are declining. What learning strategies can Elaine use to combat the problems she has encountered in the first half of this term?

CASE STUDY 2: Conor is enrolled in a poetry class to complete one of his program requirements. He has never enjoyed poetry, but this class is even more challenging for him because there is little activity or interaction in class. Students take turns reading verses, and then individual students are called on to answer questions posed by the instructor. Conor is an athlete and is not used to sitting in what seems to be an inactive environment. One student suggests that he switch to a different section with a different instructor. What type of classroom environment and teaching approach would be better suited for this kinesthetic learner?

Access Chapter 1 Textbook Case Studies in your College Success CourseMate, accessed through *CengageBrain.com.*

Multiple Intelligences

Define the term intelligences *and describe the common characteristics of each of Howard Gardner's eight intelligences.*

Theory of Multiple Intelligences is a cognitive theory that proposes that individuals have at least eight kinds of intelligences.

An **intelligence** is the potential to take in and process information that can then be used or activated to solve problems or create products that are valued in a specific culture.

Traditional intelligence, or IQ (intelligence quotient), tests basically measure linguistic, logical-mathematical, and spatial abilities. The Stanford-Binet Intelligence Scale is an intelligence test that consists of verbal and nonverbal questions for different age groups. The results of the test provide a single IQ score for the individual. The Wechsler Intelligence Scale is another test used to measure intelligence and yields a general intelligence score. IQ scores are derived by comparing a person's mental age to his or her chronological age. An IQ of 100 (an average IQ) means that chronological age equals mental age.

In 1983, Howard Gardner, a noted Harvard University psychologist, presented a new theory of cognitive development in his book *Frames of Mind: The Theory of Multiple Intelligences.* Gardner's ***Theory of Multiple Intelligences*** (MI) is a cognitive theory that proposes that individuals have at least eight kinds of intelligences. According to Gardner, an ***intelligence*** is the potential to take in and process information that can then be used or activated to solve problems or create products that are valued in a specific culture. Gardner established specific scientific criteria to identify seven intelligences; however, in 1996, Gardner used the same criteria

3 Using Time Effectively

© iStockphoto.com/Viorika

Time management is perhaps the most essential of all study skills because it lays the foundation for you to have adequate time and structure to utilize all other study skills. Knowing how to maintain a focus and concentrate on tasks leads to greater productivity, more successes, and less stress. Time management skills paired with concentration strategies result in taking better control of time and your ability to balance the academic, work, and leisure areas of your life. Time is a precious commodity, and you will benefit by managing time effectively.

CHAPTER OUTLINE

1 **SKILLFUL TIME MANAGERS**

Time Management with Personality Types

The Pie of Life

Strategies for Skilled Time Managers

2 **SCHEDULES AND STRATEGIES**

Term Schedules

Weekly Schedules

Daily Schedules

3 **FOCUS AND CONCENTRATION**

An Ideal Study Area

Essential Concentration/Focusing Strategies

Manage Distractors

Access Chapter 3 Expanded Chapter Outline in your College Success CourseMate, accessed through *CengageBrain.com*.

YOUR CHAPTER MAPPING

After reading information under each heading, return to the chapter visual mapping below. Add key words to show subheadings and important details related to each heading.

Access Chapter 3 Visual Mapping in your College Success CourseMate, accessed through *CengageBrain.com*.

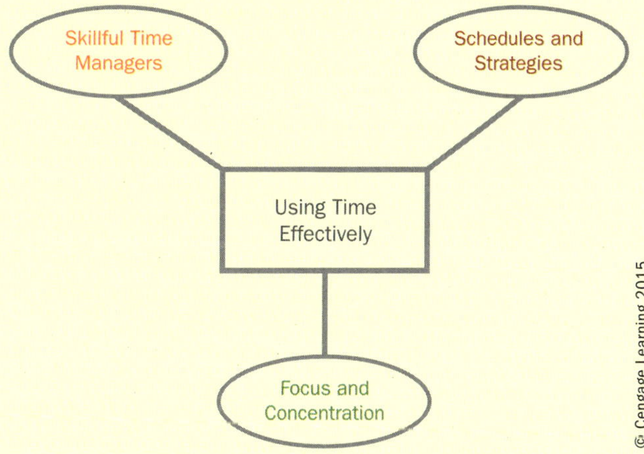

LEARNING OBJECTIVES

1 *Discuss how skillful time managers create balance, prioritize tasks, and use task schedules in their approaches to managing time.*

2 *Create and use effective term, weekly, and daily schedules to manage your time.*

3 *Explain how to create an ideal study area, use time effectively by maintaining a focus and concentrating, and manage internal and external distractions.*

Using Time Effectively

ANSWER, SCORE, and **RECORD** your profile before you read this chapter. If you need to review the process, refer to the complete directions given in the profile for Chapter 1 on page 4.

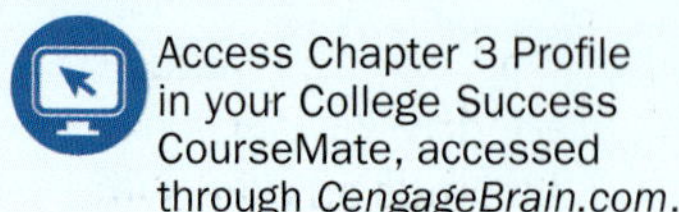
Access Chapter 3 Profile in your College Success CourseMate, accessed through *CengageBrain.com*.

ONLINE: You can complete the profile and get your score online in this textbook's College Success CourseMate.

	YES	NO
1. I use strategies to create a comfortable balance in my school, work, and leisure life.	______	______
2. I make a list of things I need to do and then start with the tasks that seem the easiest or most interesting to do.	______	______
3. I create a specific task schedule or list of steps to use to work on a task or project during a specific period of time.	______	______
4. I organize my activities and my time by making and following a weekly time-management schedule.	______	______
5. I usually study for two or three hours during the week for every class.	______	______
6. I often study for three hours or more in a row so I can stay current with my reading and homework assignments.	______	______
7. I have little control over the people or things that break my concentration or disrupt my study time.	______	______
8. I use effective strategies to concentrate and block out internal and external distractors when I study.	______	______
9. The places where I study have a low noise level, at least two sources of lighting, and an uncluttered workspace.	______	______
10. I am confident that I have the skills necessary to manage my time effectively and maintain a focus and concentrate on the work that I am doing.	______	______

QUESTIONS LINKED TO THE CHAPTER LEARNING OBJECTIVES:

Questions 1–3: objective 1

Questions 4–6: objective 2

Questions 7–9: objective 3

Question 10: all objectives

Skillful Time Managers

Discuss how skillful time managers create balance, prioritize tasks, and use task schedules in their approaches to managing time.

Everyone faces demands on their time. Students, parents, professors, secretaries, delivery drivers, CEOs, accountants, researchers, and anyone else you can name face demands on time. Our lives are busy, and for many people responsibilities and expectations are high. To use time the most effectively, to get the most out of each day, and to manage daily obligations and still enjoy free time require taking control of the hours so your days are meaningful and rewarding. By becoming an effective time manager, you experience or do the following:

- Increase awareness of time and how you use it
- Gain sense of control by identifying what needs to be done and making time to do it
- Gain more time by not wasting time, floundering or spinning aimlessly in circles
- Get started more quickly on projects or tasks and procrastinate less
- Increase productivity by setting time aside to do what needs to be done
- Boost confidence and self-esteem each time you complete goals on time
- Increase motivation when you begin to see progress and results
- Become more punctual, meet deadlines, and complete goals
- Establish structure for your daily routines
- Take responsibility by valuing your time and that of others
- Learn faster and more efficiently during focused, specific study blocks
- Improve grades by making more time available to study and review
- Meet obligations and commitments with less stress and frustration
- Recognize and stop unproductive use of time when you have time pressures
- Enjoy and appreciate social, family, and recreational time and events
- Organize priorities and show results
- Increase confidence in your ability to take charge of your life in an orderly way
- Strengthen time-management skills valued in the world of work

CONCEPT CHECK 3.1

If you were asked to describe the benefits of becoming a skilled time manager, how would you respond? What would you gain by knowing how to manage time effectively?

With so many advantages and benefits of managing time, why would anyone not want to improve time-management skills? Some people are resistant to time management for a variety of reasons, such as not wanting to be "controlled by a schedule" or "bound to something that takes away spontaneity." Often times, however, people resist becoming time managers due to a lack of time-management strategies or lack of know-how to change well-established personal patterns and routines. They are comfortable with the way they move through the days and the weeks and are not all that interested in changing what is familiar. Use **Exercise 3.1** to self-assess your time-management skills and the need for new strategies.

Time Management with Personality Types

As you recall from Chapter 1, the Myers-Briggs Type Indicator instrument discusses eight different personality preferences that combine in various ways to represent sixteen personality types. Four of these personality preferences may affect the

EXERCISE 3.1

Time-Management Inventory

DIRECTIONS:

To assess your time-management skills or need for new time-management strategies, go to Exercise 3.1: Time-Management Inventory in Appendix C, page C4.

manner in which a person views time and time-management strategies: Sensing, Intuition, Judging, and Perceiving.

Sensing and Intuition: How You Prefer to Take In Information

Students with the *Sensing personality preference* tend to display the following characteristics related to time-management concepts and strategies:

- Prefer factual, concrete, and realistic approaches to take in information
- Show interest in the accuracy of details
- Value established, proven methods
- Work in a logical, sequential way
- Take in information through the senses; for time management, prefer to see a schedule or a plan that shows how they intend to use time

Students with a Sensing personality preference tend to accept and even embrace creating and following time-management schedules. They use specific blocks of time to complete assignments, and they use the guidelines to schedule sufficient study blocks to meet the requirements of their courses. They get a sense of comfort, control, and confidence knowing that they have control of their time and have created plans of action that work and create balance in their lives.

Students with the *Intuition personality preference* tend to display the following characteristics related to time-management concepts and strategies:

- Rely on hunches or guesses for how to process information
- Use imaginative, creative, or inventive ways to perform tasks
- Tend to create unique personal strategies or approaches
- Focus on big picture and develop details during a process

Students who find that the most natural or comfortable way to process information is to let details or steps unfold once they get started, or students who use hunches or intuition to figure out how to organize time or work on assignments, may find scheduling and using time-management schedules uncomfortable or difficult. This does not mean that they should forego creating a schedule. The time-management schedules or task schedules for students with the Intuition personality preference may be more "big picture" or "global" in nature. Their schedules may simply label blocks of time, but their intuitive approaches come into play when they sit down to begin working on a specific subject in a specific block of time. Their approach may be to start on the assignment and figure out how to get to the outcome as they explore various possibilities. They may choose not to create task schedules because the steps unfold as a part of the process and are not anticipated or planned in advance.

CONCEPT CHECK 3.2

How does your personality preference or learning style preference affect your attitude and approach toward time management? Be specific.

Judging and Perceiving: How You Prefer to Approach or Structure Your Life

Students with the *Judging personality preference* tend to display the following characteristics related to time-management concepts and strategies:

- Prefer organized, structured, orderly approaches
- Organize using systematic, methodical strategies
- Make short-term and long-term goals with plans of action to complete
- Use lists to plan time, projects, or assignments
- Avoid completing projects at the last minute

Students with a Judging personality preference tend to accept and even embrace creating and following time-management schedules. They work steadily to complete goals and complete assignments before the deadlines occur. They are most comfortable with clear expectations and feel that the most natural way to approach life is to be organized, goal-oriented, and structured. They experience a sense of comfort and confidence knowing that they have control over their time and have created plans of action that work. Notice that this personality preference mirrors the characteristics of the Sensing personality preference.

Students with the *Perceiving personality preference* tend to display the following characteristics related to time-management concepts and strategies:

- Prefer to be more spontaneous and flexible
- Feel constrained and even stressed by schedules
- Are energized by last-minute pressure to meet deadlines
- Perform with bursts of energy

Students with a Perceiving personality personality preference tend to be the most resistant to using time-management strategies and schedules. These students often think about or ponder their approach to assignments, but they wait to start closer to the deadlines. They are not, however, starting cold; they have thought about the assignment, but they postpone getting down to the nitty gritty details of working on the assignment itself. The productive final burst of energy close to deadlines often results in work getting done on time. This last-minute approach has its drawbacks. If the student underestimates the time needed for the assignment or gets sidetracked by other activities, the assignment may be late or not reflect the quality work that the student is capable of doing. Students with this Perceiving personality preference benefit by doing the following:

- Accept that their approach to life works for many things but not necessarily for academic requirements and performance
- Show a willingness to incorporate modified time-management strategies and schedules into their approach for dealing with commitments and obligations

- Use the earlier blocks of time on a time-management schedule to examine the topic, understand the assignment, and begin to think about how to proceed to complete the assignment
- Schedule longer or more frequent blocks of time close to the deadline to use the bursts of energy to complete the assignment on time

CONCEPT CHECK 3.3

Personality and learning style preferences often indicate the most comfortable way to do things. Why is it important at times to explore strategies that are not within your comfort zones or preferred methods?

Learning Flexibility

Effective learners are able to adapt or modify their approaches to learning. Acquiring new skills from other learning styles or personality preferences strengthens students' abilities to handle a greater variety of learning situations, processes, and assignments. Following are examples of students acquiring skills or strategies from a different or opposite preference style:

- A student with the Extraversion personality preference can learn to become more reflective and refrain from being so open. A student with the Introversion personality preference can learn to become more sociable and comfortable discussing with others.
- A student with the Sensing personality preference can learn to become more flexible and open to more creative ways. A student with the Intuition personality preference can learn to give more attention to details and concrete information.
- A student with the Thinking personality preference can learn to be less rigid or fixed in logic and more open to compassion and feelings. A student with the Feeling personality preference can learn to use more logic and less empathy to make decisions.
- A student with the Judging personality preference can learn to be more flexible and spontaneous. A student with the Perceiving personality preference can learn to add more structure and organization by planning tasks.
- A visual learner can learn to incorporate more auditory and kinesthetic strategies. An auditory learner can learn to incorporate more visual and kinesthetic strategies. A kinesthetic learner can learn to incorporate more visual and auditory strategies.

In other words, all types of learners benefit by expanding their range of strategies and approaches. Making a conscious effort to use a variety of strategies, some of which are not from your learning style preferences, strengthens your ability to perform effectively in different situations and with various tasks, assignments, or requirements. In terms of using time-management strategies, it is important to remember that we live in a world that revolves in many ways around time. Being punctual, meeting deadlines, and organizing study or work demands reflect your character and influence the impression you make on others you encounter. Learning to manage time is essential to function in our time-oriented world.

The Pie of Life

Time management is a set of skills designed to help you monitor and use time effectively to increase performance, gain a sense of control over many aspects of your life, and achieve goals. As a student, you must continually balance three main areas in your life: school, work, and leisure. How you spend your time in these three main areas will vary term by term and will be influenced by your personal goals, needs, and interests. Imbalances in these three areas of life can lead to an array of negative consequences, including frequent frustration, low productivity, resentment, confusion, or a lack of motivation.

Time management is a set of skills designed to help you monitor and use time effectively to increase performance, gain a sense of control over many aspects in your life, and achieve goals.

CHAPTER 3 REFLECTIVE WRITING 1

On separate paper, in a journal, or in this textbook's College Success CourseMate, respond to the following questions.

1. How do you see yourself as an effective time manager? If you are effective, what habits or processes do you use that build your confidence that you are an effective time manager? If you do not see yourself as an effective time manager, what attitudes or behaviors do you demonstrate that lead to limited or weak skills as a time manager?

2. What do you see as benefits for learning to become an effective time manager? How would it affect your performance as a student? How would it affect your personal life? How would it affect you on a job or in your career?

Access Chapter 3 Reflective Writing 1 in your College Success CourseMate, accessed through *CengageBrain.com*.

The ***Pie of Life*** is a graphic that shows how much time you dedicate to each of the three main areas of your life: *school*, *work*, and *leisure*. **Figure 3.1** shows the activities, responsibilities, and commitments that are a part of each section of the Pie of Life. A balanced Pie of Life is not necessarily divided into three equal parts. The amount of time dedicated to school, work, and leisure vary according to an individual's circumstances, goals, and values. Consider the different Pies of Life for the following students:

The **Pie of Life** is a graphic that shows how much time you dedicate to each of the three main areas of your life: school, work, and leisure.

- A student who lives in a dorm and does not work while attending school
- A student who works a graveyard shift and attends college full time
- A student who lives at home and has few responsibilities other than school
- A student who attends school full time on an athletic scholarship
- A student who is a single parent and is enrolled in college part time
- A full-time student who has three children and family responsibilities

FIGURE 3.1 Three Main Areas of the Pie of Life

School	Work	Leisure
Classes	*Work/Job*	*Family time*
Homework	*Parenting*	*Social time with friends*
Study/review time	*Household chores*	*Recreation*
Tutoring	*Errands, shopping*	*Exercise*
Study groups	*Volunteer work*	*Personal "alone" time*
Test preparation	*Committee work*	*Hobbies*
Lab projects		*Television, movies, music*
Meetings		*Computer time*
Conferences		*Church*
Team practices/games		

Access Chapter 3 Topics In-Depth: Interactive Pie of Life in your College Success CourseMate, accessed through *CengageBrain.com*.

FIGURE 3.2 Pies of Life

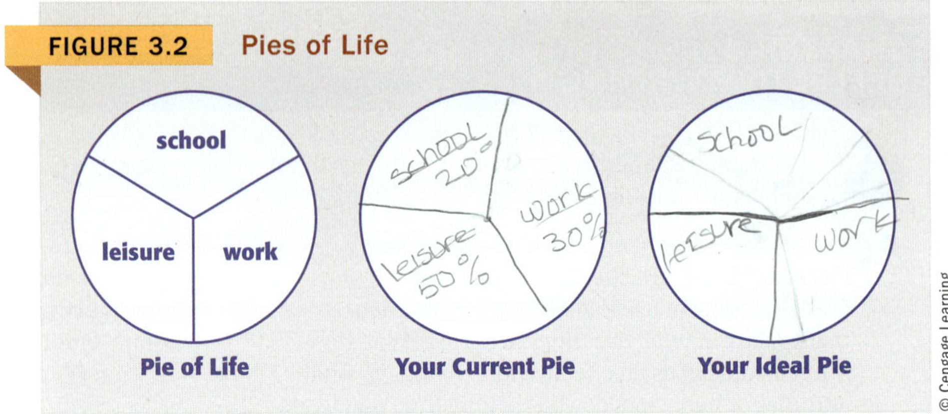

In **Figure 3.2**, the first circle shows a Pie of Life divided into three equal parts for school, work, and leisure. Think about your current use of time for these three main areas of the Pie of Life. Then divide the second circle to show the *estimated amount of time* you currently spend per week in each of the three areas. In the last circle, adjust the lines to show your *ideal* Pie of Life that reflects the balance that you wish to obtain.

CONCEPT CHECK 3.4

What does it mean to have a "balanced Pie of Life"? What would your balanced Pie of Life look like?

Achieving your ideal Pie of Life requires a willingness to examine the ways you currently use time and to commit to exploring new strategies that will improve your time-management skills. Change is not always easy, but the benefits of having a more balanced life make the process rewarding and worthwhile. In **Exercise 3.2** you will have the opportunity to complete a three-day time log to examine how you use time.

EXERCISE 3.2

How to Use Time: A Three-Day Time Log

PURPOSE: Creating a more effective balance of time in your life begins with an awareness of your daily patterns, habits, and priorities for using time. Keep a log of how you spend your time for three complete days. After analyzing the results of your three-day time log, you can begin applying time-management strategies to create a more effective balance in your life. (A form for a 7-day time log is available in this textbook's College Success CourseMate.)

DIRECTIONS: Go to Exercise 3.2 in Appendix C, pages C5–C6. Complete the following steps:

1. **Step 1:** On the chart, record all your activities for three days. *Be specific.* For example, you might write: in class, met with tutor, lab work, team practice, job, laundry, television, gym, hobby, e-mail, talked on phone, commuted, napped, or ate dinner.
2. **Step 2:** After completing your three-day log, count the number of hours spent each day in the areas shown on the final chart. Some activities may fit into more than one category; however, count them only once in the most appropriate category.
3. **Step 3: Class Discussion:** How do the results of your three-day log match your ideal Pie of Life as shown in Figure 3.2? Explain.

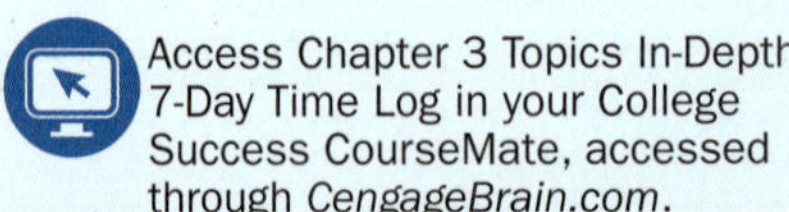

Access Chapter 3 Topics In-Depth: 7-Day Time Log in your College Success CourseMate, accessed through *CengageBrain.com*.

© PNC/Digital Vision/Getty Images

What time-management strategies help you break inertia and get you moving on a productive path? What are common consequences of not using effective time-management strategies in all three areas of your life: school, work, and social settings?

Strategies for Skilled Time Managers

Skilled time managers demonstrate a confidence in dealing with demands on time and meeting important deadlines and obligations. Skilled time managers rely on their ability to create well-planned, balanced schedules and use the schedules to organize time and tasks. Effective time-management strategies guide you through the process to produce the desired results.

Create Better Balance

You only have so many hours in a week. If your Pie of Life is unbalanced, you have two choices:

1. **Learn more efficient ways to do things.** Explore more efficient ways to study, to avoid wasting time during study blocks, to organize tasks at school and work, and to complete daily chores. Use goal-setting strategies to organize, finish projects, and achieve goals in less time without reducing the quality of the finished product. Spend less time floundering and more time using strategies that organize you in an efficient, focused, and productive way. Become an "efficiency manager" as well as a "time manager."
2. **Use the Increase-Decrease Method to change the boundaries in your Pie of Life.** The ***Increase-Decrease Method*** involves increasing or decreasing time used in one area of life in order to make more time for another area of life. Begin by identifying the section of your Pie of Life that needs more time to create a better balance in your life. As you increase time in this section, you will need to decrease time allocated to one or both of the remaining sections of your pie. For example, if your goal is to increase the amount of time allocated to *school*, you will need to decrease the time you spend in the area of *work* or *leisure* or both. Do not be too quick to say, "That won't work" or "That's not possible in my situation." Finding a better balance involves a willingness to change old behaviors and routines and to give possibilities a chance to work for you.

The **Increase-Decrease Method** involves increasing or decreasing time used in one area of life in order to make more time for another area of life.

FIGURE 3.3 ABC Method to Prioritize Tasks

1. List all the tasks that you want to achieve within a specific time period.
2. Use the letter "A" to label your highest-priority tasks—the most important or the most urgent tasks on your list to complete.
3. Use the letter "B" to label the tasks of medium importance and less urgency to complete.
4. Use the letter "C" to label the tasks of lowest importance and urgency—the ones you wish to complete but only after the higher-priority A and B tasks are achieved.
5. Return to the "A" list to prioritize these tasks. Identify the order in which you plan to complete these tasks.
6. Continue prioritizing your "B" and "C" lists of tasks to complete.
7. Use goal-setting and motivational strategies to begin working on your sequenced list of tasks. As you complete one task, start on the next.

CONCEPT CHECK 3.5

In the ABC Method to prioritize tasks, what do the letters A, B, and C represent? How does this method work?

Prioritize Tasks

Having multiple tasks to manage, goals to achieve, and projects to tackle is a situation that many people face. Sometimes multitasking is possible, but trying to multitask often results in a lack of productivity or a variety of tasks that are started but are not completed. The lack of success results in feelings of being overwhelmed, frustrated, or defeated. Skilled time managers know the importance of organizing and prioritizing what needs to be done. It takes only a few minutes to organize tasks from most important or urgent to the least important or least urgent. The result is a logically sequenced list of tasks or goals that serve as a road map for greater productivity and success. The ***ABC Method*** is a strategy to prioritize tasks or projects according to rank of importance or urgency. **Figure 3.3** shows the steps to use in the ABC Method.

The **ABC Method** is a strategy to prioritize tasks or projects according to rank of importance or urgency.

Create Task Schedules

A ***task schedule*** is a step-by-step plan for completing a specific task in a specific block of time. Taking a few minutes at the beginning of a block of time to create a task schedule structures the block of time. **Figure 3.4** shows a task schedule for a study block. Task schedules help you to do the following:

- Increase your efficiency by organizing the process before your begin
- Waste less time trying to decide where to begin or what to do next
- Motivate you to identify what you need to do and to create a plan of action
- Increase motivation by planning a reward upon completion of the task
- Perform in a time-efficient and an organized, logical manner
- Set immediate goals for study blocks, job-related tasks, personal responsibilities, or household chores

A **task schedule** is a step-by-step plan for completing a specific task in a specific block of time.

CONCEPT CHECK 3.6

How can you use task schedules with your weekly schedule? What is the value of using task schedules?

FIGURE 3.4 Task Schedule for a Study Block

Step 1: Specific goal: Review math class and do math homework pp. 26–33.

Step 2: Target date and time: Wednesday, 10:00–11:00 AM

Step 3: Individual steps:

1. Review class notes and rework class problem sets.
2. Read pages 26–32. Highlight key points. Study examples.
3. Do even-numbered problems on p. 33.
4. Check answers with answer key. Study/rework any incorrect problems.

Step 4: Reward: Extrinsic: Watch my favorite show on television.

EXERCISE 3.3

Transfer These Skills: Prioritizing and Creating a Task Schedule

PURPOSE: Using the ABC Method to prioritize important things you need to accomplish and creating task schedules to use as you work on prioritized items are effective strategies skillful time managers rely on to be productive and efficient.

DIRECTIONS: Complete the following steps to demonstrate your use of these strategies.

1. Make a list of your upcoming assignments, obligations, projects, and goals for your academic, personal, and work life.
2. Use the ABC Method. Group the tasks into A, B, C groups.
3. Within each A, B, C group, number the order or sequence you will use to tackle and complete the tasks within each group.
4. Select one item in the "A" list. Create a task schedule that shows step-by-step what you need to do to complete the task in a timely manner.

CHECK POINT 3.1

Answers appear on page B3.

True or False? See Test-Taking Strategies 1–9 in Appendix A.

___ 1. Balance in the areas of school, work, and leisure often results in less stress, greater productivity, and a more positive lifestyle.

___ 2. For realistic balance in one's daily life, a person should allocate equal time to school, work, and leisure activities.

___ 3. The majority of *school* time in the Pie of Life occurs within the classroom.

___ 4. The main goal of the Increase-Decrease Method is to decrease social and leisure time.

___ 5. A task schedule should be used only for "A" level tasks or projects.

___ 6. A person who attempts to begin too many tasks simultaneously would benefit from using the ABC Method.

Access Chapter 3 Practice Quiz 1 in your College Success CourseMate, accessed through *CengageBrain.com*.

Schedules and Strategies

2 *Create and use effective term, weekly, and daily schedules to manage your time.*

Well-designed schedules serve as road maps to guide you through the months of an academic term, through each week, and through each day. Rather than being at the mercy of time, schedules empower you with the ability to take control of time. With schedules, *you* decide and plan how you wish to spend your time. Your skills as a time manager become lifelong skills that benefit you well in school, at home, and in your chosen career.

Term Schedules

A **term schedule** is a month-by-month calendar that shows important events and deadlines for the entire term.

A ***term schedule*** is a month-by-month calendar that shows important events and deadlines for the entire term. You can use a regular calendar, a monthly planner, an electronic organizer, or a computer calendar program for each month in your current academic term. At the beginning of each term, create your term schedule; include the items that appear in **Figure 3.5**.

CONCEPT CHECK 3.7

What system will you use to create a term schedule? What specific details from Figure 3.5 will appear on your term schedule?

FIGURE 3.5 Items to Include on Your Term Schedule

1. Important deadlines for special projects, reports, and writing or lab assignments that appear on your course syllabi
2. Scheduled tests, midterms, and final exams
3. Special events, meetings, workshops, or conferences
4. Holidays
5. Scheduled times for tutors, study groups, or other support services
6. Personal appointments on or off campus

EXERCISE 3.4

Create a Term Schedule

PURPOSE: Create a term schedule that provides you with an overview of the term and serves as a guide when you create your weekly schedule.

DIRECTIONS: Gather together your campus calendar, the syllabus from each of your courses, and your personal calendar of events to create a term schedule.

1. Use a month-by-month planner or calendar. On your calendar, enter the items shown in Figure 3.5.
2. Place your month-by-month calendars in the front of your notebook, or if you are using an electronic calendar program, refer to the monthly calendar at the beginning of each week when you create your weekly schedule.
3. Update your term calendar throughout the term with deadlines for new assignments or significant events.

Access Chapter 3 Topics In-Depth: Quick Start Forms in your College Success CourseMate, accessed through *CengageBrain.com*.

Weekly Schedules

A ***weekly schedule*** is a detailed plan that serves as a guide for creating a manageable plan for each day of the week. While term schedules provide you with an overview of important events and deadlines on a month-to-month basis, weekly schedules focus your attention on details and requirements for the upcoming week. Using a weekly schedule helps you to maintain a focus and to organize, monitor, and regulate your use of time.

A **weekly schedule** is a detailed plan that serves as a guide for creating a manageable plan for each day of the week.

Unlike a time log made *after* you complete activities or tasks, a weekly time-management schedule is made *before* you engage in the activities. The weekly schedule becomes your plan, your guide, and your structure for the week. **Figure 3.6** shows a well-planned weekly schedule. A well-planned weekly schedule includes the following characteristics:

- **A realistic, balanced Pie of Life for school, work, and leisure**
- **Adequate time for study blocks:** Study blocks are scheduled throughout the week so you study on a regular basis, not just when you have assignments due or an upcoming test.
- **Sufficient time for online courses:** You will need to spend time listening to or viewing lectures, watching instructional videos, working and reworking problems, submitting written work, corresponding with the instructor, or engaging in discussion boards.
- **Effective use of all blocks of time:** Tighten up your schedule to avoid wasted blocks of time, such as an hour between classes or an hour or two after dinner.
- **Blocks of time for work and for leisure activities:** Your schedule shows your hours of employment. If your work hours change weekly, your weekly schedule reflects these changes. Your weekly schedule also shows time set aside for household chores, errands, exercise, recreation, social and family time, and daily routines, such as getting ready in the morning, commuting, or preparing and eating meals.
- **Strong, consistent patterns:** Patterns, such as specific times for studying specific classes, eating meals, doing chores, or engaging in recreation help you follow your schedule to the point that it becomes routine and habitual.
- **Time allocated to work on personal goals or prioritized items:** For example, if you want to jog three times a week or spend time in the park with your children twice a week, your schedule shows time set aside for those goals. Your schedule also shows adequate time to complete the steps on a task schedule for school, work, or personal life.
- **A routine time to sleep each night:** Going to bed about the same time each night helps stabilize your internal clock and your sleep-awake patterns. Short nights occasionally followed by long nights of sleep disrupt your normal rhythm and your natural flow of energy.

CONCEPT CHECK 3.8

How do you know if your weekly schedule is effective? What criteria could you use to assess your or another student's weekly schedule?

Five Steps to Create a Weekly Time-Management Schedule

Using a systematic approach to create your weekly time-management schedule helps you plan sufficient time for important areas of your daily life. **Figure 3.7** explains a five-step approach for developing your weekly time-management

FIGURE 3.6 Example of a Weekly Time-Management Schedule

WEEKLY TIME-MANAGEMENT SCHEDULE

For the week of ____________

Time	Monday	Tuesday	Wednesday	Thursday	Friday	Saturday	Sunday
12–6 AM	SLEEP →						
6–7:00	SLEEP →						
7–8:00	Get up, get ready, eat breakfast →					SLEEP	SLEEP
8–9:00	Commute to school →					Get up	Get up
9–10:00	PE Class	Online Math Course	PE Class	Online Math Course	PE Class	Breakfast	Breakfast
10–11:00	Online Math Course		Online Math Course		Study Math with TUTOR	Career Class	Get ready
11–12 NOON		LUNCH		LUNCH		Study Career	CHURCH
12–1:00	LUNCH	Computer Class	LUNCH	Computer Class	LUNCH	ERRANDS	CHURCH
1–2:00	Reading Class	Computer Class	Reading Class	Computer Class	Reading Class	LUNCH	LUNCH
2–3:00	Study Reading	Lab-Study Computer	Study Reading	Lab-Study Computer	Study Reading	CHORES	LEISURE
3–4:00	Study Reading	Lab-Study Computer	FLEX	Lab-Study Computer	FLEX	CHORES	LEISURE
4–5:00	Commute home →					Study Math	Online Math Course
5–6:00	DINNER →						
6–7:00	LEISURE	LEISURE	LEISURE	LEISURE	WORK	WORK	DINNER
7–8:00	Study Reading	WORKOUT ↓	Study Computer	WORKOUT ↓	WORK	WORK	Study Math
8–9:00	Study Reading		Study Computer		WORK	WORK	Study Computer
9–10:00	LEISURE		LEISURE		WORK	WORK	FLEX
10–11:00	LEISURE		LEISURE		WORK	WORK	PLAN WEEK
11–12 AM	SLEEP →				WORK	WORK	SLEEP

FIGURE 3.7 Five Steps for Creating a Weekly Time-Management Schedule

1. Write in all your fixed activities.
2. Write in your fixed study blocks for each class.
3. Add two or three flexible study blocks.
4. Add time for personal goals and personal responsibilities.
5. Schedule leisure, family, and social time.

Access Chapter 3 Topics In-Depth: Quick Start Forms in your College Success CourseMate, accessed through *CengageBrain.com*.

schedule. The following points will help you develop and use your weekly schedule effectively:

- Each Sunday spend a few minutes planning your schedule for the upcoming week.
- Keep your weekly schedule in the front of your notebook or in your electronic organizer. Refer to your weekly schedule whenever you wish to make new plans or set up appointments.
- Use your schedule for the entire term. On occasion, you may need to make minor changes in your schedule to accommodate special events or work schedules.
- Apply the strategies discussed in the following five steps for creating a weekly time-management schedule.

Step 1: Write your fixed activities. **Fixed activities** are those activities that do not vary much from week to week. On your weekly schedule, write the following fixed activities in the appropriate time blocks:

1. Class times
2. Work schedule (employment)
3. Daily routines: getting ready in the morning, commuting
4. Meals: breakfast, lunch, and dinner
5. Special appointments
6. Sleep

Fixed activities are those activities that do not vary much from week to week.

Step 2: Write your fixed study blocks. **Fixed study blocks** are well-planned blocks of time set aside to study specific subjects during the course of the week. By having effective fixed study blocks, you place a high priority on having sufficient time to complete your reading and homework assignments, create study tools, use elaborative rehearsal, and practice retrieving information through ongoing review.

Fixed study blocks are well-planned blocks of time set aside to study specific subjects during the course of the week.

Step 3: Add several flexible study blocks. **Flex study blocks** are flexible blocks of time on a weekly schedule that you use only when you need them. Flex blocks are safety nets for extra study time. Identify two or three hours each week that

Flex study blocks are flexible blocks of time on a weekly schedule that you use only when you need them.

you can hold in reserve in case you need additional time to study for a specific class, prepare for a test, or complete a special project. On your weekly schedule, write *FLEX* for these time blocks. Unlike fixed study blocks, which you should use each time they appear on your schedule, if you do not need to use the flex blocks, *convert them to free time.*

Step 4: Add time for personal goals and responsibilities. Schedule time blocks to work specifically on important goals or personal responsibilities. If you do not set aside time specifically for these important goals, tasks, or responsibilities, you may find yourself postponing or procrastinating about them or ignoring them completely.

Step 5: Schedule leisure, family, and social time. Label the remaining time on your schedule as *family, social,* or *leisure.* For the upcoming week, you can specify plans for time blocks, such as "swimming," "movie," or "entertaining," or you can leave the time blocks open and flexible to do whatever you decide to do on that day in that time block. Having family, social, and leisure time is important for mental and physical health as well as for strong relationships. If you do not have adequate time on your schedule for these activities, explore ways to use the Increase-Decrease Method to find more social and leisure time.

CONCEPT CHECK 3.9

What are the five steps to use to create a weekly schedule? Why are the first three steps important to you as a student?

Five Basic Time-Management Strategies

The following five strategies provide additional guidelines for organizing your study blocks and using your time wisely for academic success.

The **2:1 ratio** is a time-management technique that involves studying two hours for every one hour in class.

1. **Use the 2:1 ratio to schedule fixed study blocks.** The ***2:1 ratio*** is a time-management technique that involves studying two hours for every one hour in class. For example, if your writing class meets for three hours each week, schedule six hours of studying *for the writing class* each week. Studying in college means more than just doing homework. The 2:1 ratio provides you, in most cases, with sufficient time not only to read, take notes, memorize, and elaborate on course work, but also to rehearse or review to keep information in long-term memory fresh and accessible.

The **3:1 ratio** is a time-management technique that involves studying nine hours a week for three-credit independent study or online courses.

2. **Use the 3:1 ratio for independent study or online courses.** The ***3:1 ratio*** is a time-management technique that involves studying nine hours a week for three-credit independent study or online courses. Even though independent study and online courses offer students flexibility, they often require a higher level of self-discipline and time commitment to complete successfully. For three-credit independent study or online courses that have few or no in-class hours, you need to schedule a minimum of *nine hours* per week for coursework. Use the course syllabus to create a term schedule and your personal week-by-week schedule of assignments to ensure that you complete the course in a timely manner.

Spaced practice, also known as *distributed practice*, is a time-management strategy that involves making multiple contacts with new information and spreading this contact over several days or weeks.

3. **Use spaced practice.** ***Spaced practice***, also known as *distributed practice*, is a time-management strategy that involves making multiple contacts with new information and spreading this contact over several days or weeks. Spaced practice limits the length of a study block and spreads study blocks out over time. Using spaced practice increases comprehension, retention, motivation, concentration, and productivity. You will spend less time rereading and relearning information. Following are important points to understand about spaced practice:

- You will understand and recall information better for a subject if you study it for one hour six times a week, or two hours three times a week, rather than study it for six hours on the same day.
- The breaks or rest intervals between every fifty-minute study block give your memory system time to sort, process, and connect information.
- After studying two or three hours (with short breaks between each fifty-minute study block), change to a different kind of activity, such as a leisure or social activity. Your thinking processes do not shut down when you step away from the books for a few hours. When you return to studying, you will be more alert and receptive to new information.

4. **Avoid marathon studying.** ***Marathon studying***, also known as *massed practice*, occurs when you study more than three hours in a row. Three or more continuous hours of studying without a break leads to problems with productivity, concentration, and retention. Avoiding marathon studying will also help you avoid overloading your memory system.

   Marathon studying *is* acceptable in some learning situations that involve a creative flow of ideas or energy. Marathon studying may be appropriate for learning tasks such as painting, sculpting, constructing a model, or writing a research paper because tapping into the same channel of creativity and thought patterns at a later time may be more difficult to achieve. In such situations, scheduling longer study blocks is acceptable.

5. **Use trading time sparingly.** ***Trading time*** is a time-management technique that allows you to trade or exchange time blocks for two activities within the same day. Use this strategy when you need flexibility in your schedule to adjust to a special event. For example, if you want to participate in an unexpected social activity that will occur during your 7:00–9:00 PM study block, trade the study block with a 2:00–4:00 PM block of time you had set aside to spend with friends. Use trading time cautiously. If you trade time blocks too frequently, you will lose the sense of routine, and your self-discipline to follow your schedule may decline.

Marathon studying, also known as *massed practice*, occurs when you study more than three hours in a row.

CONCEPT CHECK 3.10

What is the difference between the 2:1 ratio and the 3:1 ratio? What is the difference between spaced practice and massed practice?

Trading time is a time-management technique that allows you to trade or exchange time blocks for two activities within the same day.

GROUP PROCESSING

A Collaborative Learning Activity

Form groups of three or four students. You will need to have a chart to record information. Select one member of your group to be the group recorder. Complete the following directions.

1. Divide a large chart into two columns. In the left column write all the problems the members of your group have encountered with managing time. List as many different ideas or problems as possible.
2. After you have a list of common problems, brainstorm possible solutions. Write the possible solutions in the right column. You may provide more than one possible solution for each problem. Be prepared to share your list of problems and possible solutions with the class.

FIGURE 3.8 Essential Strategies for Scheduling Fixed Study Blocks

- Label and use each study block for one specific subject.
- Schedule at least one study block every day of the week.
- Schedule a math study block every day.
- Study during your most alert times of the day.
- Schedule your hardest or least-liked subject early in the day.
- Schedule a study block right *before* a class that involves discussions or student participation.
- Schedule a study block right *after* a lecture or a math class.

Essential Strategies for Scheduling Fixed Study Blocks

Learning to become a time manager involves a willingness to adjust behaviors, attitudes, and ways you use time. To succeed as a time manager, you will need to anticipate change, be willing to relax or replace your old patterns, and be patient with yourself as you make the necessary adjustments. As you learn to use your weekly schedule, you may at times recognize that you are wandering from your time-management plan. Do not be hard on yourself or discard the schedule. Instead, recognize that change requires adjustments. Return to your schedule and get yourself back on track.

Creating an effective weekly schedule helps you get off to a good start and experience the benefits of using time management. **Figure 3.8** provides you with seven essential strategies to use as you schedule your fixed study blocks.

Label and use each study block for one specific subject. Labeling a block "study" does not provide you with a specific study plan and tends to promote an ineffective habit of studying whatever feels to be of the greatest urgency. Instead, use specific labels such as *Study English*, *Study Math*, or *Study Psychology*. Plan to use the entire study block for one subject. Jumping from one subject to another within a one-hour block disrupts the process of creating a "mindset" for the subject matter. Use the entire fifty-minute study block to review previous work, complete the current assignment, make notes or other study tools, and review. At the end of fifty minutes, give yourself a ten-minute break before moving into the next hour of studying.

Schedule at least one study block every day of the week. Spreading your study times throughout the entire week is a good spaced practice strategy, and you will experience less stress and frustration. Studying long hours during the weekdays and then engaging mainly in leisure or social activities on the weekend is ineffective.

CONCEPT CHECK 3.11

What specific strategies or guidelines can you use to schedule study blocks for your most difficult class, a Spanish class, a math class, and a history lecture class?

Schedule a math study block every day. Math involves working with steps and processes, the kind of knowledge that requires repetition, repetition, and more repetition. Studying math on a daily basis provides essential time for repetition and to practice increasing problem-solving speed and accuracy. When possible, schedule a math study block right after your math class; on the days of the week that you do not have a math class, schedule your math study block during your alert times of the day.

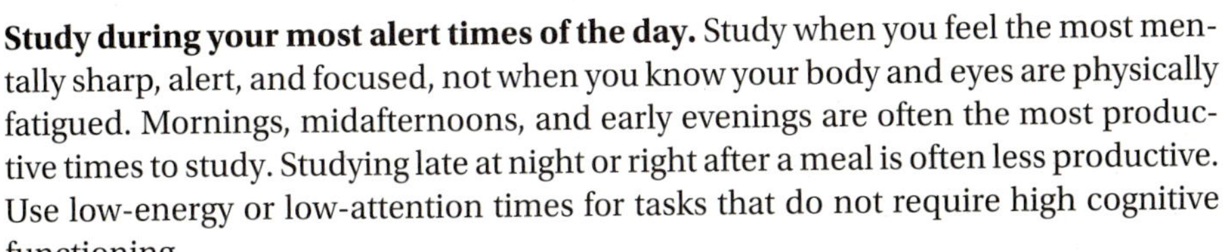

Study during your most alert times of the day. Study when you feel the most mentally sharp, alert, and focused, not when you know your body and eyes are physically fatigued. Mornings, midafternoons, and early evenings are often the most productive times to study. Studying late at night or right after a meal is often less productive. Use low-energy or low-attention times for tasks that do not require high cognitive functioning.

Schedule your hardest or least-liked subjects early in the day. By placing the hardest or least-liked subjects first on your study priorities, you are able to use a more alert mind and focused attention to tackle the assignments and process new information.

Schedule a study block right before a class that involves discussion or student participation. This puts you in the mindset for the course, refreshes your memory of key concepts, and provides you with time to rehearse as needed.

Schedule a study block right after a lecture or a math class. Taking notes is your main task during a lecture class. By scheduling a study time right *after* the class, you can review your notes, compare them with other students' notes, fill in missing details, and reorganize your notes in more meaningful ways while the information is still fresh in your mind. Scheduling a study time right after a math class reinforces the processes and provides immediate practice working problem sets or applications while the class explanations or examples are fresh in your memory.

Exercise 3.5 guides you through the process of creating your weekly time-management schedule. Examine the effectiveness of your schedule during the first three weeks of using it. If you do not follow your plans for some of the scheduled blocks of time, analyze the situations to identify what happened. Adjust your schedule the following week if necessary. As you learn these skills, remember that the time-management skills you learn now are highly prized skills recognized and admired in both the work force and the academic world.

EXERCISE 3.5

Creating a Weekly Schedule

DIRECTIONS: Go to Exercise 3.5 in Appendix C, pages C7–C8, for a weekly time-management form and a Time-Management Self-Assessment Checklist. Photocopy the weekly schedule form to use for this exercise or download the form from online Chapter 3 in the Topics In-Depth: Quick Start Forms. Complete the following directions.

1. **Step 1: Use the steps diagrammed on the following page to create a weekly time-management schedule.** Use a pencil at first so you can rearrange time blocks and make adjustments as needed to create a manageable and realistic schedule.
2. **Step 2: Mentally walk through each day** on your schedule to determine that it is realistic. Make adjustments if necessary.
3. **Step 3: Complete the Time-Management Self-Assessment Checklist** on page C8 in Appendix C. Use that information to make any necessary adjustments on your schedule.
4. **Step 4: Color-code your schedule** so it is easier to see at a glance. Use one color for your classes; another for study times; and a third for leisure, family, and social time. Use a fourth color for work or leave the spaces without color coding.

(continued)

Exercise 3.5 (continued)

5. **Step 5: Make a copy of your schedule** to keep in the front of your notebook if your instructor asks you to turn in your original schedule and the Time-Management Self-Assessment Checklist.
6. **Step 6: Begin following your schedule** as soon as possible. Several times during the day, indicate on your schedule how often you followed it as planned. Create a code system such as using stars for blocks that worked as planned and checks for blocks that you did not follow according to the plan.
7. **Step 7: Use your schedule for a full seven days.** After you have used your schedule for a full week, your instructor may ask you to turn in your first schedule and the Time-Management Self-Assessment Checklist.

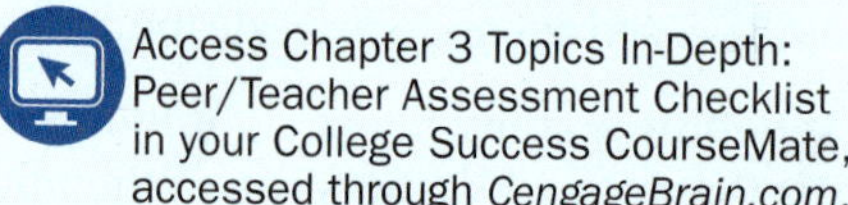

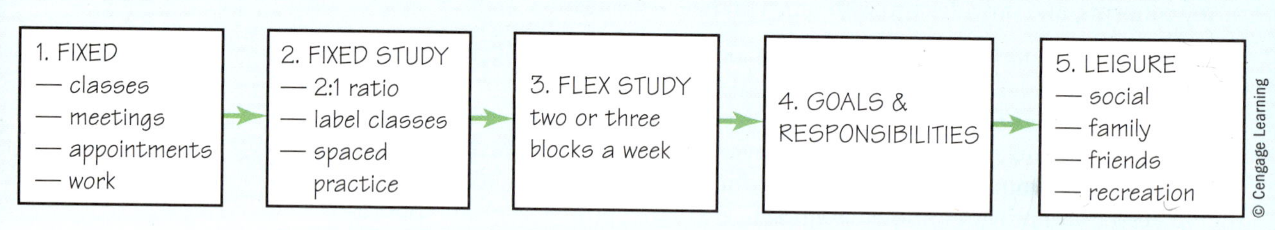

A **daily schedule** is a specific list of tasks that you plan to achieve over the course of a day.

Daily Schedules

A ***daily schedule*** is a specific list of tasks that you plan to achieve over the course of a day. It is your to-do list that helps you move through the day efficiently. Use an index card, a daily planner, or an electronic organizer for your daily schedule. Each night before you go to bed, take a few minutes to prepare your daily schedule for the next day's activities. Keep the schedule in a convenient place for quick reference. **In Figure 3.9, after examining the example of the daily schedule on the left, make a daily schedule for yourself in the box on the right.**

FIGURE 3.9 Example of a Daily Schedule

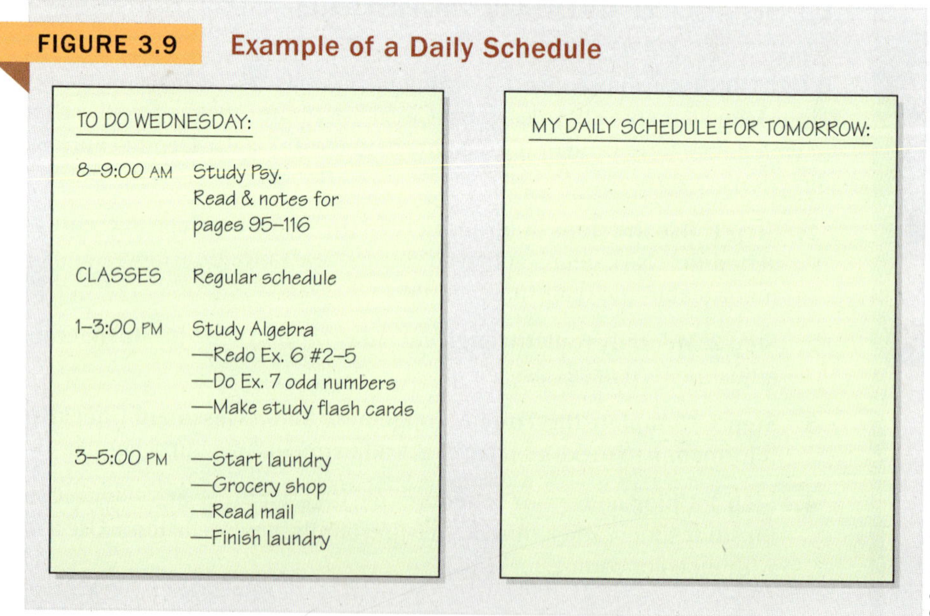

CHECK POINT 3.2

Answers appear on page B3.

Matching See Test-Taking Strategies 16–20 in Appendix A.

Match the terms on the left with the shortened definitions or descriptions on the right. Write the letter of the definition next to the word in the left column.

____ 1. flex blocks	a. often require more than the hours associated with the 2:1 ratio
____ 2. 2:1 ratio	b. occurs with marathon studying
____ 3. spaced practice	c. best to schedule study block right before class
____ 4. massed practice	d. distributed practice
____ 5. trading time	e. study blocks set to study specific courses
____ 6. online courses	f. set of monthly calendars with deadlines and events
____ 7. lecture classes	g. two or three blocks of time set aside as "safety nets"
____ 8. speech classes	h. best to schedule study block after class
____ 9. fixed study blocks	i. a formula for allocating sufficient time to study in most courses
____ 10. term schedule	j. an exchange of two blocks of time within the same day

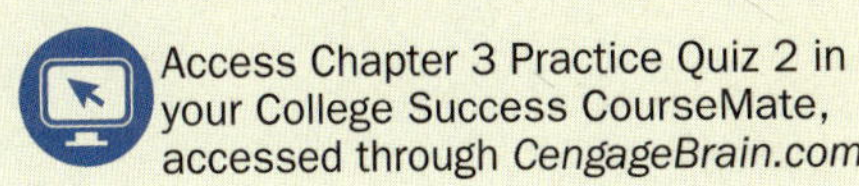
Access Chapter 3 Practice Quiz 2 in your College Success CourseMate, accessed through *CengageBrain.com*.

EXERCISE 3.6

Textbook Case Studies

DIRECTIONS:

1. Read each case study carefully. Respond to the question at the end of each case study by using *specific* strategies discussed in this chapter. Answer in complete sentences.
2. Write your responses on paper or online in the College Success CourseMate, Textbook Case Studies. You will be able to print your online response or e-mail it to your instructor.

CASE STUDY 1: Julian always seems to be caught off-guard. He is surprised when he arrives in class and hears that a specific assignment is due that day. He seldom has his assignments done on time. Sometimes he does not remember them, and other times he runs out of time. He prefers to do all his studying on the weekends, so when an assignment is due in the middle of or at the end of the week, he never has it completed. What suggestions would you give to Julian so he might modify his approach to his assignments?

(continued)

Exercise 3.6 (continued)

Case Study 2: Melissa is a very spontaneous, creative person who likes to march to her own drum. She feels that she works well under pressure and can pour on the energy to do what it takes to finish things and make deadlines. However, in reality, her work is "hit and miss." Sometimes it is creative and well done, and other times it is thrown together too quickly to show quality. A bigger problem is that she is often stressed and exhausted because she uses marathon studying to meet deadlines. What changes in attitudes and behaviors would benefit Melissa as a student?

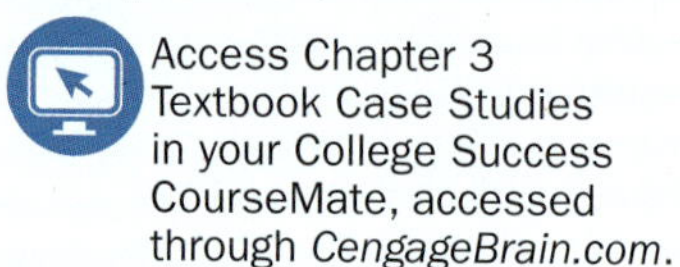

Access Chapter 3 Textbook Case Studies in your College Success CourseMate, accessed through *CengageBrain.com*.

Focus and Concentration

Explain how to create an ideal study area, use time effectively by maintaining a focus and concentrating, and manage internal and external distractions.

Creating well-planned schedules lays the foundation for managing time effectively and accomplishing important goals and tasks. However, to make the very best use of the time you schedule to be productive involves acquiring skills and strategies to keep your mind focused—to concentrate on your intended plan of action.

Concentration is the ability to block out *external* and *internal distractors* in order to stay focused on one specific item or task.

Concentration is the ability to block out *external* and *internal distractors* in order to stay focused on one specific item or task. Concentration is a flighty process; you can concentrate one minute and then easily become distracted and lose that concentration. The following are important points about concentration:

CONCEPT CHECK 3.12

What are common external and internal distractors you encounter when you study? What effects do they have on your thought processes?

- Concentration requires a concerted effort on your part to train or discipline your mind.
- Concentration involves monitoring your thoughts and emotions as well as your environment.
- External and internal distractors consume space in your memory system, disturb your brainwave patterns, and affect the flow of stimuli throughout your memory system (see Chapter 5). You can use effective strategies to train your mind and your attention to not respond to external and internal distractors.
- ***External distractors*** are disruptions caused by things in your physical environment. Noises, people, music, television, enticing or harsh weather, clutter, and lighting are examples of external distractors. If you are working online, e-mail, social media, and instant messaging can quickly become external distractors.
- ***Internal distractors*** are disruptions that occur inside you physically or emotionally. Worry, stress, anxiety, depression, sickness, hunger, pain,

External distractors are disruptions caused by things in your physical environment.

Internal distractors are disruptions that occur inside you physically or emotionally.

daydreams, and anticipation of upcoming events are examples of internal distractors.

An Ideal Study Area

An ideal study area is a specific area designated as your place in which to concentrate and focus on studying. You should have an ideal study area on campus and one at home so you have an organized area in both locations that is conducive to learning, has few or no distractions, and helps you focus your attention on your learning tasks. Creating ideal study areas will help you do the following:

- Increase your ability to concentrate
- Promote the use of selective attention on specific tasks and goals
- Increase motivation and academic performance
- Reduce the tendency to procrastinate
- Reduce or eliminate the effects of internal and external distractors

CONCEPT CHECK 3.13

What constitutes an ideal study area? How do the elements in your study environment affect your thinking and memory processes?

Creating an ideal study area may require some thoughtful planning and rearranging of furniture or materials, but the time spent will bring positive results. During this process, pay careful attention to three elements in your physical environment: the noise level, the lighting, and the workspace.

The Noise Level

Even though people have different tolerance levels for noise, research shows that noisy environments interrupt the steady flow of thought processes and brainwave patterns, thus causing concentration to turn on and off and on and off in split-second intervals. External noise takes up space in your memory system, thus reducing the amount of memory available to process information efficiently. A noisy study environment impacts the quality of learning, so consciously increase your awareness of the noise level around you and be willing to change your study location or adjust your existing learning space. **Check the following items that describe your current study spaces at home and on your campus:**

Television is turned off.	Home:_____ Campus: _____
No music is playing.	Home:__✓__ Campus: _____
Little or no movement is present.	Home:__✓__ Campus: _____
Minimal or no noises are present.	Home:__✓__ Campus: _____
People refrain from interrupting you.	Home:__—__ Campus: _____

The Lighting

Proper lighting is important in any study area. If you have too little light, your eyes can easily become strained and tired. Some lighting can create shadows or glare on your books or your digital monitors. To avoid many of the problems created by poor lighting, have *two* sources of light in your study area. These light sources may include overhead lights, desk lamps, or floor lamps. **Check the following items that describe your current study spaces:**

Two sources of lighting are used.	Home:______ Campus: ______
No glare appears on textbook pages or on a monitor.	Home:______ Campus: ______
Computer monitor is bright and easy to read.	Home:______ Campus: ______
Computer resolution level is "easy on the eyes."	Home:______ Campus: ______

The Workspace

Trying to study in an area that lacks sufficient space to spread out your textbooks, open your notebooks, access a computer, take notes as you read, or use other study materials and supplies creates distractions. Trying to study on the floor, in a recliner, on a couch, on a bed, or outdoors tends to create unnecessary distractions. **Check the following items that describe your current study spaces:**

No clutter to create distractions is present.	Home:______ Campus: ______
Space has limited visual stimuli (posters or pictures).	Home:______ Campus: ______
Space has a work surface with ample room for your notebooks, textbooks, computer, and supplies.	Home:______ Campus: ______
Space has a comfortable chair that is an appropriate height for the table or desk and for you.	Home:______ Campus: ______

Essential Concentration/Focusing Strategies

As you will learn in Chapter 6, concentration is a memory principle that promotes effective use of your memory in the learning process. **Figure 3.10** summarizes six essential concentration strategies for studying. After reading explanations of each strategy, return to **Figure 3.10** and recite what you remember about each strategy.

FIGURE 3.10 Essential Concentration Strategies for Studying

- Set learning goals with plans of action.
- Be an active learner.
- Chunk information.
- Create a study ritual.
- Begin with a warm-up activity.
- Use mental rehearsal.

Set Learning Goals

Knowing *what* you plan to do and *how* you plan to achieve your goals gives you a purpose, a motivation to stay focused, and a mission to achieve. At the beginning of a study block, create a task schedule that identifies your specific intentions for your study block. Setting learning goals and creating task schedules activate your memory and initiate the plan of action to achieve the goals.

Be an Active Learner

Active learning is a process of engaging in the learning process instead of working in a detached, mechanical way. Active learning increases concentration and helps you avoid internal distractors, such as sleepiness, boredom, or disinterest. Be an active learner by studying with a pen in hand, taking notes, highlighting textbooks, writing questions, and creating study tools, such as diagrams, flashcards, and visual notes.

Active learning is a process of engaging in the learning process instead of working in a detached, mechanical way.

Chunk Information

Chunking down is the process of breaking larger assignments or sections of information into smaller, more manageable units that memory can process. Trying to take in too much information too rapidly overloads your memory and results in loss of concentration and ineffective learning. When you feel distracted by the demands of an assignment, the complexity of a project, or a task such as reading a long chapter, take a deep breath and methodically identify the steps or parts that you need to complete. Breaking an overwhelming assignment, project, or task into smaller units boosts your confidence level, and you find that the task is manageable and less intimidating.

Chunking down is the process of breaking larger assignments or sections of information into smaller, more manageable units that memory can process.

Create a Study Ritual

A ***study ritual*** is a series of steps or a consistent routine that helps you start quickly on a task. Instead of wasting time trying to decide what to do or where to begin, a study ritual moves you directly into the mindset of studying. For example, your study ritual might be to use a quick relaxation or visualization technique, create a task schedule, and do a warm-up activity.

A **study ritual** is a series of steps or a consistent routine that helps you start quickly on a task.

CONCEPT CHECK 3.14

What strategies can you use within the first five minutes of a study block to help you focus your mind on the assignment? Can you name all six strategies?

Begin with a Warm-Up Activity

Warm-ups are activities at the beginning of a study block that shift thoughts and create a mindset for studying and concentrating. Warm-ups activate memory and set up frameworks, schemas, or big pictures in your memory for new information. *Previewing* (skimming through a new chapter or assignment to get an overview) and *reviewing* previous work are effective warm-up activities.

Warm-ups are activities at the beginning of a study block that shift thoughts and create a mindset for studying and concentrating.

Use Mental Rehearsal

Mental rehearsal is the process of creating a picture or a movie in your mind that shows you performing effectively. The image that you hold of yourself as a learner often affects the behaviors you exhibit. Use mental rehearsal to replace any negative images of yourself as a learner with positive images of yourself as a learner who stays focused and achieves learning goals. For example, picture yourself beginning an assignment, working with ease, writing answers on a test with confidence, or studying without distractions.

Mental rehearsal is the process of creating a picture or a movie in your mind that shows you performing effectively.

CHAPTER 3 REFLECTIVE WRITING 2

On separate paper, in a journal, or online in this textbook's College Success CourseMate, respond to the following questions:

1. *When* and *where* do you have the most problems concentrating when you study? How can you change the study environment so it is more conducive for concentrating and focusing on learning?
2. What concentration strategies work best for you to help you keep your mind focused when you are studying? Describe strategies with details.

Access Chapter 3 Reflective Writing 2 in your College Success CourseMate, accessed through *CengageBrain.com*.

Manage Distractors

When you find yourself distracted and unable to concentrate, the first step is to analyze the situation to determine the source of your distraction. Is it caused by an *internal distractor* or an *external distractor?* The second step is to select an appropriate technique to address the concentration problem. **Figure 3.11** summarizes six quick, easy-to-use techniques to reduce or eliminate distractors. After reading about each technique, return to **Figure 3.11** and recite what you remember about each technique. Then practice using the techniques several times to increase your ability to stay focused and manage distractors.

The **Say No Technique** involves resisting the urge to participate in an external or internal distraction.

The **No Need Technique** is the process of training yourself not to look up and not to break your concentration to attend to minor, familiar distractions.

The ***Say No Technique*** involves resisting the urge to participate in an external or internal distraction. Assertively *say no* when friends or family members ask you to drop your study schedule and participate in an activity with them. Train yourself to *say no* and to stay focused when you want to get a snack, turn on the television, daydream, text friends, or check social media accounts.

The ***No Need Technique*** is the process of training yourself not to look up and not to break your concentration to attend to minor, familiar distractions. Wherever you

CONCEPT CHECK 3.15

Which of the techniques in Figure 3.11 work to reduce or eliminate external distractors? Which work to eliminate internal distractors? Which work best for you?

FIGURE 3.11 Techniques to Manage Distractors

- Say No
- No Need
- Do Not Disturb Symbol
- Check Mark
- Mental Storage Box
- Take Charge

are studying, you know minor distractions and predictable noises will occur. Force yourself to keep your eyes and your attention on your own work. Tell yourself, "There is *no need* to look."

The ***Do Not Disturb Symbol Technique*** involves using a symbol, such as a sign or a red bow, to signal to others that you do not want to be interrupted or disturbed. Place this symbol on your door or in your work area to indicate to others that they should not disturb you.

The **Do Not Disturb Symbol Technique** involves using a symbol, such as a sign or a red bow, to signal to others that you do not want to be interrupted or disturbed.

The ***Check Mark Technique*** involves keeping a score card to record and reduce the number of distractions that you allow to disrupt your concentration. Each time you lose your concentration during a study block, make a check mark on a score card you keep on your desk. At the end of your study block, count the number of checks. Set a goal each time you study to reduce the number of check marks.

The **Check Mark Technique** involves keeping a score card to record and reduce the number of distractions that you allow to disrupt your concentration.

The ***Mental Storage Box Technique*** involves placing any internal distractors into an imaginary box, putting a lid on the box, and setting that box aside to be dealt with at a later time. Before you begin studying, identify any concerns, worries, or emotions that might interrupt your concentration. Place them inside your mental storage box. Tell yourself that you will deal with the contents of the box at a more appropriate time, and then do so later.

The **Mental Storage Box Technique** involves placing any internal distractors into an imaginary box, putting a lid on the box, and setting that box aside to be dealt with at a later time.

The ***Take Charge Technique*** involves taking responsibility for your environment by seeking an alternative place to study or by modifying the existing environment so it has few or no distractions. You do not want to waste your valuable time trying to study in an environment filled with distractions. Taking charge of your environment exhibits a willingness to let go of old habits and try new strategies to increase your ability to concentrate and your overall performance. Use this technique to eliminate a pattern of blaming others for your situation. You are in control by taking charge and making necessary adjustments.

The **Take Charge Technique** involves taking responsibility for your environment by seeking an alternative place to study or by modifying the existing environment so it has few or no distractions.

CHECK POINT 3.3

Answers appear on page B3.

True or False? See Test-Taking Strategies 1–9 in Appendix A.

T 1. Using concentration strategies effectively increases memory space for cognitive functions.

T 2. You can focus your mind more quickly on studying when you create plans of action, create a study ritual, and do a warm-up activity.

F 3. A person's physical environment has less of an impact on concentration than his or her emotional state of mind.

F 4. The Take Charge, Mental Storage Box, and the Say No techniques are designed to deal only with external distractors.

Access Chapter 3 Practice Quiz 3 in your College Success CourseMate, accessed through *CengageBrain.com*.

ACTIVITY

Chapter 3 Critical Thinking

PURPOSE: The term "chunking down" refers to breaking larger sections of information into smaller, more manageable units of information that memory can process. The excerpt below discusses the power of chunking; however, this refers to the process of "chunking up."

DIRECTIONS: After you read the excerpt, answer the following critical thinking questions.

1. What is your definition of **chunking up**? refers to

2. What is the purpose or value of using a **chunking up** process?

3. How do the processes of **chunking down** and **chunking up** differ?

4. What do the processes of **chunking down** and **chunking up** have in common?

5. Brainstorm applications. List ways you could apply the **chunking up** process to a variety of situations.

6. Brainstorm applications. List ways you could apply the **chunking down** process to a variety of situations.

The Power of Chunking

Chunks of information can be quite complex. If you heard someone say, "The boy in the red shirt kicked his mother in the shin," you could probably repeat the sentence perfectly. Yet it contains twelve words and forty-three letters. How can you repeat the sentence so effortlessly? The answer is that you are able to build bigger and bigger chunks of information (Ericsson & Staszewski, 1989). In this case, you might represent "the boy in the red shirt" as one chunk of information rather than as six words or nineteen letters. Similarly, "kicked his mother" and "in the shin" represent separate chunks of information.

Learning to use bigger and bigger chunks of information can improve short-term memory. In fact, children's short-term memories improve partly because they gradually become able to hold as many as seven chunks in memory and also because they get better at grouping information into chunks (Servan-Schreiber & Anderson, 1990). Adults also can greatly increase the capacity of their short-term memory by using more efficient chunking. For example, after extensive training, one college student increased his immediate memory span from seven to eighty digits (Neisser, 2000a). So although the capacity of short-term memory is more or less constant (from five to nine chunks of meaningful information), the size of those chunks can vary tremendously.

Learning Objectives Review

1 ***Discuss how skillful time managers create balance, prioritize tasks, and use task schedules in their approaches to managing time.***

- Knowing how to control and manage time has many benefits.
- Two personality preferences tend to embrace scheduling and using time-management strategies: Sensing and Judging. Two other personality preferences tend to resist and have more difficulties learning to structure time: Intuition and Perceiving.
- The Pie of Life represents three main areas of life that people need to learn to manage and balance: school, work, and leisure.
- Skilled time managers find more efficient ways to do things, use the Increase-Decrease Method, prioritize tasks by using the ABC Method, and create task schedules to be more productive.

2 ***Create and use effective term, weekly, and daily schedules to manage your time.***

- Term schedules provide a method to plan for important events and deadlines month-by-month for an entire term.
- Weekly schedules serve as a guide for managing daily plans for a week.
- A variety of strategies are available to create a well-planned weekly schedule with individual blocks of time dedicated to specific subjects, tasks, or obligations.
- Five steps to create a weekly time-management schedule include identifying fixed activities, fixed study blocks, flexible study blocks, personal goals, and time for leisure, family, and social activities.
- Five important strategies for scheduling study blocks involve using the 2:1 ratio, the 3:1 ratio, spaced practice, trading time, and avoiding marathon studying.
- Daily schedules are a form of to-do lists to organize time for a day.

3 ***Explain how to create an ideal study area, use time effectively by maintaining a focus and concentrating, and manage internal and external distractions.***

- Concentration is the ability to block out external and internal distractors.
- An ideal study area has little or no noise, two or more sources of lighting, and an uncluttered work area.
- A variety of concentration strategies help you focus and stay on task: setting learning goals, being an active learner, chunking information, creating a study ritual, using a warm-up activity, and using mental rehearsal.
- To maintain a focus and concentrate require using strategies to manage or eliminate internal and external distractors. Six strategies are recommended to manage distractors.

Terms to Know

By yourself or with a partner, practice reciting or writing definitions for the following terms. You may also practice defining these terms by using the online flashcards or comparing your answers to the online glossary.

time management p. 74
Pie of Life p. 75
Increase-Decrease Method p. 77
ABC Method p. 78
task schedule p. 78
term schedule p. 80
weekly schedule p. 81
fixed activities p. 83
fixed study blocks p. 83
flex study blocks p. 83
2:1 ratio p. 84
3:1 ratio p. 84
spaced practice p. 84
marathon studying p. 85
trading time p. 85
daily schedule p. 88
concentration p. 90
external distractors p. 90
internal distractors p. 90
active learning p. 93
chunking down p. 93
study ritual p. 93
warm-ups p. 93
mental rehearsal p. 93
Say No Technique p. 94
No Need Technique p. 94
Do Not Disturb Symbol Technique p. 95
Check Mark Technique p. 95
Mental Storage Box Technique p. 95
Take Charge Technique p. 95

Access Chapter 3 Flashcards and Online Glossary in your College Success CourseMate, accessed through *CengageBrain.com.*

Chapter 3 Review Questions

Answers appear on page B3.

Multiple Choice See Test-Taking Strategies 10–15 in Appendix A.

1. A well-planned term schedule
   a. shows only midterm and final exams.
   b. reflects academic and personal timelines and commitments.
   c. states your weekly goals and shows your daily homework assignments.
   d. accomplishes all of the above.

2. When you use a fifty-minute study block effectively, you
   a. spend time reviewing each of your courses.
   b. create a mindset that focuses on only one subject.
   c. cover as many textbook pages as possible by reading fast.
   d. begin by identifying which class has an assignment due the next day.

3. An effective weekly time-management schedule includes
   a. eight hours of studying on weekends.
   b. three or more flex blocks and three times set aside for trading time.
   c. adequate time to use the 2:1 ratio, elaborative rehearsal, and spaced practice.
   d. all study blocks completed by 9:00 PM.

___ 4. A person with an Intuition or Perceiving Myers-Briggs personality preference often does not tend to
   a. feel comfortable establishing structure, schedules, and predictable routines.
   b. prefer more creative or open-ended ways of approaching assignments.
   c. explore different ways to work through the steps of an assignment.
   d. make any effort to manage time or try to create a usable schedule.

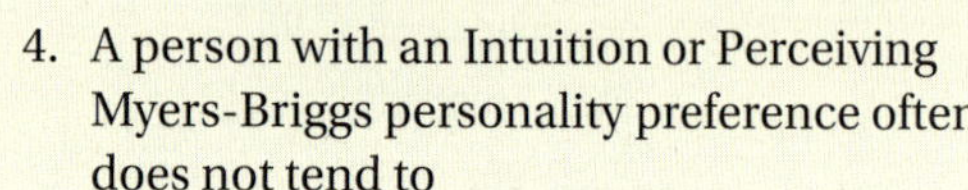

5. The primary purpose of the Increase-Decrease Method is to
   a. help you find ways to increase your social time each week.
   b. find a more satisfying and productive balance in your Pie of Life.
   c. move you toward having a Pie of Life that shows an equal amount of time each week for school, work, and leisure.
   d. decrease the amount of time you need to study each day.

6. Concentration is
   a. the ability to block out distractions and focus on only one item or task.
   b. a process that affects memory.
   c. a mental discipline that involves training your mind to maintain a focus.
   d. all of the above.

7. Which techniques would not work well for a student who wants to stop wasting the first half hour of a study block trying to "get started" on studying?
   a. Warm-up activities and using the Take-Charge Technique.
   b. Chunking technique and mental rehearsal.
   c. Setting learning goals and creating a task schedule.
   d. Looking through assignments for each course to decide where to begin.

8. The ABC Method is used to
   a. make a single list numbered from one to ten to show things you need to do daily.
   b. learn how to recite the alphabet.
   c. identify, classify, organize, and prioritize tasks based on importance or urgency.
   d. do all of the above.

Fill-in-the-Blanks See Test-Taking Strategies 21–24 in Appendix A.

1. The 2:1 ratio and the 3:1 ratio are used to determine the amount of time on a weekly schedule to set aside for study practice.
2. Marathon studying is also known as massed practice practice.
3. Spaced practice is also known as distibuted pra practice.
4. Disruptions or distractions that occur within you are called enternal distractors.
5. The process of breaking larger assignments or sections of information into more manageable units is called the process of chucking down
6. The take - charge Technique involves assuming responsibility for situations, being willing to make changes, and not blaming others for your circumstances.

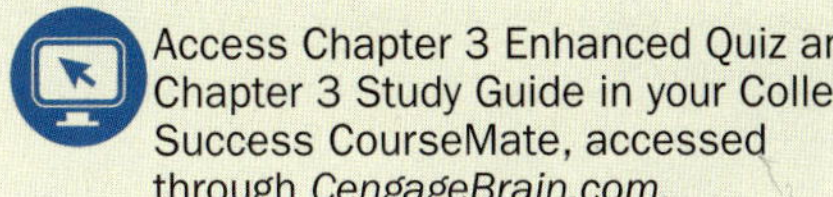

Access Chapter 3 Enhanced Quiz and Chapter 3 Study Guide in your College Success CourseMate, accessed through *CengageBrain.com.*

Access all Chapter 3 Online Materials in your College Success CourseMate, accessed through *CengageBrain.com*.

4 Creating and Achieving Goals

© iStockphoto.com/szefei

Learning to set goals provides you with well-defined plans of action to achieve specific results. Learning strategies to motivate and energize yourself to achieve your goals is rewarding and productive. In this chapter you will learn to become a skillful goal setter as well as learn strategies for becoming a stress manager and a procrastination manager. As you work with these skills, you will realize that goal setting involves lifelong skills that will benefit you in your academic, professional, and personal life.

CHAPTER OUTLINE

Access Chapter 4 Expanded Chapter Outline in your College Success CourseMate, accessed through *CengageBrain.com*.

YOUR CHAPTER MAPPING

After reading information under each heading, return to the chapter visual mapping below. Add key words to show subheadings and important details related to each heading.

Access Chapter 4 Visual Mapping in your College Success CourseMate, accessed through *CengageBrain.com*.

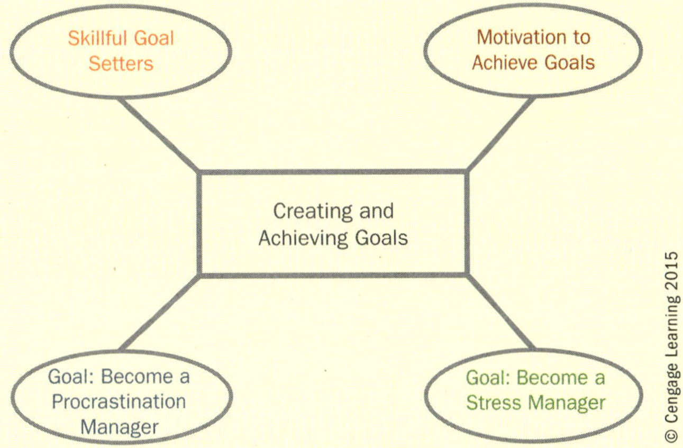

LEARNING OBJECTIVES

1. *Explain how to use the GPS Strategy, visualization, extrinsic and intrinsic rewards, and other strategies to create a plan of action for term-long projects and for immediate, short-term, intermediary, and long-term goals.*

2. *Discuss ways to achieve goals by using intrinsic and extrinsic motivation, the Incentive Theory, the Expectancy Theory, and Maslow's Hierarchy of Needs.*

3. *Explain how to become a stress manager by using coping, relaxation, and intrapersonal strategies to combat stressors.*

4. *Explain how to become a procrastination manager by using effective strategies to identify and reduce procrastination.*

CHAPTER 4 PROFILE

Creating and Achieving Goals

ANSWER, SCORE, and **RECORD** your profile before you read this chapter. If you need to review the process, refer to the complete directions given in the profile for Chapter 1 on page 4.

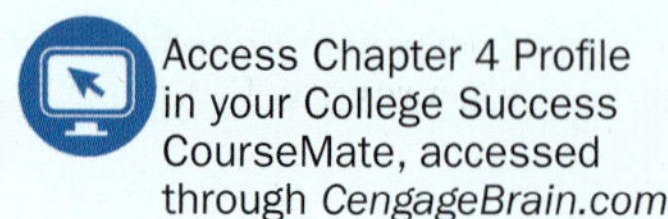

ONLINE: You can complete the profile and get your score online in this textbook's College Success CourseMate.

		YES	NO
1.	I use a systematic approach for planning and achieving goals.		
2.	I tend to have difficulty completing term-long projects on time.		
3.	I use goal setting for immediate tasks I need to do, but I do not use goal setting for assignments or projects that are not due for several weeks.		
4.	I am self-motivated when I have a purpose or a reason to work hard to achieve goals.		
5.	I am only motivated when I know I will receive something like a good grade, money, recognition, or some incentive for my effort and work.		
6.	I use effective strategies, such as relaxation or coping strategies, to manage my stress levels.		
7.	My level of stress often reduces my performance or ability to complete my goals.		
8.	I prolong starting on goals that relate to tasks that are difficult or unpleasant to do.		
9.	I recognize when and why I procrastinate, and then I select strategies to get back on track and moving forward.		
10.	I am confident that I have the skills necessary to become a skillful goal setter.		

QUESTIONS LINKED TO THE CHAPTER LEARNING OBJECTIVES:

Questions 1–3: objective 1

Questions 4–5: objective 2

Questions 6–7: objective 3

Questions 8–9: objective 4

Question 10: all objectives

Skillful Goal Setters

1 *Explain how to use the GPS Strategy, visualization, extrinsic and intrinsic rewards, and other strategies to create a plan of action for term-long projects and for immediate, short-term, intermediary, and long-term goals.*

Goals are well-defined plans of action aimed at achieving specific outcomes or results.

Goals are well-defined plans of action aimed at achieving specific outcomes or results. Effective goal setting requires effective time management because you need to be aware of time and allocate sufficient time to work through the steps to complete your goals. Your goals become your road maps to guide you to your desired outcomes.

Many people have good intentions and a strong desire or motivation to succeed by achieving their goals; however, many of these same people fall short of making their goals a reality. Frequently, the inability to achieve goals begins with the lack of a sound process or strategy to write and plan effective goals. In other cases, people shy away from goal setting because of attitudes such as the following:

- *I have a fear of failure*, or *I have a fear of success.*
- *It's better not to try than to try and not succeed.*
- *I'll just get discouraged, frustrated, or embarrassed, so why bother?*
- *I've never been a goal setter and I'm doing okay.*
- *I have never learned how to set goals and don't know where to start.*

Fortunately, you can learn strategies to write effective goals and achieve those goals or desired outcomes. How effective are you as a goal setter? **Exercise 4.1** gives you an opportunity to examine your current goal-setting skills and achievements.

CONCEPT CHECK 4.1

Why are some people all talk but no results? What are possible consequences for people who set goals but do not complete them?

EXERCISE 4.1

Goal-Setting Inventory

DIRECTIONS: Go to Exercise 4.1 in Appendix C, page C9 to complete the Goal-Setting Inventory. This inventory provides the opportunity to examine your current goal-setting skills and achievements. This nongraded inventory provides you with insights about yourself as a skillful goal setter.

Long-Term and Intermediary Goals

A ***long-term goal*** is a well-defined plan of action to achieve a specific result after two or more years. To complete a long-term goal usually involves completing a series of smaller subgoals called *intermediary goals.*

An ***intermediary goal***, a subgoal or a stepping stone to a long-term goal, is a well-defined plan of action to achieve a specific result within a time period of one or two years. For example, a long-term goal to complete a four-year degree in computer science requires other, smaller steps or stepping stones, such as completing required courses as a freshman, completing a 2-year transfer degree, and then completing 2 years of course requirements to receive a bachelor of science degree. **Exercise 4.2** encourages you to think about long-term and intermediary goals important to you in several areas of your life.

A **long-term goal**, is a well-defined plan of action to achieve a specific result after two or more years.

An **intermediary goal**, a subgoal or a stepping stone to a long-term goal, is a well-defined plan of action to achieve a specific result within a time period of one or two years.

CONCEPT CHECK 4.2

How are intermediary goals related to long-term goals? Do long-term goals always have intermediary goals? Explain your answer.

goal and its subgoals, their importance, and a well-defined plan of action to guide the process through its many steps.

The GPS Strategy for Setting Goals

GPS Strategy is a systematic three-step goal-setting process to create a plan of action to achieve desired outcomes or goals.

Many cars and smartphones have GPS (Global Positioning System) navigational systems to navigate roads and freeways and to find convenient, direct routes to get people to where they want to go. The ***GPS Strategy*** is a systematic three-step goal-setting process to create a plan of action to achieve desired outcomes or goals. This GPS Strategy is your roadmap or navigational system to use for immediate, short-term, intermediary, and long-term goals. **Figure 4.2** shows the three steps in the GPS Strategy for setting goals.

Step One: GOAL

CONCEPT CHECK 4.5

What does each letter in the GPS Strategy represent (G-P-S)? Why is each step important for successful goal setting?

Begin by identifying a specific, well-defined goal that is clear, realistic, and has a definite target date and time for completion. To simply say, "I will do better" or "I want something new" results in vague wishes that are not specific, meaningful, or measureable. To say, "I will be a millionaire tomorrow" is not realistic for most people. To say, "I would like to do that whenever I have some time," or "I will start but have no idea when I'll finish it" does not set a specific or definite timeline (date and time) to finish the steps and achieve the goal. A well-defined target date and time work as a form of motivation to keep you moving forward and on time.

Step 2: PURPOSE

Identifying a purpose for your goal shows that you understand the importance, relevance, and value of the outcome. Having a specific purpose in mind adds motivation, intensity, and commitment to the process of achieving your goal. Goals, especially long-term goals, can become outdated due to changes in values or life circumstances. If a goal is no longer of value to you, replace it with a new, more significant goal. After you identify a specific goal, examine its purpose by asking yourself the following questions:

- Why is this goal important to me?
- What benefits will I gain when I achieve this goal?
- Is this goal compatible with other goals of mine?
- Is this goal an intermediary goal or a step essential for a long-term goal?
- Why am I motivated to follow the steps and complete this goal?
- Do I want to complete this goal for my own satisfaction or to please someone else?
- What consequences will I encounter if I do not achieve this goal?

FIGURE 4.2 The GPS Strategy for Goal Setting

G = **GOAL** with target date and time of completion

P = **PURPOSE** stating importance, relevancy, value

S = **STEPS** to complete to achieve the outcome

When a goal is right for you, you are motivated to get started, feel a sense of excitement, anticipation, and commitment to achieve the outcome. You can vividly picture or create a vision of the desired outcome and know that the goal is important and right for you. When you acknowledge that a goal is important to you, but you need to increase motivation, select one or more of the goal-setting strategies on pages 110–112.

Step 3: STEPS

On paper, in chronological order, list the individual steps you need to work through to achieve your goal. Be specific in naming the steps and the details. Next to each step, jot down any special supplies, materials, or resources you will need to complete that step. Jotting down this information helps you organize yourself so the process does not get interrupted due to poor planning or lack of access to items you need to complete the step. For steps that are spread across different time blocks, days, weeks, or months, schedule the dates on a calendar to show when you will complete each step. Following are additional strategies to use to plan the steps in your GPS Strategy for setting goals:

- **Break larger goals into smaller subgoals.** By using the *chunking down technique*, your larger goal becomes a series of smaller, more manageable, and realistic subgoals. As you check off and complete each smaller subgoal, you gain momentum and motivation and realize you are moving toward completion of the larger goal.
- **Schedule time to complete each step.** Use your weekly schedule to identify blocks of time you can use to work on one or more steps of your goal.
- **Use a goal organizer.** A ***goal organizer*** is a chart that consists of six questions to help plan a course of action to achieve a specific goal. **Figure 4.3** shows the questions used in a goal organizer. As you use a goal organizer, you will find that it helps you do the following:
  - Identify a specific goal and its importance to you
  - Increase awareness and prepare you to deal with possible obstacles you may encounter as you work on your goal
  - Utilize the support of other people and resources

A **goal organizer** is a chart that consists of six questions to help plan a course of action to achieve a specific goal.

CONCEPT CHECK 4.6

What is the value of a goal organizer? How can it assist you in achieving a specific goal?

FIGURE 4.3 The Goal Organizer

1. What is your goal?
2. What benefits will you gain by achieving this goal?
3. What consequences will you experience by *not* achieving this goal?
4. What obstacles might you encounter while working on this goal?
5. How can you deal with the obstacles effectively if they occur?
6. What people or resources could help you with achieving this goal?

EXERCISE 4.3

Achieving an Immediate Goal

PURPOSE: Select an immediate goal that you can complete within the next day or two. Use the GPS Strategy steps to tackle a small task that you would like to accomplish but keep putting off doing.

DIRECTIONS: On a separate piece of paper, complete each of the following steps.

1. **Complete the following steps of the GPS Strategy.**

   Step 1: What is your specific goal, with a specific target date and time to complete? Write a clear, specific goal complete with a completion date and time.

   Step 2: What is the purpose of this goal? Why is it important? Why do you want it done? Write a clear statement that explains your purpose for this goal.

   Step 3: What are the individual steps you must complete to achieve the goal? Are there subgoals with separate timelines? Are there specific supplies, materials, or resources you need to have available for one or more of the steps? Write the specific steps you need to work through to achieve your goal.

2. **Implement your plan of action**. Begin working to complete each step as soon as possible.
3. **After your target date and time pass, respond to the following questions:**

   Did you achieve your goal by the target date and time? If yes, explain what contributed to your success. If no, describe the obstacles that interfered with the process.

CONCEPT CHECK 4.7

What potential problems can you avoid by using all five steps to set goals and create a plan of action for a term-long project?

Goals for Term-Long Projects

Term-long projects occur when early in the term instructors assign a project, such as a research report, a group project, or a portfolio project, that is not due until later in the term. Following are situations students often face with term-long projects:

- **False sense of time:** Rather than start immediately, they believe the project will not take long, so they start on the project too close to its due date, often neglecting their other study times and classes in order to meet the deadline.
- **Procrastination:** Not sure how to manage the project, they postpone starting. Instead of identifying the steps that need to be done and beginning the project as soon as it is assigned, they wait too long to begin, and they run out of time. This creates unnecessary stress and may lower the quality of the work.

When faced with term-long projects, use the strategies in **Figure 4.4** to guide you through the steps to complete your project on time. Taking time to create and then follow your plan of action results in completion of your project on time. This process also provides you with sufficient time to produce quality work that reflects your abilities. **Figure 4.5** shows the format to use to create your plan of action for a term-long project.

FIGURE 4.4 Setting Goals for a Term-Long Project

Step 1: Break the assignment into specific tasks. Analyze the project carefully until you can identify the individual tasks involved for the entire project. List these tasks or steps on paper.

Step 2: Estimate the time needed for each task. Estimate the number of hours you think you will need to complete each task. Base this estimate on your past experiences with similar projects. Write the estimates next to each task.

Step 3: Double the estimated time needed for each task. To avoid running short on time or to counteract underestimating the time you will need, double your estimate. Doubling your estimated time also gives you a safety net to deal with any unforeseen problems. Planning too much time for a project always is better than running out of time to finish a project or having too little time to produce quality work that you are proud to turn in.

Step 4: Record target dates on your term calendar for each task. Plan target dates and times to complete each step. Identify time each week on your weekly schedule to work on specific steps for the term-long project. If you finish a task ahead of schedule, adjust your calendars and begin working on the next task.

Step 5: Begin immediately. Do not waste time or add unnecessary stress by procrastinating. Give yourself all the time possible to produce a quality project that reflects your abilities.

FIGURE 4.5 Example of Format for Planning a Term-Long Project

STEP 1: List the tasks	STEP 2: Estimated time	STEP 3: Doubled time
1.	3 hrs.	6 hrs.
2.	3 hrs.	6 hrs.
3.	2 hrs.	4 hrs.
4.	4 hrs.	8 hrs.
5.	5 hrs.	10 hrs.
	Time Needed:	34 hrs.

STEP 4: Schedule time on your term schedule and your weekly time-management schedule to complete each task.

Weeks 1 and 2: Do Task 1 (6 hours).

Weeks 3 and 4: Do Task 2 (6 hours).

Week 5: Do Task 3 (4 hours).

Weeks 6 and 7: Do Task 4 (8 hours).

Weeks 8 and 9: Do Task 5 (10 hours).

STEP 5: Begin immediately.

EXERCISE 4.4

Transfer These Skills: A Term-Long Project

DIRECTIONS: In Figure 4.4, you learned five steps for setting goals for a term-long project. Complete the following steps.

1. Identify a term-long project you have in one of your classes this term. The term-long project may be a research paper, compiling a portfolio for the term, or completing some other individual or group project. If you do not have a term-long project, you can select the "Optional Term-Long Project" included here.
2. Use the five steps for setting a goal for a term-long project. Write your plan of action with these five steps. Your instructor may ask you at the end of the term to discuss your success in achieving the goal you identified.

OPTIONAL TERM-LONG GOAL: CREATE AN ESSENTIAL STUDY SKILLS STRATEGY RESOURCE NOTEBOOK

1. Create your own *Essential Study Skills Strategy Notebook* to use as a reference resource for future classes throughout your college years.
2. Throughout the term, identify essential strategies from each chapter in your textbook that are useful to you. You may photocopy any charts, forms, or lists that you would like to have in your resource notebook for future use or reference.
3. Remove the Essential Test-Taking Skills Guide in Appendix A. Include it in your notebook.
4. Organize your notebook so it is functional, useful, and easy to manage. Use dividers to label different sections of information.

Strategies to Achieve Goals

Task schedules and the GPS Strategy for setting goals are plans of action to achieve specific outcomes. Creating plans of action for any goal increases the likelihood that you will complete the goal. However, knowing *how to write or create goals* is only the first step to becoming a skillful goal setter. Knowing *how to complete or achieve goals* is the true sign of an effective, skillful goal setter. **Figure 4.6** summarizes strategies to achieve goals.

The following strategies from Figure 4.6 provide an extra boost, motivation, or direction for turning your plan of action into reality with successful completion of your goals.

- **Use positive self-talk and affirmations.** Create a positive mindset to increase motivation.
- **Use the ABC Method.** List and prioritize tasks for assignments and goals.
- **Use visualization.** ***Visualizing Success*** is a strategy to strengthen your self-image and belief in your abilities to behave in a specific way, perform at a desired level, and achieve specific goals. Visualizing and then experiencing the completing of goals improves self-image, increases self-confidence, and motivates you to create plans of action and make changes in your life. Use the following steps to imprint positive images of yourself into your memory:

Visualizing Success is a strategy to strengthen your self-image and belief in your abilities to behave in a specific way, perform at a desired level, and achieve specific goals.

1. Close your eyes. Create a picture or an image of yourself, and "watch yourself" performing effectively the steps you identified for a specific goal. Acknowledge the emotions attached to performing well.

FIGURE 4.6 **Strategies to Achieve Goals**

- Use positive self-talk and affirmations.
- Use the ABC Method to prioritize.
- Use visualization and the Visualizing Success strategy.
- Use extrinsic and intrinsic rewards.
- Plan and expect to succeed.
- Evaluate the importance of a goal.
- Analyze your goal-setting strategies.
- Monitor your progress.
- Keep your goals in the forefront.

2. Visualize or "see" yourself receiving the rewards for your behavior, performance, and completion of the goal. Feel the sense of pride, accomplishment, or success.
3. Practice "rerunning" the visualization several times and recalling it from memory to use as a motivator.

- **Use extrinsic and intrinsic rewards.** Plan a reward to celebrate the completion of a goal. You can use that reward as an incentive—a motivator—to achieve your goal. For any rewards to work as motivators, the rewards should truly represent what you *want* and look forward to receiving. You can use two kinds of rewards in your goal-setting plan: extrinsic rewards and intrinsic rewards.
  - ***Extrinsic rewards*** are material things, incentives, or activities that are awarded when a goal is achieved. Buying a CD, going to a movie, going out to dinner, or planning a short trip are examples of extrinsic rewards. An extrinsic reward is a strong motivator only if you use it *after* you achieve the goal. You must also withhold the reward if you do not achieve or complete the goal.
  - ***Intrinsic rewards*** are emotions or feelings that a person experiences when a goal is achieved. Increased self-esteem, pride, relief, joy, confidence, or immense satisfaction are examples of intrinsic rewards.
- **Plan and expect to succeed.** Success seldom "just happens." Take the time to plan clear, specific goals and clear, specific plans of action. Develop a mindset that shows you expect to succeed and achieve your goals. Erase doubts, hesitations, negative self-talk, and lack of initiative.
- **Evaluate the importance of a goal.** Goals, especially long-term goals, can become outdated due to changes in values or life circumstances. If a goal is no longer of value to you, replace it with a new, more significant goal. Do not, however, abandon a goal because it is more difficult to achieve or requires more from you than you had originally anticipated.
- **Analyze your goal-setting strategies.** When you do not achieve a goal by a specific target date or do not get the desired outcome, turn such situations into

Extrinsic rewards are material things, incentives, or activities that are awarded when a goal is achieved.

Intrinsic rewards are emotions or feelings that a person experiences when a goal is achieved.

CONCEPT CHECK 4.8

Summarize the strategies to use to increase your likelihood of achieving specific goals. Which strategies work most effectively for you?

learning experiences. Ask yourself the following kinds of questions, and then use your responses to adjust your approach the next time you set goals:

> *Was the goal that I set unrealistically high or too low?*
>
> *Did I feel a lack of purpose or unchallenged?*
>
> *Was the goal high on my priority list of importance?*
>
> *Did I think through the steps carefully when I planned the goal?*
>
> *Did I allot sufficient time on my weekly schedule to work on the goal?*
>
> *Was I sufficiently motivated? Were the incentives valued?*
>
> *Was I motivated by intrinsic or extrinsic motivation?*
>
> *Did I really apply effort and follow my plan of action?*
>
> *What would I do differently if I were to set this goal again?*

- **Monitor your progress.** Create an easy-to-use method, such as checkmarks or stars, to track your progress and show that you are meeting target dates and completing the steps of a goal. Using a calendar, a checklist, or a personal journal can help you monitor your progress and motivate you to stay on course to achieve your goals.
- **Keep your goals in the forefront.** If on occasion you find yourself struggling with your goal-setting plans, your motivation dwindles, your momentum temporarily stalls, or you find yourself ignoring your goals, write your goals on index cards. Place these cards around your house and in your notebook as a constant reminder to spend time each day working toward the outcome.

CHECK POINT 4.1

Answers appear on page B3.

True or False? See Test-Taking Strategies 1–9 in Appendix A.

____ 1. Setting a specific target date to complete a goal can help reduce or eliminate procrastination.

____ 2. Extrinsic rewards include positive feelings, a sense of pride, and relief.

____ 3. Not all immediate and short-term goals are subgoals of long-term goals.

____ 4. The GPS Strategy is ineffective for planning immediate or short-term goals.

____ 5. Lack of goal-setting strategies, lack of a clear direction, and lack of procrastination are the three main reasons people do not complete goals.

____ 6. When planning a term-long project, you should double the estimated time you anticipate needing for only the most difficult tasks on your plan of action.

Access Chapter 4 Practice Quiz 1 in your College Success CourseMate, accessed through *CengageBrain.com*.

Motivation to Achieve Goals

Discuss ways to achieve goals by using intrinsic and extrinsic motivation, the Incentive Theory, the Expectancy Theory, and Maslow's Hierarchy of Needs.

Motivation is the driving force that moves a person to take action, create plans of action, and persevere to achieve goals. Motivation is the feeling, emotion, or desire that becomes the internal driving force to help you achieve goals, change behaviors, and "push on" and not give up. The strength of your motivation to achieve a specific goal or task often determines the intensity and persistence for achieving the goal. Following are important points about motivation:

Motivation is the driving force that moves a person to take action, create plans of action, and persevere to achieve goals.

- Goals motivate. When you use the GPS Strategy to set goals, you identify a purpose for achieving a specific outcome. As you focus on a goal with its desired outcomes, your desire to achieve increases. This motivation increases the likelihood of success.
- High motivation equates to success; low motivation equates to lower achievement, lower performance, and incompletion of goals.
- High motivation results in high self-esteem and self-confidence. Low motivation results in negative results, lack of effort, and low self-confidence.
- Individuals with a high sense of self-efficacy set goals, aim high, and work diligently to achieve goals. With each success, they become even more motivated to continue on a positive path of achievement and productivity.
- Individuals with a low sense of self-efficacy tend not to set goals; they feel frustrated and increasingly become unmotivated. They often feel stuck in a negative pattern without realizing there are ways to get out of the downward spiral.

Intrinsic and Extrinsic Motivation

Two forms of motivation drive people to achieve their goals: intrinsic and extrinsic motivation. ***Intrinsic motivation*** is the driving force to take action that comes from within oneself. Intrinsic motivation, also known as *self-motivation*, uses *intrinsic rewards* (emotions or feelings that a person experiences when a goal is achieved).

Extrinsic motivation is the driving force to take action that comes from incentives outside of oneself. Extrinsic motivation uses *extrinsic rewards*: material things, incentives, feedback, or activities awarded when a goal is achieved.

Intrinsic motivation is the driving force to take action that comes from within oneself.

Extrinsic motivation is the driving force to take action that comes from incentives outside of oneself.

Intrinsic Motivation

Intrinsic motivation is the most powerful and effective form of motivation because you "own" it, give it personal meaning, importance, and conviction. The outcome is rewarding and personally fulfilling. Intrinsic motivation often provides the platform for achieving peak performance, striving for a new, meaningful experience, or embracing personal growth. The following are common sources of intrinsic motivation:

- A desire to fulfill a basic need, such as food, shelter, or financial security
- A personal commitment to take action to change and improve some area of your life that is significant and important to you
- A personal challenge to move outside your comfort zone to take on something new without a fear of failure or self-doubt

- An internal desire and personal choice to engage in behaviors or actions that bring feelings of pride, joy, victory, sense of accomplishment, increased self-esteem, or uplifting personal satisfaction (intrinsic rewards)
- A desire to affirm your self-image, live by your values, and prove your abilities to yourself

Extrinsic Motivation

CONCEPT CHECK 4.9

How do intrinsic and extrinsic motivation differ? Why is intrinsic motivation so powerful?

The second type of motivation is extrinsic motivation. Rewards, recognition, praise, prizes, or income are typical motivators for extrinsic motivation. Another common form of extrinsic motivation is a desire to please or meet expectations of parents, family members, friends, employers, or colleagues. You look to them for approval, praise, positive feedback, and acknowledgment of your own value. For many people, work or employment is driven by the extrinsic motivation to earn an income, make money to pay bills, and acquire sufficient funds to enjoy other activities, such as entertainment or travel. Many business models use extrinsic motivation by offering incentives to encourage employees to develop specific behaviors, increase work performance, or achieve company goals. Special programs, such as acknowledging an employee of the month, awarding a prime parking space to a top performer, presenting a plaque for achievement, or providing salary increases based on performance, are all incentives designed to boost extrinsic motivation. Following are important points about extrinsic motivation:

CONCEPT CHECK 4.10

What is extrinsic motivation? When might it be effective? What extrinsic rewards motivate you?

- To work effectively, the incentives need to be meaningful and valued. Incentives with low value or interest are not motivators. Incentives with high value are motivators that energize individuals to apply effort and perform.
- Incentives become goals as individuals strive to excel or to receive an award, recognition, praise, pay raise, promotion, or prize.
- Extrinsic rewards such as praise, positive feedback, or acknowledgment need to be sincere, honest, and based on genuine accomplishments to work as extrinsic motivators.
- Extrinsic motivation often relies on someone else to provide the motivation; consequently, individuals may focus their attention on extrinsic rather than intrinsic rewards.
- You can convert extrinsic motivation to intrinsic motivation by shifting your focus and attaching a personal value, interest, or importance to the goal. In other words, strive to convert your extrinsic motivation to intrinsic motivation so your main purpose is to achieve for yourself and for intrinsic rewards—not for the main purpose of pleasing others.

Three Theories of Motivation

Motivation is the driving force that moves a person to take action, create plans of action, and persevere to achieve goals. Positive results build self-confidence, boost self-esteem, and strengthen motivation to take on new goals. Thus, it should not be surprising that researchers, educators, corporate managers, counselors, and motivational speakers continue to explore ways to understand and tap into the power of motivation.

Three theories provide informative perspectives on motivation: The Incentive Theory, the Expectancy Theory, and Maslow's Hierarchy of Basic Needs.

EXERCISE 4.5

Textbook Case Studies

DIRECTIONS:

1. Read each case study carefully. Respond to the question at the end of each case study by using *specific* strategies discussed in this chapter. Answer in complete sentences.
2. Write your responses on paper or online in this textbook's College Success CourseMate, Textbook Case Studies. You will be able to print your online response or e-mail it to your instructor.

CASE STUDY 1: Cary really wants to change his lifestyle. He wants to quit smoking, and he wants to manage his assignments with less stress. He says he wants to feel more in control of his life. When asked how he is going to accomplish these resolutions, he says he's going to quit smoking "cold turkey" when he's ready because his girlfriend complains about the smell and about his coughing. He's going to try using different strategies for his assignments to see if he can find ways that work better and produce less stress. He wants less chaos and more control. What advice could you give Cary to help him set and achieve his goals?

CASE STUDY 2: Amy is the first to admit that she always runs out of time to complete assignments on time. She's concerned about a research project that is due in eight weeks. She has to create a list of questions, interview four experts in the world of business, summarize findings, explain the outcomes, and relate them to textbook concepts. What strategies could Amy use to set and achieve the goal of completing this assignment on time?

Access Chapter 4 Textbook Case Studies in your College Success CourseMate, accessed through *CengageBrain.com*.

The Incentive Theory of Motivation

The ***Incentive Theory of Motivation*** states that incentives and rewards are the driving forces behind people's choices and behaviors. The incentive or motivation behind specific behaviors may be to receive a desired reward or a positive consequence or to avoid some type of punishment or negative consequence. The following points provide further clarification about the Incentive Theory:

- Incentives motivate people to behave in positive ways. For example, children behave in specific ways to receive a treat or praise. The incentive for many working adults is to receive a decent paycheck. The incentive for many students to study hard is to receive good grades, meet scholarship requirements, be admitted to a desired program, or earn a degree.
- Incentives also motivate people to refrain from negative behaviors that may have negative consequences. A student is motivated *not* to cheat on a test or plagiarize a research paper because of potentially severe consequences.
- Incentives become strong motivators only when the individual places a high value on the incentive and is willing to take action to obtain the reward. Effective incentives energize people and instill a desire to excel.
- To work as motivators, the incentives and rewards must be obtainable. For example, most employees would not be highly motivated by an employer's offer of a week's paid vacation (incentive) if the goal set to receive the award is unrealistically high and most likely unobtainable.

The **Incentive Theory of Motivation** states that incentives and rewards are the driving forces behind people's choices and behaviors.

CONCEPT CHECK 4.11

Why do you think business models tend to use the Incentive Theory to motivate employees? What makes incentives work effectively as motivators?

- You use this Incentive Theory of Motivation each time you use a goal organizer or the GPS Strategy. Asking questions such as the following focus your attention on the value, importance, and consequences of striving to achieve a specific goal.
  - *What benefits will I gain by achieving this goal?*
  - *What is the purpose, value, or meaning of this goal?*
  - *What negative consequences will I experience by not achieving this goal?*
  - *Will not achieving this goal hurt me or my future opportunities in any way?*

CONCEPT CHECK 4.12

Why is the self-fulfilling prophecy concept an integral part of the Expectancy Theory of Motivation? In what ways do your beliefs affect your ability to complete goals?

The Expectancy Theory of Motivation

The **Expectancy Theory of Motivation** states that the degree of motivation is determined by a person's belief in the likelihood, desire, and ability to achieve a specific outcome or goal. This theory is based on the concept of *self-fulfilling prophecy*. **Self-fulfilling prophecy** is a belief that what one thinks or believes is what will become reality. In other words, "What you think is what you get." When you exhibit self-confidence to succeed, and you believe you are worthy and capable of achieving a specific goal, your attitude and expectancy to succeed motivate you to give your very best to achieve that goal. However, if you exhibit hesitancy or self-doubt, or question your ability or interest in achieving a goal, the result is lower motivation and the expectancy not to achieve the goal. The excerpt in **Figure 4.7** explains the Expectancy Theory.

The **Expectancy Theory of Motivation** states that the degree of motivation is determined by a person's belief in the likelihood, desire, and ability to achieve a specific outcome or goal.

Self-fulfilling prophecy is a belief that what one thinks or believes is what will become reality.

FIGURE 4.7 Expectancy Theory of Motivation

Expectancy Theory, developed by Victor Vroom, is a very complex model of motivation based on a deceptively simple assumption. According to the expectancy theory, motivation depends on how much we want something and on how likely we think we are to get it. Consider, for example, the case of three sales representatives who are candidates for promotion to one sales manager's job. Bill has had a very good sales year and always gets good performance eval- uations. However, he isn't sure he wants the job because it involves a great deal of travel, long working hours, and much stress and pressure. Paul wants the job badly but doesn't think he has much chance of getting it. He has had a terrible sales year and gets only mediocre performance evaluations from his present boss. Susan wants the job as much as Paul, and she thinks she has a pretty good shot at it. Her sales have improved significantly this past year, and her evaluations are the best in the company.

Expectancy theory would predict that Bill and Paul are not very motivated to seek the promotion. Bill doesn't really want it, and Paul doesn't think he has much of a chance of getting it. Susan, however, is very motivated to seek the promotion because she wants it *and* thinks she can get it.

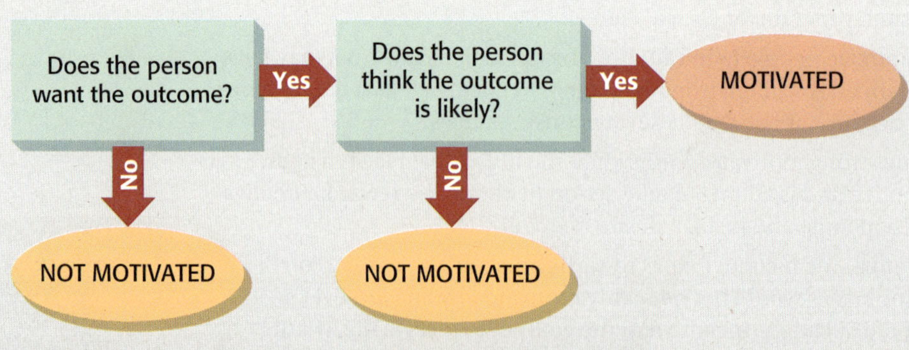

From Pride/Hughes/Kapoor, *Business*, 12E. © 2014 Cengage Learning

Maslow's Hierarchy of Needs for Motivation

In 1970, American psychologist Abraham Maslow suggested that human behavior is influenced or motivated by categories of needs. ***Maslow's Hierarchy of Needs*** is a theory that identifies five categories of human needs, from the most basic to the most difficult to achieve. The lowest level of needs is level 1, physiological survival needs; individuals are motivated to fulfill those needs first. According to Maslow's theory, as lower level needs are fulfilled, individuals become motivated to fulfill the needs on the higher levels. **Figure 4.8** (page 118) shows the order of needs that motivate human behavior. Following are important points about Maslow's Hierarchy of Needs:

- Even though Maslow's hierarchy has been referred to extensively in many fields of study, some critics believe the hierarchy is too simplistic and argue that one level of needs does not need to be completely fulfilled before working on higher levels of needs. For example, can a person be motivated to meet the need of love and belonging if he or she is still working on goals to feel safe and secure?
- Another point of discussion is whether the levels of needs must be satisfied in a specific order. Could it be that individuals are motivated by different levels of needs as they move from one situation to another? For example, if a person feels defeated after losing a job or after going through a divorce, could that person possibly become motivated to improve esteem needs before applying for a new position or looking for a new relationship?
- Being familiar with the levels of needs may help explain why you are motivated to achieve specific goals. When you set a goal and strive to identify the purpose of the goal, ask yourself, *Why is this important to me?* Your answer may relate directly to one of the five levels of needs in Maslow's Hierarchy.

Maslow's Hierarchy of Needs is a theory that identifies five categories of human needs, from the most basic to the most difficult to achieve.

CONCEPT CHECK 4.13

Do you believe you must fulfill the needs on a specific level in Maslow's Hierarchy before you are motivated to move up to the needs on the next higher level? Explain your answer.

CHECK POINT 4.2

Answers appear on page B3.

True or False? See Test-Taking Strategies 1–9 in Appendix A.

____ 1. Extrinsic motivation based on physical, monetary, or intrinsic rewards tends to be the most powerful form of motivation for adults.

____ 2. As extrinsic motivators gain momentum, a person may convert them to intrinsic motivators to attach more meaning, purpose, or value to them.

____ 3. Incentives may motivate people to behave in positive ways or refrain from behaving in negative ways with negative consequences.

____ 4. The self-fulfilling prophecy concept reflects a person's attitudes and beliefs.

____ 5. A person can refer to Maslow's Hierarchy of Needs to try to understand what needs he or she is trying to fulfill when striving to achieve a specific goal.

____ 6. Setting goals, using a goal organizer, and boosting a sense of self-efficacy can work as motivators to persevere to achieve goals.

Access Chapter 4 Practice Quiz 2 in your College Success CourseMate, accessed through *CengageBrain.com*.

FIGURE 4.8 Maslow's Hierarchy of Needs

If you were very hungry and very lonely at the same time, which need would you satisfy first, your biological need (hunger) or your social need (affiliation)? One answer to this question can be found in Maslow's (1970) hierarchy of needs.

Maslow's hierarchy of needs is an ascending order, or hierarchy, in which biological needs are placed at the bottom and social needs at the top.

Level 5 Self-Actualization: Fulfillment of One's Unique Potential

According to Maslow, the highest need is self-actualization, which involves developing and reaching our full potential as unique human beings. However, Maslow cautioned that very few individuals reach the level of self-actualization because it is so difficult and challenging.

Level 4 Esteem Needs: Achievement, Competency, Approval, and Recognition

During early and middle adulthood, people are especially concerned with achieving their goals and establishing their careers. As we develop skills to gain personal achievement and social recognition, we turn our energies to Level 5.

Level 3 Love and Belonging Needs: Affiliation with Others and Acceptance by Others

Adolescents and young adults, who are beginning to form serious relationships, would be especially interested in fulfilling their needs for love and belonging. After we find love and affection, we advance to Level 4.

Level 2 Safety Needs: Protection from Harm

People who live in high-crime or dangerous areas would be very concerned about satisfying their safety needs. After we find a way to live in a safe environment, we advance to Level 3.

Level 1 Physiological Needs: Food, Water, Sex, and Sleep

People who are homeless or jobless would be especially concerned with satisfying their physiological needs above all other needs. We must satisfy these basic needs before we advance to Level 2.

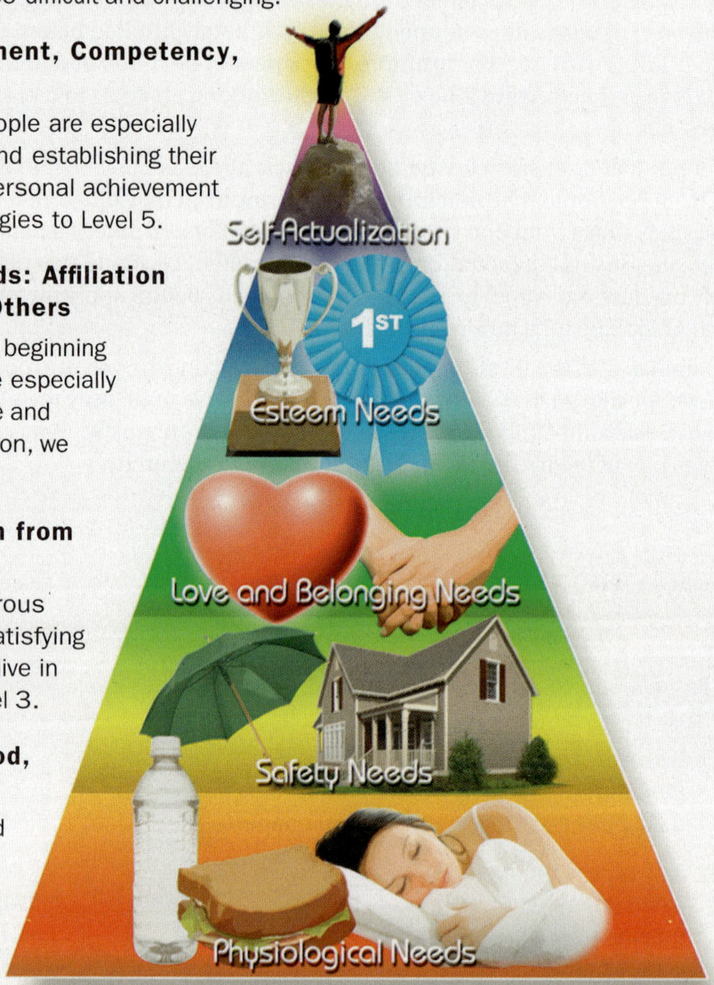

Goal: Become a Stress Manager

Explain how to become a stress manager by using coping, relaxation, and intrapersonal strategies to combat stressors.

Stress is a reaction or response to events or situations that threaten or disrupt a person's normal patterns or routines. Stress is the wear and tear on our bodies due to physical, emotional, cognitive, and behavioral responses. The following are important points about stress:

- Some stress is normal as we move through life, making decisions and changing directions in our personal, work, and academic lives.
- In some situations, stress is beneficial. Stress can compel us to take action and to move in new directions. The increased adrenaline from stress can help us perform at higher levels.
- As stress increases, our ability to deal with and control the stress decreases.
- Early warning signs that stress is becoming more intense and moving into the danger level include headaches, backaches, insomnia, fatigue, anxiety attacks, mood swings, depression, forgetfulness, carelessness, and irritability.
- You can learn more about stress by reading Excerpt 1: Understanding Stress and Stressors in Appendix D.

Stress is a reaction or response to events or situations that threaten or disrupt a person's normal patterns or routines.

Creating a Goal to Reduce Stress

If you experience stress on a regular basis or stress seems to increase in intensity or frequency, creating a goal to change patterns or behaviors to reduce stress is important. Learning to manage stress is a lifelong skill that affects the quality of life and longevity. It is not something you simply accomplish in one week and then set aside as a completed goal. Reducing stress is important for a variety of reasons:

- Excessive stress hinders performance and affects cognitive functions. Excessive stress affects memory processes and reduces the ability to concentrate, solve problems, and make wise decisions.
- Excessive stress from unresolved issues has physical consequences: increased pulse rate, faster breathing, higher blood pressure, a weakening of the immune system, a decrease in the production of endorphins (a neurochemical that makes us feel happy), ulcers, heart attacks, strokes, and clinical depression.
- Excessive stress may turn into anxiety. Test anxiety, which hinders performance and results in physical, emotional, cognitive, and behavioral consequences, is one of several kinds of anxiety that results from excessive stress.

Stressors

To create a goal to manage stress more effectively, begin by identifying your stressors. **Stressors** are situations or actions that cause stress. How you *perceive* and *handle* external situations or stressors—rather than the situations themselves—is the cause of stress. Taking some form of action to reduce or eliminate stressors empowers you to have greater control over your stress and to alter your perception of external situations. For example, if an upcoming test is a stressor, you can create a plan of action and use specific techniques to take control of the situation. Other stressors, such as the terminal illness of a loved one, are out of

Stressors are situations or actions that cause stress.

EXERCISE 4.6

Stress Test

DIRECTIONS: Go to Exercise 4.6 in Appendix C, page C10, to complete the Social Readjustment Rating Scale (Stress Test). You will be asked to circle all the events (stressors) you have experienced in the past 12 months. Each event has a point value. After totaling all the point values for events, you will be able to identify your stress level score.

CONCEPT CHECK **4.14**

Is stress always bad? Explain. What might happen if you experience stress but do not create goals to manage your stress?

your immediate control; the only control you have is how you handle your reaction to the stressor.

Stressors may be positive or negative. Divorce, personal injury, loss of a job, or family problems are negative stressors. Events such as marriage or a vacation may be positive stressors. The number of stressors you face at one time, both positive and negative, affect your overall stress level. In 1967, Dr. Thomas H. Holmes and Dr. Richard H. Rahe developed a "stress test," the Social Readjustment Rating Scale (SRRS), to help individuals identify their stress levels. The stressors and the stress scores on SRRS remain applicable today. (See **Exercise 4.6**.)

Essential Strategies for Managing Stress

Managing stress involves active participation on your part to change habits, behaviors, and emotional attitudes. After identifying your stress levels and stressors, create a plan of action to implement the effective stress-management strategies that appear in **Figure 4.9**.

FIGURE 4.9 Essential Strategies for Managing Stress

- Use coping strategies. (See Figure 4.10.)
- Use positive self-talk, affirmations, and visualizations.
- Seek social support from family and friends.
- Use time management and goal setting to organize yourself.
- Avoid chaos, clutter, and confusion by setting priorities.
- Engage in physical activity.
- Choose a healthy lifestyle. (See Excerpt 3 in Appendix D.)
- Use relaxation strategies.
- Calm yourself with meditation, guided imagery, Visualizing Success, yoga, or soothing environments.
- Keep a journal; sort your feelings out by writing and expressing ideas.

FIGURE 4.10 Methods for Coping with Stress

Type of Coping Method	Examples
Cognitive	Thinking of stressors as challenges rather than as threats; avoiding perfectionism
Emotional	Seeking social support; getting advice
Behavioral	Implementing a time-management plan; when possible, making life changes to eliminate stress
Physical	Using progressive relaxation; meditation; exercise

Source: Bernstein/Nash, *Essentials of Psychology*, 4e, Houghton Mifflin Company, © 2008, p. 414. Reprinted with permission.

Coping Strategies

Coping strategies are cognitive, emotional, behavioral, and physical strategies used to manage and overcome stressors and difficult situations. **Figure 4.10** shows examples of the four main coping methods.

- ***Cognitive coping strategies*** involve changing the way a person thinks and perceives stressors. Instead of perceiving a situation as hopeless, frightening, or insurmountable, use motivational strategies, such as positive self-talk, affirmations, and Visualizing Success, to alter your perception of the situation. Look at the situation as an opportunity to use your problem-solving skills to create a plan of action to overcome the situation.
- ***Emotional coping strategies*** involve identifying and expressing emotions to other people. Having a strong, positive social support network of friends, family, and coworkers provides you with an outlet to share your emotions, analyze the reality of situations, brainstorm solutions, and receive support and encouragement. Many research studies show that social interaction can reduce stress, improve overall health and the immune system, stimulate cognitive processes, and stave off depression. Not sharing your stress and frustrations may result in *catastrophic thinking*, a state of mind in which your perception of the problem and its severity becomes distorted and greatly exaggerated. Left unchecked, your stress level increases and your ability to manage stress decreases.
- ***Behavioral coping strategies*** involve changing patterns or behaviors to address the source of stress. For example, you can use a time-management schedule as well as goal-setting and test-preparation strategies to reduce stress about an upcoming test. If the source of your stress includes procrastinating about doing a specific task, such as finalizing financial aid papers, applying for a scholarship, or filing your taxes, using goal-setting strategies helps you deal with the source of the stress. Changing your behavior by using strategies to increase motivation, set goals, and stop procrastination will eliminate the stressor.
- ***Physical coping strategies*** involve the use of physical activity to reduce or eliminate a person's response to specific stressors. Engaging in activities that create positive emotions reduces the intensity of your emotional reaction to stress and the tendency to dwell on negative situations. Redirecting your

Coping strategies are cognitive, emotional, behavioral, and physical strategies used to manage and overcome stressors and difficult situations.

Cognitive coping strategies involve changing the way a person thinks and perceives stressors.

Emotional coping strategies involve identifying and expressing emotions to other people.

Behavioral coping strategies involve changing patterns or behaviors to address the source of stress.

CONCEPT CHECK 4.15

Describe the four categories of coping strategies and one specific technique or strategy for each category.

Physical coping strategies involve the use of physical activity to reduce or eliminate a person's response to specific stressors.

emotions by spending time on a favorite hobby, exercising, or using relaxation techniques reduces the physiological effects of stress.

Relaxation Techniques

Relaxation techniques can help reduce stress levels, improve emotional health, and create a state of mind and body that perhaps can best be described as "Ahhhhhhh." In a relaxed state, the body is not tense and the mind is not wandering; you are alert and ready to learn. Relaxation techniques help you manage emotional situations, such as anxiety, nervousness, tension, stress, apprehension, hyperactivity, restlessness, and feelings of defeat, frustration, or being overwhelmed. The following six easy-to-use relaxation techniques require only a few minutes of your time. Try each technique, select ones that work well for you, and use them on a regular basis.

CONCEPT CHECK 4.16

What is the value of using relaxation techniques? Which of the specific relaxation strategies work most effectively for you to reduce your stressors?

The **perfect place technique** involves taking a mental vacation and visualizing a perfect, stress-free place to relax.

- The ***perfect place technique*** involves taking a mental vacation and visualizing a perfect, stress-free place to relax. Use the following steps for this technique:
  1. Close your eyes, breathe in slowly, and visualize a perfect place where you feel relaxed, confident, safe, comfortable, and content.
  2. Continue breathing in and out slowly as you create this mental picture of a perfect place. Make your image more vivid by adding sounds, smells, sights, tastes, and tactile sensations.
  3. Use the power of association to recall the mental picture and the soothing sensations of this perfect place whenever you need to separate yourself in a healthy way from stress and stressful situations.

The **soothing mask technique** involves using imagination to create and pull a mask over your face to block out reactions to stress.

- The ***soothing mask technique*** involves using imagination to create and pull a mask over your face to block out reactions to stress. Use the following steps for this technique:
  1. Close your eyes and place your hands on the top of your head.
  2. Slowly move your hands down your forehead, down your face, and to your neck. As you do this, picture your hands gently pulling a *soothing mask* over your face, removing worries, fears, or stresses from your mind.
  3. Keep your eyes closed for another minute. Feel the soothing mask resting on your face, blocking out stressful thoughts or feelings. As you practice this technique, you will be able to visualize the soothing mask without using your hands.

The **relaxation blanket technique** involves visualizing pulling a soft, warm blanket up to your neck to release tension.

- The ***relaxation blanket technique*** involves visualizing pulling a soft, warm blanket up to your neck to release tension. Use the following steps for this technique:
  1. Sit comfortably in your chair, close your eyes, and focus your attention on your feet.
  2. Imagine pulling a soft, warm blanket up over your feet, up over your legs, lap, and chest until the blanket is snuggled around your shoulders and against your neck. Focus on the way your body feels warm and relaxed.
  3. Keep your eyes closed for another minute as you enjoy the warmth and comfort of the blanket. Recall this feeling during times of stress.

- The ***breathing by threes technique*** involves inhaling and exhaling slowly as a way to reduce stress. Use the following steps for this technique:
  1. Count to three as you inhale slowly through your nose. Count to three as you hold your breath. Finally, count to three as you exhale slowly.
  2. Repeat this several times. You will feel your body begin to slow down and relax. Use this any time you feel an onset of stress.

The **breathing by threes technique** involves inhaling and exhaling slowly as a way to reduce stress.

- The ***deep breathing technique*** involves taking deep breaths and exhaling slowly as a way to reduce stress. Use the following steps for this technique:
  1. Take a deep breath to fill your lungs. You may think your lungs are full, but there is room for one more breath of air. Inhale once again.
  2. Now slowly exhale and feel your body relax.
  3. Repeat this deep breathing several times. If you feel lightheaded or dizzy after trying this exercise, discontinue and use an alternative relaxation technique.

The **deep breathing technique** involves taking deep breaths and exhaling slowly as a way to reduce stress.

- The ***deep muscle relaxation technique*** involves tensing and releasing different groups of muscles as a way to reduce stress. Use the following steps for this technique:
  1. Identify the areas of your body where you feel tension.
  2. Make a clenched fist tight enough so that you can feel your fingers pulsating. Breathe several times, feel the tension in your fingers and your hands, and then breathe slowly as you uncurl your fists until they are totally relaxed. Pay close attention to the different sensations as you go from tense to relaxed.
  3. Continue this with other muscle groups that tend to hold tension: shoulders, arms, lower back, legs, chest, fingers, or face. As you work to release tension from your different muscle groups, your total body moves into a state of greater relaxation.

The **deep muscle relaxation technique** involves tensing and releasing different groups of muscles as a way to reduce stress.

Intrapersonal Strategies

Intrapersonal intelligence involves developing skills related to personal growth, self-understanding, self-motivation, intuition, and spirituality. Using intrapersonal skills shifts your focus from the outside world to your inner world—your thoughts, feelings, inspirations, and goals. Following are three ways to use your intrapersonal skills to reduce or eliminate stress.

1. **Take time to center yourself.** Engage in a mind-calming activity such as meditation, yoga, prayer, or biofeedback to center yourself and return to a state of calmness and serenity. Sitting in a sauna, soaking in a hot tub or warm bath, or sitting near a fountain of water can also be a mind-calming experience. Centering activities provide a way to block out and temporarily shield yourself from the rest of the world.
2. **Keep a journal.** In a journal, describe your feelings or concerns privately and tap into some of your innermost thoughts in a nonthreatening way. Putting your emotions on paper often reduces the intensity of the emotions, disperses some of the negative energy, and helps you discover solutions or new directions to take with the situation.

3. **Strive to strengthen self-esteem.** As you recall from Figure 2.3, positive self-talk, high achievement, positive perception of self and others, rewarding relationships, and improved self-confidence are characteristics of high self-esteem, which often reflect fewer stressors than the characteristics associated with low self-esteem. Using strategies to boost your confidence, your self-perception, and your self-esteem provides you with additional coping strategies to reduce the effects of stressors.

CHECK POINT 4.3

Answers appear in B3.

Multiple Choice See Test-Taking Strategies 10–15 in Appendix A.

 1. Which statement is *not* true about stress?
   a. Excessive stress hinders performance and cognitive abilities.
   b. With effective stress-management skills, a person can avoid experiencing stress.
   c. In some situations, stress can be beneficial.
   d. Stress is caused by the ways you perceive and handle stressors.

 2. You can learn to handle or manage stress by
   a. using relaxation strategies and shifting your focus from a negative stressor to a more positive activity.
   b. creating a strong support network.
   c. using cognitive or behavioral coping strategies.
   d. doing all of the above.

 3. Which of the following statements is inaccurate?
   a. Stressors are often created by external situations.
   b. Ignoring stress is often an effective strategy to help it go away.
   c. Excessive stress may become anxiety and may cause physical illnesses.
   d. Both positive and negative stressors can disrupt a person's normal daily pattern or routine.

Access Chapter 4 Practice Quiz 3 in your College Success CourseMate, accessed through *CengageBrain.com*.

Goal: Become a Procrastination Manager

4 *Explain how to become a procrastination manager by using effective strategies to identify and reduce procrastination.*

Procrastination is a learned behavior that involves putting off or postponing something until a later time.

Procrastination is a learned behavior that involves putting off or postponing something until a later time. Chronic procrastinators have ingrained certain behavioral and cognitive patterns into their way of "doing life." They consistently choose low-priority tasks over high-priority tasks. Fortunately, because procrastination is a learned behavior, it can be unlearned, reduced, or eliminated.

Do you know any procrastinators? Procrastinators often exhibit the following characteristics:

- Accept and even boast about being procrastinators
- Pride themselves on being able to do things quickly, at the last minute, and under pressure

- Often wait for a "push," a threat of a specific consequence, a crisis, or some outside force to get the momentum to do what needs to be done
- Focus on proving they can complete a task in a short time frame, but may show little concern about the quality of the final product
- Use their procrastination as a legitimate excuse for not performing on high levels or not completing projects

Habitual or chronic procrastinators can create new behavioral and cognitive patterns that place a higher value on working first on high-priority tasks—even when they may not be as exciting or enjoyable as the low-priority tasks. Managing and reducing procrastination begins by understanding when and why procrastination occurs.

Stockbyte/Getty Images

Procrastinators put off or postpone tasks for a variety of reasons and tend to choose low-priority tasks. Often they attempt to rationalize or justify their behavior. When and why do you procrastinate?

When You Procrastinate

Any time you find yourself avoiding a specific task or making statements such as "I'll do it when I am in the mood," "I have plenty of time to do it later," "I can let it slide a few more days," or "I will wait because I work better under pressure," recognize that you most likely are procrastinating. Become aware of your procrastination patterns and *when* you procrastinate. **Place a check next to the statements that describe you.**

____**I tend to procrastinate when faced with specific kinds of tasks.** Any time you procrastinate, examine the task that you are postponing or avoiding. You may find yourself procrastinating about doing tasks that are uninteresting, too challenging or confusing, or difficult. For example, do you plan and follow through with studying for your computer class but procrastinate about studying for your writing or your math class? Do you empty the dishwasher but procrastinate when faced with doing the laundry? Examine the tasks involved when you procrastinate to look for patterns or kinds of tasks that trigger your procrastination. Formulate a plan of action to change your attitude and reaction to the task.

____**I tend to procrastinate about beginning a specific task.** If you drag your feet and make excuses to avoid beginning a task, the source of your procrastination may be due to lack of motivation, lack of confidence in your ability to do the work, confusion about what steps are involved, or uncertainty about how to begin to tackle the task. Breaking the task down, setting goals, using the GPS Strategy, identifying incentives, and placing the task higher on your priority list can help you break through your procrastination pattern.

____**I tend to start tasks but then procrastinate during the middle of the process.** When procrastination sets in during the middle of a process, you may have lost interest, motivation, or a sense of purpose in persevering to completion. Other times you may find procrastination in the middle of a process occurs due to time-related issues: you underestimate the length of time needed, you have other demands on your time that seem more urgent, or you fail to use your time-management skills and schedules. As soon as your momentum starts to shift, create a plan of action that utilizes strategies to boost your time-management, goal-setting, and motivation skills.

CONCEPT CHECK 4.17

What are common learned behaviors of procrastinators that would be beneficial to "unlearn"?

____**I procrastinate close to the end of the completion of a task.** Procrastinating close to the completion of a task or project is a way to quit and to avoid the final results. The underlying cause may be related to fear: fear of being evaluated or judged on your work, fear of failure, or fear of success. People who fear success become concerned that excellence on performance will put pressure on them to repeat that level of excellence on future tasks as well. Use strategies such as visualizing success, positive self-talk, incentives, and a goal organizer to motivate yourself to finish the task.

____**I tend to start multiple tasks, jumping from one to another, and making less important tasks seem more important or urgent.** This behavior is a common sign of the onset of procrastination. Procrastinators can get so caught up in this whirlwind behavior that they do not realize all the busy work is a mask for avoiding specific tasks. When you find yourself scurrying around, sometimes aimlessly keeping busy, take time to identify the task you are avoiding. Use the ABC Method for prioritizing the tasks you need to accomplish. Focus your attention on the tasks with highest importance and refrain from dedicating time to the less urgent or low-priority tasks.

CONCEPT CHECK **4.18**

Why is it important to analyze behavior patterns to identify when and why you procrastinate? Give examples of when and why you sometimes procrastinate.

Why You Procrastinate

Reasons for procrastinating vary for different tasks, situations, and individuals. In some cases, procrastinating will not have any serious consequences. For example, procrastinating about moving a stack of magazines to the garage or putting your CDs back in their cases has no dire consequences. In other cases, procrastinating leads to increased stress and additional problems. Procrastinating about paying your bills, studying for a test, or filling your tires with air will have more serious consequences, some of which could alter your goals or course for the future.

We all procrastinate at one time or another. When you are aware of *why* you procrastinate, dig deep to discover your reason for putting off something important that needs to be done. **Check all of the following behaviors or underlying beliefs that tend to trigger your procrastination:**

____Lack of interest, motivation, or purpose

____Lack of confidence or low self-confidence

____Lack of strategies or skills for the assignment

____Difficulty, complexity, or length of an assignment

____Confusion or lack of know-how

____Weak time-management skills

____Poor judgment of time needed (overestimate or underestimate)

____Fear of failure or fear of success

As you conduct an honest search for the reasons you procrastinate, you may discover additional behaviors or beliefs that trigger this self-defeating pattern of behavior. Understanding both *when* and *why* you procrastinate is the first step to overcome the learned behavior of postponing or avoiding productive activity. **Figure 4.11** summarizes common causes of procrastination.

FIGURE 4.11 Causes of Procrastination

Essential Strategies to Combat Procrastination

Learning to reduce or eliminate procrastination can empower you, enhance your self-esteem, strengthen your self-discipline, and put you in greater control of your life. In addition to the time-management, goal-setting, motivation, and other self-management strategies that you have already learned, you can use the following ten recommended strategies to combat procrastination.

- **Strategy 1: Use your intrapersonal intelligence.** Explore *when* and *why* you procrastinate about a specific task. Use those insights to identify appropriate strategies to deal directly with the underlying issues.

GROUP PROCESSING

A Collaborative Learning Activity

DIRECTIONS: Form groups of three or four students. Each group needs to have a chart to record information. Select one group member to be the group recorder. Complete the following directions.

1. Create a two-column chart. In the left column, brainstorm and list any ten reasons people experience stress or procrastinate about assignments or tasks.
2. In the second column, brainstorm as a group. List as many different strategies a person could use to become a stress manager or a procrastination manager by combating the problems in the left column.

Reason	Strategies
Lack of motivation	• *Use goal organizer to identify importance* • *Break task into steps; use rewards for completing each step*

- **Strategy 2: Identify a purpose and meaning.** Avoid labeling a task as "meaningless, stupid, or boring" or expressing a negative attitude toward a task, as these attitudes and behaviors lower motivation and create a negative mindset. Find a purpose or a valid reason for the task. Use a goal organizer and use the GPS Strategy; identify the benefits.
- **Strategy 3: Create an interest.** Engage a family member, a tutor, or a study group to work with you on the task. Seek alternative sources of information, such as a video, Internet searches, magazines, or books related to the topic. Once you become familiar with the topic, interest often increases.
- **Strategy 4: Take charge of the situation.** Identify and list the steps you need to perform to break the cycle of procrastination about a specific task. Gather up all the supplies or materials you need to get started. Create a goal or a plan of action. Select an appropriate work environment. *Take charge* and take responsibility of the situation.

CONCEPT CHECK 4.19

Explain which strategies to combat procrastination you can use to manage your procrastination. What additional strategies can you suggest to combat procrastination?

- **Strategy 5: Prioritize and stick to the order.** When you feel overwhelmed or overextended, make a list of tasks that must be done. Use the ABC Method to prioritize them by their importance or prioritize them by completion date requirements. Tackle the high-priority tasks first. Schedule time on your weekly schedule to work on these tasks.
- **Strategy 6: Use the GPS Strategy to set goals.** Set goals with due dates and timelines. Identify the goal, the purpose or importance, and the steps to use to get you started and keep you going.
- **Strategy 7: Relax your personal standards.** If you tend to be a perfectionist, lower your unrealistically high standards or expectations. You can continue to produce quality work without always having to be the "best." Avoid spending

excessive time redoing parts of a task or the final outcome, such as a paper, when your work already shows quality.

- **Strategy 8: Be flexible and willing to change.** Be willing to give up the attitude that "I have always done things this way" or the false belief that "I work best under pressure or stress." Be willing to try new strategies and to create new behavior patterns that have the potential to produce higher quality work and reduce stress.
- **Strategy 9: Face your fear of failure.** Focus on your positive traits, your accomplishments, and the skills you have acquired. Use positive self-talk to negate self-doubts, silence self-criticism, and combat the fear of failure. Build your self-confidence by mentally rehearsing the steps of the task several times before you begin.
- **Strategy 10: Visualize success.** Create a mental picture of yourself working through a task, feeling positive about your work, and completing the task on time.
- **Strategy 11: Make a contract with yourself.** Make a contract with yourself to stop using excuses for not getting things done. Begin by creating a plan of action (a goal). Push yourself to "just do it." Finish your contract with an incentive, such as an extrinsic or an intrinsic reward.
- **Strategy 12: Use your interpersonal skills.** Seek the help, advice, and support of friends, family, and other students in class. If you feel you lack the skills or the know-how to do an assignment, meet and discuss the assignment with other students. If your work environment is not conducive to getting tasks done, discuss the situation with family or friends and make the necessary adjustments.

CHECK POINT 4.4

Answers appear on page B3.

True or False? See Test-Taking Strategies 1–9 in Appendix A.

____ 1. Procrastination is a learned behavior that can be reduced or eliminated.

____ 2. Students with a Perceiving personality preference always have problems with procrastination because of their preferred way to structure assignments.

____ 3. If a person starts a task and later procrastinates, he or she may fear failure or find the task to be too complex or difficult.

____ 4. Procrastination often involves selecting high-priority tasks over low-priority tasks.

____ 5. For a chronic procrastinator, procrastination always begins right before he or she is close to completing the task.

____ 6. Low levels of interest, self-confidence, and motivation may all be triggers that cause procrastination.

Access Chapter 4 Practice Quiz 4 in your College Success CourseMate, accessed through *CengageBrain.com*.

Chapter 4 Review Questions

Answers appear on page B3.

Fill-in-the-Blanks See Test-Taking Strategies 21–24 in Appendix A.

1. Visualizing ______________ is the name of a strategy that involves visualizing your performance or completion of a goal.

2. ______________ rewards are not physical incentives but instead are internal feelings, emotions, and responses that motivate a person to perform and achieve goals.

3. The driving force that moves a person to take action, create plans, and persevere to achieve goals is called ______________.

4. To reduce stress, people can learn to use cognitive ______________ strategies to change the way they think about and perceive situations or stressors.

5. The deep ______________ technique to reduce stress involves inhaling and exhaling slowly and with control.

Multiple Choice See Test-Taking Strategies 10–15 in Appendix A.

____ 1. A(n) ______________ goal is a plan of action to achieve specific results within one or two years and possibly be a subgoal for a long-term goal.
   a. short-term
   b. immediate
   c. intermediary
   d. long-term

____ 2. Identifying a ______________ is the second step in the GPS Strategy for goal setting.
   a. goal
   b. part of a goal
   c. purpose
   d. priority

____ 3. The ______________ Theory of motivation involves extrinsic or intrinsic rewards.
   a. Rewards
   b. Hierarchy
   c. Expectancy
   d. Incentive

____ 4. A ______________ organizer helps you plan and think about goals.
   a. short-term
   b. goal
   c. time-manager
   d. priority

____ 5. Setting goals for a term-long project
   a. begins by listing all the tasks or steps required to finish the project.
   b. includes doubling the amount of time you estimate you need for each task.
   c. involves writing target dates on your term calendar and your weekly schedule.
   d. involves all of the above.

____ 6. Which of the following names the levels of needs, from basic to complex, in Maslow's Hierarchy of Needs?
   a. physiological, belonging, esteem, safety, self-actualization
   b. self-actualization, esteem, love and belonging, physiological, safety
   c. physiological, safety, love and belonging, esteem, self-actualization
   d. physiological, love and belonging, safety, esteem, self-actualization

7. Which of the following is *not* a recommended goal-setting strategy to keep yourself motivated?
   a. Visualize yourself achieving your goal.
   b. Use a checklist or a journal to track your progress.
   c. Select meaningful intrinsic or extrinsic rewards that motivate you.
   d. Write your goals in a safe place so other people cannot see them and possibly discourage you from achieving your goals.

8. Procrastination
   a. may stem from lack of interest, fear of failure, or faulty beliefs.
   b. occurs when low-priority tasks take the place of high-priority tasks.
   c. is a learned behavior that can be altered by using effective strategies.
   d. involves all of the above.

Short-Answer Questions See Test-Taking Strategies 32–36 in Appendix A.

On separate paper, answer the following questions. Use complete sentences and terminology from this chapter in your answers.

1. Define any one theory of motivation. Explain how it works to motivate people to move forward and work to achieve goals.
2. In your opinion, what are the five most important strategies to use to become an effective goal setter? Briefly explain why each is important.

Access Chapter 4 Enhanced Quiz and Chapter 4 Study Guide in your College Success CourseMate, accessed through *CengageBrain.com*.

Access all Chapter 4 Online Materials in your College Success CourseMate accessed through *CengageBrain.com*.

7 Preparing for Upcoming Tests

ImageSource/Getty Images

Tests in college are a standard method to assess your understanding of course material. As you approach the middle of a term and midterm exams, laying a strong foundation to perform well on tests involves exploring test-preparation strategies, kinds of test questions, and test-taking strategies. When faced with apprehension or test anxiety, using the skills you learned and becoming familiar with additional strategies can reduce or eliminate test anxiety. This chapter also refers to the removable Essential Test-Taking Skills guide in Appendix A, which provides you with specific strategies and skills for objective, recall, math, and essay tests.

CHAPTER OUTLINE

1 **ESSENTIAL TEST-PREPARATION STRATEGIES AND TIPS**
- *Using Appendix A: Essential Test-Taking Skills*
- *Organizing Your Materials*
- *Organizing Your Time*
- *Creating a Five-Day Study Plan*
- *Creating Summary Notes*
- *Using Effective Memory Strategies to Review*

2 **KINDS OF TEST QUESTIONS**
- *Important Terminology for Objective Questions*
- *True-False Questions*
- *Multiple-Choice Questions*
- *Matching Questions*
- *Important Terminology for Recall Questions*
- *Fill-in-the-Blanks Questions*
- *Listing Questions*
- *Definition Questions*
- *Short-Answer Questions*
- *Important Terminology for Math Questions*
- *Problem-Solving Questions*
- *Important Terminology and Test Formats for Essay Questions*
- *Essay Questions*

3 **ESSENTIAL TEST-TAKING STRATEGIES AND TIPS**
- *Creating a Plan of Action to Begin a Test*
- *Answering Questions*
- *Learning From Your Tests*
- *Computerized Tests*

4 **TEST-ANXIETY MANAGEMENT SKILLS**
- *Sources of Test Anxiety*
- *Strategies to Reduce Test Anxiety Before a Test*
- *Strategies to Reduce Test Anxiety During a Test*

YOUR CHAPTER MAPPING

After reading information under each heading, return to the chapter visual mapping below. Add key words to show subheadings and important details related to each heading.

Access Chapter 7 Visual Mapping in your College Success CourseMate, accessed through *CengageBrain.com*.

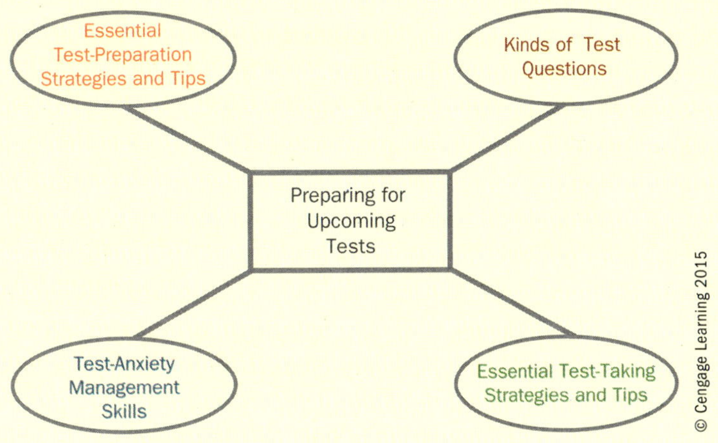

Access Chapter 7 Expanded Chapter Outline in your College Success CourseMate, accessed through *CengageBrain.com*.

LEARNING OBJECTIVES

1. *Discuss effective strategies to organize materials and time, create a five-day study plan and summary notes, and use memory strategies to review for upcoming tests.*
2. *Identify the different kinds of objective, recall, math, and essay questions that appear on tests, and explain at least two strategies for answering each type of question.*
3. *Describe effective test-taking strategies to increase your performance on classroom, online, and computerized tests.*
4. *Identify the four main sources of test anxiety, and summarize strategies to reduce or eliminate test anxiety before and during the taking of tests.*

CHAPTER 7 PROFILE

Preparing for Upcoming Tests

ANSWER, SCORE, and **RECORD** your profile before you read this chapter. If you need to review the process, refer to the complete directions given in the profile for Chapter 1 on page 4.

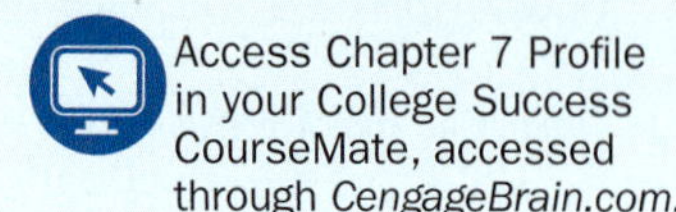

ONLINE: You can complete the profile and get your score online in this textbook's College Success CourseMate.

	YES	NO
1. When I start studying for tests, I organize my materials, use special time-management schedules, and predict possible test questions.	______	______
2. I reread chapters multiple times and rewrite all my notes as a way to prepare for upcoming tests.	______	______
3. I make a five-day study plan and summary notes to prepare for major tests.	______	______
4. On multiple-choice questions, I select the first answer or option that seems to answer the question.	______	______
5. I create an outline or plan for an essay before I begin developing the individual paragraphs.	______	______
6. On tests, I answer or guess at an answer, and then move systematically to the next question.	______	______
7. I learn from my graded tests by looking for patterns of errors, correcting errors, and adjusting my study and test-taking strategies.	______	______
8. My grades are lower than they should be because I struggle with test anxiety.	______	______
9. I deal with test-anxiety issues by being prepared for tests and controlling attitudes and beliefs that otherwise could hinder my test-taking skills.	______	______
10. I am confident in my test-preparation and test-taking skills and abilities.	______	______

QUESTIONS LINKED TO THE CHAPTER LEARNING OBJECTIVES:

Questions 1–3: objective 1
Questions 4–5: objective 2
Questions 6–7: objective 3
Questions 8–9: objective 4
Question 10: all objectives

Essential Test-Preparation Strategies and Tips

1 *Discuss effective strategies to organize materials and time, create a five-day study plan and summary notes, and use memory strategies to review for upcoming tests.*

Tests are inevitable in the college setting as well as in many workplace settings. No one wants to be caught off guard, unprepared, or lack the necessary skills to perform well on tests. Test-preparation skills involve organizing materials, organizing time, creating a positive mindset to perform well, and using effective test-preparation strategies that bring good results. Following are important points to keep in mind before beginning the review process to prepare for an upcoming test:

- Complete all reading or homework assignments so you do not need to mix review time with new learning time.
- If you have used ongoing review prior to the announcement of a test, you will find that preparing for a test will involve *reviewing* and not *studying to learn* information for a test.
- Preparing for tests should be a matter of "brushing up" or refreshing your memory. If you did not dedicate adequate time for ongoing review each week, you now will need to dedicate more time to prepare for a test.

EXERCISE 7.1

Academic Preparation Inventory

Your grades on tests often reflect the effectiveness of your study and review strategies. Identifying your strengths and weaknesses *before* a test and *after* you receive test results provides you with an opportunity to identify which strategies work and which you need to modify or replace. Go to Exercise 7.1 in Appendix C, page C15, to complete this inventory.

Using Appendix A: Essential Test-Taking Skills

Throughout this chapter you will be accessing important information and strategies in **Appendix A: Essential Test-Taking Skills.** For quick reference to Appendix A, consider removing Appendix A from your textbook, punching three holes in the pages, and creating a section in your notebook for this valuable resource. Appendix A provides detailed directions for performing well on all kinds of tests, so it is a resource that you will want to use not only this term, but also for future terms. Take a few minutes to survey Appendix A.

Organizing Your Materials

Preparing for a test requires additional time and organization, both of which can be demanding in a schedule that already is filled with other demands from your courses and in your personal life. The following suggestions can help you organize your materials in an efficient and effective manner.

Pay Attention to Test Details

Your goal is to be prepared and avoid, if possible, surprises or unexpected content on an upcoming test. Use the following tips to find out as much as you can about an upcoming test. Listen carefully to your instructor's description of the test and the topics or chapters that the test will cover. Take notes on materials or topics your instructor emphasizes that you should review or need to know.

1. If your instructor indicates the kinds of test questions that will appear on the test, jot these down as you may use different strategies to prepare for different kinds of test questions.
2. Talk to other students who have already completed the course and tutors who are familiar with the course. Ask them for study suggestions and about the kinds of test questions to expect. Remember, however, that instructors do change test questions and formats, so do not feel overly confident about an upcoming test based on information you obtained from previous students or from tutors.
3. If previous tests are available to examine, take the time to look at and practice with the tests.

Gather Your Course Materials

Review your course syllabus and class assignment sheets so you know specifically which chapters and topics will be included on the test. Gather together and organize your notes and assignments, chapter by chapter. Identify topics that received special attention in class or through assignments as the test may place greater emphasis on these topics. Pulling together and organizing your materials before you begin the serious review process promotes effective and efficient use of time.

Predict Test Questions

Predicting test questions is an excellent method for preparing for tests and reducing test anxiety. Predicting test questions becomes easier when you become familiar with the kinds of tests your instructor uses.

Figure 7.1 shows the kind of information to study and the type of practice to use when you predict specific kinds of question formats will appear on a test.

CONCEPT CHECK 7.1

Does knowing the type of questions that will be used on an upcoming test affect the way you study for the test? Explain.

Organizing Your Time

Preparing for upcoming tests, especially major tests such as midterm or final exams, is time-consuming and time-intensive. Using time-management skills throughout the term places you in a better position to prepare for tests, helps you avoid the need to cram, or removes the feeling of being underprepared, which is one source of test anxiety.

Use Ongoing Time-Management Strategies

In Chapter 3, you learned to use effective time-management strategies. Use the following time-management and test-preparation strategies consistently

FIGURE 7.1 Predicting and Studying for Different Kinds of Tests

If You Predict...	Study This Kind of Information:	Practice May Include:
Objective Questions	• Definitions of key terms • Categories or lists of information • Details: names, dates, theories, rules, events	• Writing and later answering true-false, multiple-choice, and matching questions • Working with a study partner to exchange practice questions
Recall Questions	• Information presented in lists • Definitions of terminology • Cornell recall columns (Chapter 9) • Questions formulated before, during, and after reading • Chapter summaries • Details on visual notes (Chapter 11)	• Reciting and using the Look-Away Technique • Writing summaries and answers to questions to practice expressing ideas • Writing and answering fill-in-the-blanks, listing, and definition questions • Working with a study partner to exchange practice questions
Math Questions	• Problem-solving examples and prototypes	• Reworking math problems • Writing the problem-solving steps
Essay Questions	• Themes • Relationships • Major concepts	• Outlining chapters to see headings and relationships • Reviewing notes for recurring themes • Using Essential Test-Taking Skills in Appendix A for all kinds of questions

throughout the term to build confidence about your ability to perform well on tests:

1. **Fixed study blocks:** Schedule sufficient fixed study blocks to complete regular assignments and review course content on an ongoing basis.
2. **Spaced practice:** Use spaced practice, not marathon studying, to learn and review information.
3. **Schedules:** Create and follow a weekly time-management schedule.
4. **Review schedules:** Add specific blocks of time on your weekly schedule specifically for review. Spread your review time out over several different time blocks and several different days.
5. **Five-day plan:** Use the *five-day study plan* in the following section to prepare for major tests.
6. **Summary notes:** Create a special set of review notes called *summary notes* during this test-preparation, review process.

Use the Recency Effect

The ***recency effect*** states that the items you will remember more easily are items that you most recently practiced. When using a five-day study plan, you utilize this recency effect when the fifth day of this plan is the day before a test. You can also

The **recency effect** states that the items you will remember more easily are items that you most recently practiced.

utilize this recency effect by reviewing summary notes one final time right before you go to bed the night before a test. For the greatest impact, avoid placing any other kinds of stimuli, such as television or a movie, between your review time and your sleep. As you sleep, your mind may continue thinking about and integrating the information you reviewed. You can also gain the benefits of the recency effect by reviewing summary notes one final time the day of the test or the hour before the test.

Creating a Five-Day Study Plan

A ***five-day study plan*** is a plan of action that helps you organize your materials and schedule time to review for a major test, such as a midterm or a final exam. This plan promotes spaced practice and ongoing review; it reduces tendencies to procrastinate, cram, or experience test anxiety. Use the following steps to create a five-day study plan:

A **five-day study plan** is a plan of action that helps you organize your materials and schedule time to review for a major test, such as a midterm or a final exam.

Step 1: Identify Specific Topics to Review

Begin by making a list of all the topics and materials that you need to review for the upcoming test. Following is an example for a sociology course.

Terminology	Lecture notes	Textbook notes
Study guides	Chapter reviews	Homework assignments
Guest speaker notes	Notes from video	Two discussion papers

Step 2: Schedule Specific Days and Times to Review

Organize specific blocks of time on days 1, 2, 3, and 4 for review sessions. On day 5, dedicate all of your study time to reviewing your *summary notes.* Mark the study/review days and times on your calendar or your weekly schedule. Coordinate these times with other students if you are going to review with a study partner or study group.

Day 1	Day 2	Day 3	Day 4	Day 5
Monday Review Times:	Wednesday Review Times:	Friday Review Times:	Saturday Review Times:	Sunday Final Review Times:
8–9:00 AM	8–9:00 AM	8–9:00 AM	10:00 AM–12:00 PM	2–4:00 PM
3–5:00 PM	3–5:00 PM	3–5:00 PM	4–6:00 PM	7–9:00 PM

Step 3: Create a Plan of Action

Identify which chapters and which materials you will review on day 1, day 2, day 3, and finally on day 4. To avoid wasting review time, create a pattern or plan for reviewing each time you sit down. For example, your plan may be to use this sequence of review activities: review study guide, review chapter summary, review textbook notes, review terminology, review homework, review class handouts, and review lecture notes. Throughout this review process, plan to make *summary notes* for the information you feel you need to review further on day 5 and right before the test. Following is an example of a plan of action.

Example of a Plan of Action

Monday	Wednesday	Friday	Saturday	Sunday
8-9:00 AM Ch. 1 class study guide homework Q handouts	8-9:00 AM Ch. 2 study guide homework Q video notes	8-9:00 AM Ch. 3 class study guide handouts homework Q	10-12:00 PM Ch. 4 study guide (no handouts) homework Q 2 short papers	2-4:00 PM Review summary notes; self-quiz on Ch. 1 & 2
3-5:00 PM Ch. 1 lecture notes textbook notes Notes-Guest speaker	3-5:00 PM Ch. 2 lecture notes textbook notes	3-5:00 PM Ch. 3 lecture notes textbook notes	4-6:00 PM Ch. 4 lecture notes textbook notes	7-9:00 PM Review summary notes; self-quiz on Ch. 3 & 4

Creating Summary Notes

Summary notes are specific notes that include concepts, definitions, details, steps, or other information that you need to review further before the day of the test. If you have used effective learning strategies and ongoing review, as you review your textbook and lecture notes, you will recognize concepts, facts, and terms that you already know well. These do not need to appear on your summary notes. Your summary notes are special sets of notes for information that you know you need to give more attention to and study further. **Figure 7.2** shows a variety of formats that are commonly used for summary notes that you create as you prepare for an upcoming test.

Summary notes are specific notes that include information that you need to review further before the day of the test.

CONCEPT CHECK 7.2

How are the summary notes you create to prepare for an upcoming test different from your regular textbook and lecture notes?

EXERCISE 7.2

Transfer These Skills: Summary Notes and Five-Day Study Plan

PURPOSE: Creating summary notes and organizing a five-day study plan are two important processes you can use to organize your materials and your time for an upcoming test. Both take time but each has the potential to increase your test-taking performance.

DIRECTIONS: Unless your instructor provides you with alternative directions, choose to do one of the following assignments to demonstrate your ability to transfer skills from this chapter to other courses. On your paper, identify the course, the instructor, and the assignment option you selected.

1. For any one of your classes, create summary notes for an upcoming test. Use a variety of summary note formats. Remember, your summary notes reflect only the information that you know you need to study further to prepare for the test.
2. For any one of your classes, create a five-day study plan that shows the specific topics you need to review, the target dates and times for reviewing, the steps, and your plan of action. Use the format shown above for each step of the five-day study plan.

FIGURE 7.2 Formats Commonly Used for Summary Notes

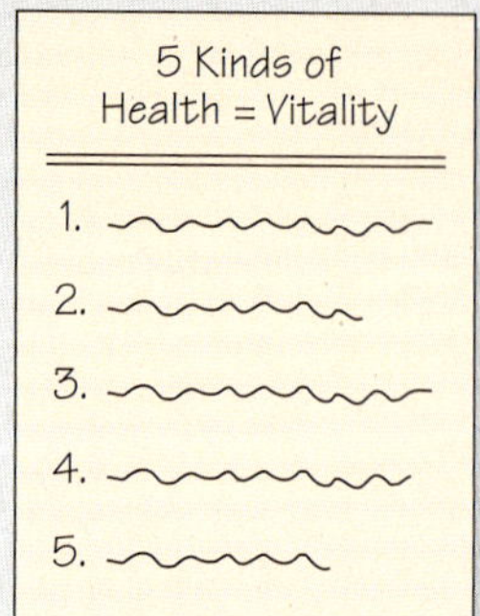

Lists/categories of information to remember

Psy. Theory	Who	Type	Char.

Comparison charts to compare or contrast different subjects studied

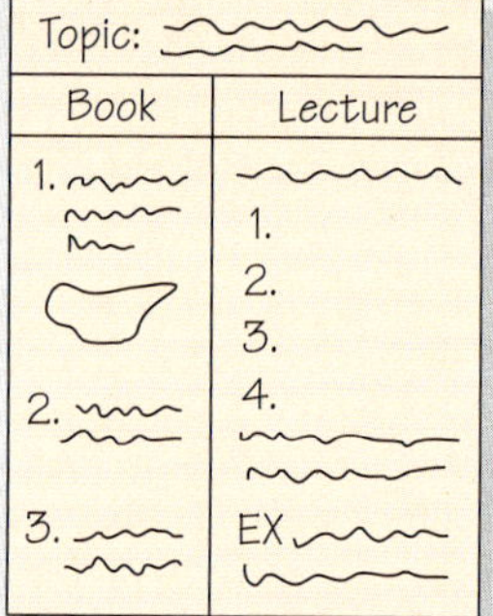

Notes based on topics that include textbook and lecture information

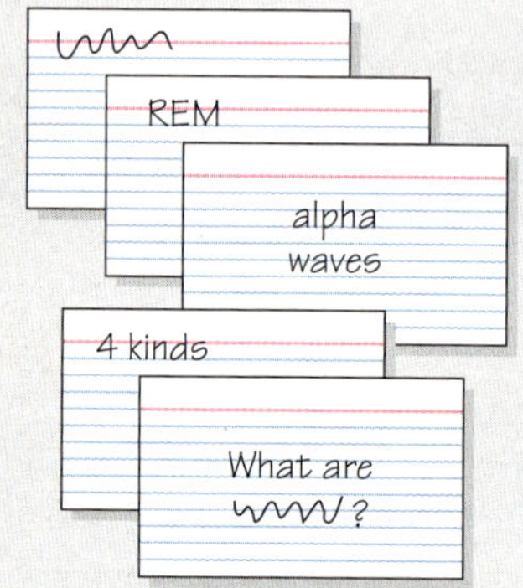

Flashcards of categories, terminology, and study questions

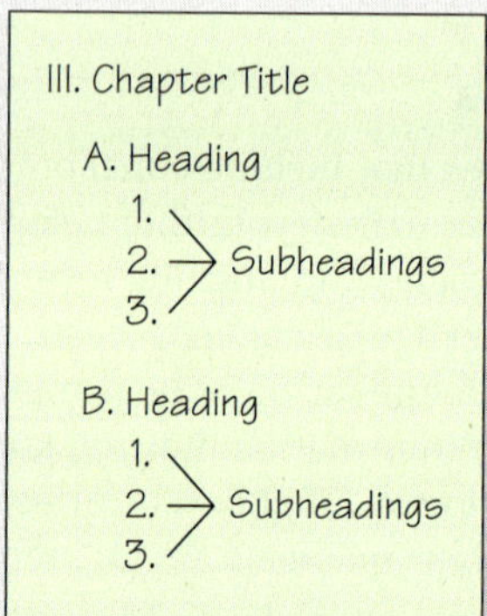

Chapter outlines made by using headings and subheadings

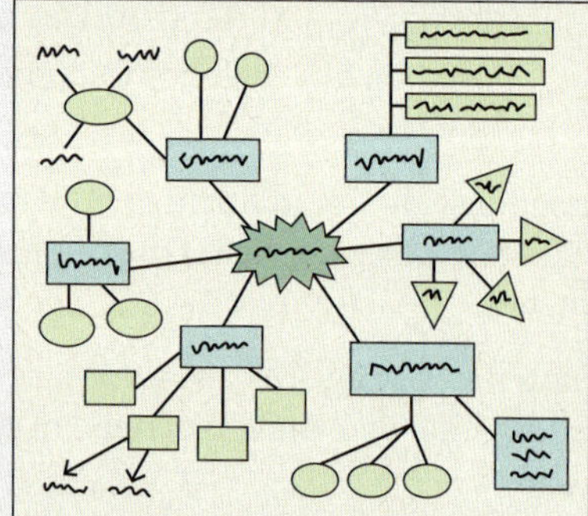

Visual mappings for individual chapters or topics that appear in several different chapters

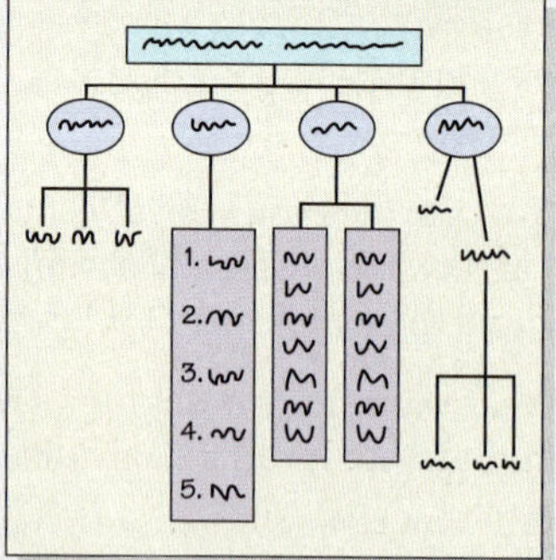

Large hierarchies made on poster paper to include several topics or chapters

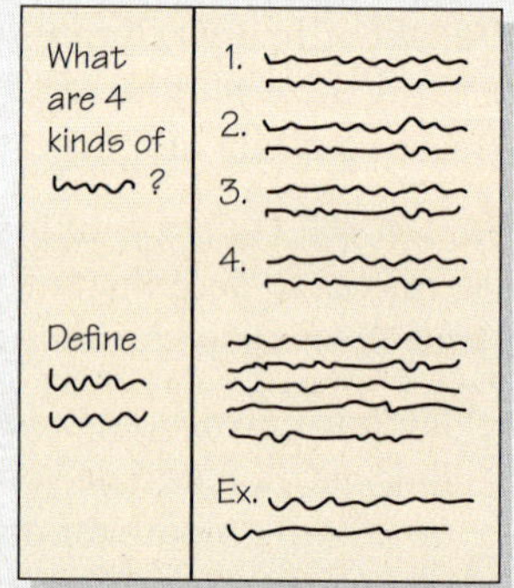

Cornell notes with study questions on the left for self-quizzing

Using Effective Memory Strategies to Review

Preparing for tests by reviewing course content activates the array of memory strategies you learned to use in Chapters 5 and 6. Preparing for tests involves revisiting concepts, main ideas, and important details through the use of the following learning and memory strategies. Use the index of this textbook to locate reference pages for each of the following topics. Review the strategies in Chapters 5 and 6 if necessary.

Twelve memory processes	**Twelve Principles of Memory**	**Positive and negative feedback**
Memory searches	**Retrieval cues**	**Mental rehearsal**
Look-Away Technique	**Mnemonics**	**Paired associations**

CONCEPT CHECK 7.3

How can the processes of visualization and recitation be used together to review material for an upcoming test? How can the memory principles of Selectivity and Big and Little Pictures be used together?

CHECK POINT 7.1

Answers appear on page B3.

True or False? See Test-Taking Strategies 1–9 in Appendix A.

_____ 1. Students who do not use a five-day study plan may need to resort to last-minute cramming.

_____ 2. The recency effect states that you will remember the first items you study at the beginning of a review session.

_____ 3. Studying throughout the day before a test and then enjoying a movie or some type of recreational activity the night before a test are effective test-preparation strategies that also reduce stress.

_____ 4. The feedback you receive from the Look-Away Technique can help you decide what information to put into summary notes.

_____ 5. It is best not to rely on learning course materials a day or two before a test.

_____ 6. In a five-day study plan, a plan of action involves identifying the topics to review, times to review, and planning a course of action with specific steps to prepare for upcoming tests.

_____ 7. It is dishonest and a form of cheating if you talk to students who previously took tests for the class you are in or if you look at tests previously used in the class.

_____ 8. Summary notes are always brief and limited to topics that you need to mentally rehearse.

Access Chapter 7 Practice Quiz 1 in your College Success CourseMate, accessed through *CengageBrain.com*.

Kinds of Test Questions

2 *Identify the different kinds of objective, recall, math, and essay questions that appear on tests, and explain at least two strategies for answering each type of question.*

Understanding types of test questions is an important step in the process of strengthening your test-preparation and test-taking skills. **Figure 7.3** provides you with information about the different formats for test questions that you may encounter on your tests. To learn more about each kind of test question, and to familiarize yourself with fifty-two easy-to-use strategies for all test question formats, refer to the Essential Test-Taking Skills guide in Appendix A. When you know an upcoming test will focus on a specific type of test question, you may refer to that specific section in

FIGURE 7.3 Test Question Formats

Kind of Question	Level of Difficulty	Includes	Requires
Recognition: Objective Questions	Easiest	True-False Multiple-Choice Matching	Read and recognize whether information is correct; apply a skill and then recognize the correct answer.
Recall Questions	More demanding	Fill-in-the-Blanks Listings Definitions Short Answers	Retrieve the information from your memory and then respond.
Math Questions	Demanding	Problem-Solving	Use procedural knowledge to complete steps of processes.
Essay Questions	Most difficult	Essays	Retrieve the information from memory, organize it, and use effective writing skills to respond.

Appendix A to prepare for the test. You can remove the Essential Test-Taking Skills guide and place it in your notebook for quick reference in any of your classes. For now, the following common test-question formats will help you begin to anticipate what to expect on upcoming tests.

Important Terminology for Objective Questions

As you work with true-false, multiple-choice, and matching questions, you will encounter important terminology. Refer to Appendix A, page A3–A4, to familiarize yourself with the following important test-question terminology for objective questions:

Modifiers	Definition clues	Relationship clues
Negatives	Stems	Options
Distractors	Levels of response	Immediate response
Delayed response	Assisted response	Educated selection

True-false questions are objective questions that require you to recognize if a statement is true or false.

True-False Questions

True-false questions are objective questions that require you to recognize if a statement is true or false. Mark a question *true* only when the complete statement is true and accurate. If any part of the statement is false or inaccurate, you must mark the statement as *false*. **See Appendix A, Test-Taking Strategies 1–9, pages A5--A12, for more details.** Following is an example of a true-false question:

_____ 1. A five-day study plan must always be scheduled for five consecutive days prior to the test day. *Answer: False*

Multiple-choice questions are objective questions that require you to select the best answer from a group of options to complete an opening statement.

Multiple-Choice Questions

Multiple-choice questions are objective questions that require you to select the best answer from a group of options to complete an opening statement. At times, more than one option may complete the statement accurately, but only one option is the best, most inclusive, or most complete answer. Multiple-choice questions may show three, four, or five options. Sometimes the last option includes "all of the above," which means every option is accurate. **See Appendix A, Test-Taking Strategies 10–15, pages A12–A19, for more details.** Following is an example of a multiple-choice question:

_____ 1. Kinds of encoding to prepare stimuli for long-term memory include:

a. linguistic and visual coding
b. kinesthetic coding
c. semantic coding
d. all of the above *Answer: d*

CONCEPT CHECK 7.4
What are the three kinds of objective test question formats? What do they have in common?

Matching Questions

Matching questions are objective questions that require you to match items in the left column with items in the right column. Matching questions often test your ability to match terminology with definitions; people, places, or dates with descriptions, characteristics, or events; or match causes and effects. **See Appendix A, Test-Taking Strategies 16–20, pages A19–A22, for more details.** Following is a partial example of the matching question format:

_____ 1. reciting	a. learning styles
_____ 2. See-Say-Do Strategy	b. multisensory learning strategy
_____ 3. learning modalities	c. explaining out loud, in your own words without referring to printed information *Answers: 1. c 2. b 3. a*

Matching questions are objective questions that require you to match items in the left column with items in the right column.

Important Terminology for Recall Questions

As you work with listing and short-answer recall questions, you will encounter important terminology. Refer to Appendix A, page A22, to familiarize yourself with the following important test-question terminology:

- ***Closed questions***: Questions that require specific answers
- ***Open-ended questions***: Questions that have a variety of possible answers
- ***Direction words***: Words in test questions that indicate what is expected in the answers

Closed questions are questions that require specific answers.

Open-ended questions are questions that have a variety of possible answers.

Direction words are words in test questions that indicate what is expected in the answers.

Fill-in-the-Blanks Questions

Fill-in-the-blanks questions are recall questions that require you to write a term or a word on each blank line to complete the statement. Words that complete these statements are often vocabulary or terminology words. Correct answers often require that you spell the words in the blanks correctly. **See Appendix A, Test-Taking Strategies 21–24, pages A22–A24, for more details.** Following is an example of a fill-in-the-blanks question:

1. __________ is the process of postponing a task for a later time.
Answer: Procrastination

Fill-in-the-blanks questions are recall questions that require you to write a term or a word on each blank line to complete the statement.

EXERCISE 7.3

Objective Test Questions

DIRECTIONS: Read and review Test-Taking Strategies 1–20 in Appendix A, pages A5–A22. Then answer the following questions.

TRUE OR FALSE?

_____ **1.** To answer true-false questions correctly, you cannot personalize the question by responding with your opinion.

_____ **2.** To be true, every part of a true-false question must be true.

_____ **3.** When you have reservations about an answer on a true-false question, you should explain your answer next to the question.

_____ **4.** Negatives are words in a sentence that make the sentence false.

_____ **5.** *Always, never, best,* and *everyone* are word definition clues.

_____ **6.** The left column in matching questions often contains course-specific vocabulary terms.

_____ **7.** In a matching test, each item in the right column must be matched up with an item in the left column.

MULTIPLE CHOICE

_____ **1.** Which of the following statements is not true?

a. Before you convert each option into a true-false statement, you should finish the stem in your mind and check if one of the options matches your preliminary answer.

b. On a multiple-choice question, when you combine the stem with each option, only one statement can be true, so all the remaining statements must be false.

c. The *best* answer will form a completely true statement.

d. To be sure you write the correct answer, you can circle the correct answer before you write the answer on the line.

_____ **2.** If a multiple-choice question has four options, how many distractors are there?

a. one

b. two

c. three

d. four

_____ **3.** Multiple-choice questions are similar to true-false questions in that both types of questions

a. may have 100 percent and in-between modifiers.

b. have only one correct answer.

c. may include a definition clue or a relationship clue.

d. show all of the above.

Listing Questions

Listing questions are recall questions that require you to generate a list of items from memory to answer a question. *Closed questions* require specific items in the answer. *Open-ended questions* have a variety of possible answers. Listing questions often begin with one of these direction words: *list, name,* or *what are.* Unless the directions ask you to add details about each item, your answer simply lists the items. **See Appendix A, Test-Taking Strategies 25–28, pages A24–A26, for more details.** Following is an example of a listing question that is a closed question that requires a specific answer.

Listing questions are recall questions that require you to generate a list of items from memory to answer a question.

1. List the three memory systems in the Information Processing Model.
   Answer: *1. sensory memory*
   2. working memory
   3. long-term memory

Definition Questions

Definition questions are recall questions that require you to define and expand upon a vocabulary term. Simply writing a word-for-word textbook definition is not sufficient. Instead, you can use a three-part definition: (1) identify the category to which the term belongs, (2) define the term, and (3) give one more detail about the term. **See Appendix A, Test-Taking Strategies 29–31, pages A26–A28, for more details.** Following is an example of a definition question.

Definition questions are recall questions that require you to define and expand upon a vocabulary term.

1. What is the definition of the Take Charge Technique?
   Answer: *The Take Charge Technique is a concentration technique. It involves taking responsibility for your environment by seeking alternative places to study or by modifying your existing place of study so you have few or no distractions. When you use this technique, you find solutions rather than blame others for your inability to concentrate.*

CONCEPT CHECK 7.5

What are the four kinds of recall question formats? Why are recall questions considered more demanding than recognition (objective) questions?

Short-Answer Questions

Short-answer questions are recall questions that require you to pull information from memory to write a short answer to a question. Often times you can answer the question in five to seven sentences. Direction words for short-answer questions include *discuss, tell, identify, describe, explain why, explain how,* and *when.* Short-answer questions may be closed or open-ended questions. **See Appendix A, Test-Taking Strategies 32–36, pages A28–A31, for more details.** Following is an example of a short-answer question.

Short-answer questions are recall questions that require you to pull information from memory to write a short answer to a question.

1. Explain what the Retrieval Failure Theory states about forgetting.
   Answer: *The Retrieval Failure Theory states that failure to locate information in long-term memory may be the result of lack of effort, memorizing details in isolation, or using a weak system to organize information. Lack of effort shows lack of intention to imprint information clearly in long-term memory. Information that is memorized in isolation rather than associating it to related schemas becomes difficult to locate. Information that is not organized in a logical way also makes locating and retrieving the information from long-term memory difficult to do.*

EXERCISE 7.4

Recall Questions

DIRECTIONS: Read and review Test-Taking Strategies 21–36 in Appendix A, pages A22–A31. Then answer the following questions.

TRUE OR FALSE?

_____ **1.** The second sentence in an answer for a definition question should state important details that show you understand the term.

_____ **2.** Well-developed answers to definition questions should consist of one or two sentences.

_____ **3.** Short-answer questions should consist of sentences written in paragraph form and not as a list of points.

_____ **4.** A closed question for a listing question allows many different answers as long as the information is course specific.

_____ **5.** In a well-written fill-in-the-blanks question, the number of blanks indicates the number of words required to complete the sentence.

FILL-IN-THE-BLANKS

1. Answers for an ______________ - ______________ question may vary from one student to another.

2. When writing an answer for a short-answer question, your ______________ sentence should be direct and to the point so your instructor knows you understand the question.

3. ______________ words in short-answer questions indicate the type of answer that is expected.

4. A well-developed answer to a definition question shows ______________ levels of information.

Important Terminology for Math Questions

When students think about math courses and math tests, they often focus on using numbers and processes to solve problems; they pay less attention to math terminology. However, understanding and knowing how to define math terminology lays the foundation for discussing math principles, understanding concepts, and working steps of problem-solving processes. Spend ample time learning definitions of math terminology you encounter in your math textbooks. Refer to Appendix A, page A31, to familiarize yourself with the following important test-question terminology for math:

Algebraic expressions	Algebraic symbols	Algorithms
Equations	Prototypes	Word or story problems

Problem-Solving Questions

Problem-solving questions are questions that require you to use procedural knowledge to apply a series of steps to solve a problem.

Problem-solving questions are questions that require you to use procedural knowledge to apply a series of steps to solve a problem. Problem-solving questions may involve story problems or solving a mathematical equation. Usually your answer must show all the steps used to solve the problem. **See Appendix A, Test-Taking**

Strategies 37–44, pages A31–A37, for more details. Following is an example of a problem-solving question:

1. Use the power rule to solve the following equation: $(2^3)^4 = ?$
   Answer: $(2^3)^4 = 2^{3\times4} = 2^{12} = 4{,}096$

Important Terminology and Test Formats for Essay Questions

As you work with essay questions, you will encounter important terminology. Refer to Appendix A, page A37, to familiarize yourself with the following important test-question terminology:

Thesis statement	Direction words	Organizational plan
Five-paragraph format	Main idea	Supporting details

Essay Questions

Essay questions require you to retrieve information from memory and organize it into several paragraphs with main ideas that are related to a thesis statement. Essay questions involve higher-level thinking, organizational skills, and writing skills. **See Appendix A, Test-Taking Strategies 45–51, pages A37–A43, for more details.** Following are examples of essay questions that require multiple paragraphs in the response.

Essay questions require you to retrieve information from memory and organize it into several paragraphs with main ideas that are related to a thesis statement.

1. Explain the meaning of the following statement: *The Myers-Briggs Personality Indicator is based on opposite poles of preferences and characteristics.*
2. How do self-talk, locus of control, and self-efficacy affect a person's academic performance?

Strengthen Your Essay Writing Skills

Do you find essay questions to be the most challenging kind of question on tests? Some students prefer objective test questions while others prefer essay questions. Students who do well on essay tests often have developed the following skills:

- Ability to answer questions directly and with the kind of information expected by the question
  - *Review Figure 13: Direction Words for Essay Questions* (Appendix A)
  - *Review Figure 14: Thesis Sentences* (Appendix A)
- Ability to organize information clearly so the reader can follow the reasoning or explanations, and ability to include main ideas (big pictures) and sufficient supporting details (little pictures)
  - *Review Figure 15: Organizational Plans for Essay Questions* (Appendix A)
  - *Review Key Elements in a Five-Paragraph Essay* (Appendix A)
  - *Review Pre-Writing Guide for Essay Question* (Appendix A)
- Ability to show the relationships between the different levels of information and use transition words to connect sentences and paragraphs together smoothly
- Ability to express ideas clearly by using effective choice of words, vocabulary, and course terminology
- Ability to use correct spelling, grammar, and sentence structures in paragraphs

EXERCISE 7.5

Essay Test Questions

DIRECTIONS: Read and review Test-Taking Strategies 45–51 in Appendix A, pages A37–A43. Then answer the following questions.

TRUE OR FALSE?

_____ **1.** A well-developed essay answer must include the "big pictures" (concepts) and the "little pictures" (supporting details).

_____ **2.** Once you have written an answer for an essay question, you should not attempt to add additional information because the results will be a difficult-to-read answer.

_____ **3.** The last paragraph of an essay answer should always emphasize your personal opinion.

_____ **4.** More in-depth details always would be required for an essay question that begins with the word *summarize* than would be required for a question that begins with the word *explain*.

_____ **5.** The thesis statement directly states the main point of the entire essay.

_____ **6.** If you make an organization plan for an essay answer, you should turn it in with your test if you run out of time and are not able to finish your essay answer.

FILL-IN-THE-BLANKS

1. The ______________________________ sentence in an essay states the main point the writer intends to develop throughout the entire essay.

2. Details used to develop the thesis appear in the ______________________________ of the essay.

3. The direction word ______________________________ requires you to identify different parts of something and discuss each part with details.

Kinds of Essay Tests

Unlike other test-taking formats, instructors may use a variety of formats for essay tests, some of which provide you with greater opportunities to prepare your essay answer in advance. Following are essay formats and situations you may encounter in your courses.

- **Topics are announced in advance.** Gather pertinent information on the announced topics. Use the index of your textbook to locate information on the topic and prepare a set of detailed notes. Predict possible questions, organize your information, and practice writing answers to the questions you predicted.
- **Questions are announced in advance.** Use the index in your textbook to locate and organize pertinent information. Create and memorize an outline or organizational plan for your answers. Practice writing essay answers for each question.
- **Essays will be completed in class.** For in-class essay tests, you may be assigned specific questions to answer or you may be given a choice of questions from which you select the questions to answer. In all cases, you will be challenged to retrieve and organize information from memory. Use the following suggestions to prepare for in-class essay tests.
    - ***Predict test questions.*** Use your course syllabus to identify concepts, trends, themes, or categories of information that you are expected to learn. Write practice test questions based on these materials.
    - ***Create summary notes.*** Essay questions often require you to compare, contrast, summarize, explain, discuss, or apply information about major topics, themes, theories, or models. Create summary notes with important supporting details for topics that you predict may be in essay test questions.

- ***Practice writing essay answers.*** Work with a partner or in a study group to create practice essay questions and answers. When you practice organizing information and presenting your ideas *before* an actual essay test, you become more comfortable with the essay-writing process.
- **Books may be used for the essay test.** Open-book essay tests require less retrieval of information from memory and more organizational skills to locate information in the textbook. Become familiar with the index of your book so you can look up topics quickly. Use a special highlighter to mark important facts (dates, names, events, statistics, and terminology) and quotations you may wish to use in your answer. Use tabs to mark significant pages such as those with important summary charts, tables, lists, steps, or visual materials.
- **Essay test is done at home.** Take-home essay tests provide you with more time to organize and develop your essay answer. Create a plan of action that provides you with sufficient time to develop a polished essay answer. Set your completed essay aside for a day; then, reread it; proofread for spelling, grammar, and mechanics; revise if you see ways to strengthen it; and type the final version.

CONCEPT CHECK 7.6

Which is a more difficult essay question test format: an in-class essay question when the topic is given in advance or a take-home essay question? Explain your answer.

CHECK POINT 7.2

Answers appear on page B3.

Fill-in-the-Blanks See Test-Taking Strategies 21–24 in Appendix A.

1. ______________________ questions, which are more demanding than recognition questions and less difficult than essay questions, require a person to retrieve information from memory in order to answer the question.
2. Both ______________________ questions and open-ended questions appear in listing, short-answer, and essay questions.
3. Well-developed answers to ______________________ questions often explain a vocabulary term by using three levels or kinds of information.

Listing Questions See Test-Taking Strategies 25–28 in Appendix A.

1. List the four kinds of questions that are categorized as *recall questions.*
2. What kinds of test questions are categorized as *objective questions*?

Access Chapter 7 Practice Quiz 2 in your College Success CourseMate, accessed through *CengageBrain.com*.

CHAPTER 7 REFLECTIVE WRITING 1

Before starting this writing assignment, complete Exercise 7.6: Test-Taking Skills Inventory, on page 212. On separate paper, in a journal, or online in this textbook's College Success CourseMate, respond to the following questions:

1. According to the inventory results in Exercise 7.6, what was your score? What strategies can you learn to use more effectively to improve your test-taking skills?
2. Based on test grades this term for your various classes, how do your grades reflect your overall progress in your courses? Explain with specific details.

Access Chapter 7 Reflective Writing 1 in your College Success CourseMate, accessed through *CengageBrain.com*.

EXERCISE 7.6

Test-Taking Skills Inventory

PURPOSE: Use the following self-assessment inventory to evaluate your general test-taking skills and identify areas you can strengthen. The perfect score is 60.

DIRECTIONS: Read each statement about test-taking skills. Circle the degree to which you use these test-taking skills.

1 = seldom or never 2 = sometimes 3 = always or almost always

1. I complete all of my assignments and reading prior to a test. 1 2 3
2. I set ample time aside to study specifically for a test. 1 2 3
3. I use self-quizzing and feedback methods when I study. 1 2 3
4. I know definitions for all course-specific terminology. 1 2 3
5. I feel confident that I studied sufficiently to do well on a test. 1 2 3
6. I use the four levels of response for answering test questions. 1 2 3
7. I rehearse factual information using a variety of strategies, and I rehearse procedural information by using ample repetition. 1 2 3
8. I read directions carefully and understand direction words. 1 2 3
9. I read carefully and pay attention to modifiers, clue words, negatives, and other details in test questions. 1 2 3
10. I use the essential strategies for answering objective questions: true-false, multiple-choice, and matching test questions. 1 2 3
11. I use educated selection (guessing) only as a last resort. 1 2 3
12. I use the essential strategies for answering recall questions: fill-in-the-blanks, definition, and listing questions. 1 2 3
13. I include sufficient details to answer short-answer questions. 1 2 3
14. I respond with the correct kind of information for closed questions and open-ended questions. 1 2 3
15. I memorize prototypes for different kinds of math problems. 1 2 3
16. I create an organizational plan for essay test answers. 1 2 3
17. I develop a strong thesis statement for essay test answers. 1 2 3
18. I include ample details in essays to support the thesis. 1 2 3
19. I use available test-taking time to check my answers and work. 1 2 3
20. I analyze error patterns and learn from my tests. 1 2 3

Your Total Score: ____________

Essential Test-Taking Strategies and Tips

3 *Describe effective test-taking strategies to increase your performance on classroom, online, and computerized tests.*

Feeling slightly nervous or apprehensive when you first enter the classroom or when the instructor distributes the test is a normal reaction to testing situations. Strive to use strategies to calm your nerves, establish a positive state of mind, and mentally prepare to do well on the test. Following are strategies to establish a positive mindset for tests:

- Arrive to class early. Rushing in at the last minute or arriving late adds stress and does not allow you time to mentally prepare.
- Use positive self-talk, a quick relaxation or visualization technique, or a concentration technique to focus your mind.
- Focus only on yourself; ignore other students and their nervous reactions to the test.
- If you have a few minutes before the test is distributed, mentally rehearse information from your summary notes. Or, if allowed, review your summary notes one final time.
- Listen carefully to the directions. Your instructor may announce corrections on the test, suggestions for completing the test, the amount of time available for the test, and other important directions.

Creating a Plan of Action to Begin a Test

Begin strengthening your test-taking skills by using the Essential Classroom Test-Taking Strategies in **Figure 7.4**. You can use these strategies from the beginning to the end of a test-taking situation. Details for each strategy appear in the following sections.

Jot Down Important Information

As soon as you receive the test, jot down important information on the back of the test, in the margins of the test, or on separate scratch paper. For example, you may

FIGURE 7.4 Essential Classroom Test-Taking Strategies

- Jot down important information.
- Survey the test and budget your time.
- Decide on a starting point.
- Use your test time wisely.
- Read directions and questions carefully.
- Answer all questions.
- Change answers carefully.
- Use the four levels of response to answer questions.

Robert Kneschke/Shutterstock

Performing well on tests involves developing effective test-preparation and test-taking skills. What strategies do you use to prepare for upcoming tests? What strategies do you use to move through tests with confidence and efficiency?

want to quickly write down formulas, mnemonics, lists, or facts that you may need to refer to quickly during the test. You may also want to add specific items that you reviewed immediately prior to the test so they will be fresh in your memory.

Survey the Test and Budget Your Time

Glance through the test to become familiar with the types of questions on the test, the point value of different questions or sections on the test, and the overall length of the test. Be sure to check to see if questions appear on the backs of the test pages.

Then, quickly estimate the amount of time you can spend on each section of the test. This is especially important if the test has short-answer or essay questions because those questions tend to take more time to write answers. If you wish, jot down estimated times to begin each section of the test.

Decide on a Starting Point

CONCEPT CHECK 7.7

What strategies can you use within the first five minutes of receiving a test? How will these strategies affect your attitude toward the test?

Many students prefer to work through the pages of the test in the order in which the questions are presented, but you do *not* have to work in this order. You can begin with the part of the test that feels the most comfortable, has the highest point value, or with which you feel most confident.

Use Your Test Time Wisely

Avoid the urge to bolt out of the classroom as soon as you finish a test. After answering all of the questions, use the remaining time to check your answers. Use all available test time to proofread, revise, or refine answers for short-answer or essay questions. Use available time to check math calculations and the steps used to show your work.

Answering Questions

When you first receive a test, you may feel somewhat overwhelmed by the number of questions and the different kinds of questions. The way you approach each question and select an answer affects your grade, so work carefully and thoughtfully by doing the following.

Read Directions and Questions Carefully

The number one cause of students making unnecessary errors on tests has to do with hastily reading directions and questions. Read directions slowly. Be sure you understand the directions before proceeding. Ask for clarification if the directions are not clear. Read questions carefully, paying close attention to key words and direction words. To help yourself stay focused on the question, *circle direction words and key words* in the questions as well as in the directions.

Answer All Questions

Do not leave answer spaces blank if you start to run out of time. In most cases, you will automatically lose points if you leave an answer space blank. When you are running out of time, pick up your pace, read faster, spend less time pondering answers, and make a quick choice or use an *educated selection* strategy for an answer if necessary. For essay questions, if you do not have time to write a complete answer, provide an outline or a list of points you would have developed further had you had sufficient time.

Change Answers Carefully

Do *not* change answers if you are panicking or feeling that time is running out. If you work carefully before answering questions, rely on your self-confidence that the answer you already selected is the best. However, sometimes other questions on the test give you clues or help you recall information that may have you questioning your original answer. In such cases, when you can clearly justify a reason to change an answer, *do* change answers.

Use the Four Levels of Response

Some students who have not yet learned effective test-taking strategies move through a test by reading a question, answering it with certainty or hesitancy, and then moving on to the next question. This approach works if students immediately know the correct answer for each question. When students are not able to answer all the questions immediately, using the four levels of response is a more effective approach that brings better results. The ***four levels of response*** are sequential steps students can use to answer test questions: *immediate, delayed, assisted,* and *educated selection.* **Figure 7.5** summarizes the four levels of response. Additional details about the four levels of response appear in Appendix A, page A4.

The **four levels of response** are sequential steps students can use to answer test questions: immediate, delayed, assisted, and educated selection.

As an effective test-taker and critical thinker, you can use a variety of questions to "jump-start" your memory as you conduct memory searches for correct answers.

FIGURE 7.5 Four Levels of Response to Answer Test Questions

1. **Immediate Response,** the first level of response to a test question, involves immediately knowing the answer.
2. **Delayed Response,** the second level of response to a test question, involves carefully rereading a question and seeking retrieval cues, associations, visualizations, or auditory cues to help you retrieve an answer from memory.
3. **Assisted Response,** the third level of response to a test question, involves using other questions in the test to assist you with answering a question.
4. **Educated Selection,** also called *educated guessing,* is the fourth level of response to a test question that involves using a variety of strategies to increase your odds in selecting the correct answer.

Following are definitions of each level of response followed by examples of questions you can use for each level.

Immediate response involves immediately knowing the answer.

Immediate response, the first level of response to a test question, involves immediately knowing the answer. When you read the question, you know the answer with certainty.

Am I sure this is correct?

Delayed response involves conducting a memory search to retrieve the answer from long-term memory.

Delayed response, the second level of response to a test question, involves conducting a memory search to retrieve the answer from long-term memory. This may involve rereading the question carefully, using retrieval cues and associations, visualizations, or auditory cues to recall learned information.

What do I know that is related to this question?
If I go into "retrieval mode," can I recall an association, visualization, or mnemonic to help me remember?
When did we discuss this? What chapter is this from?
What other things belong in a category with this term?
Is this a vocabulary term? Will recalling a definition help me answer the question?

Assisted response involves using other questions in the test to assist you with answering the question.

Assisted response, the third level of response to a test question, involves using other questions in the test to assist you with answering the question. Select key words in the question; scan other test questions to look for this word or concepts related to the word as these may trigger recall of the correct answer.

After carefully rereading the question, is the answer now more apparent?
What is a key word in the question? Can I find that word in another question somewhere in the test?
Is there another question that I can use to help me recall this answer?

Educated selection involves using a variety of strategies to increase your odds in selecting the correct answer.

Educated selection, the fourth level of response to a test question, involves using a variety of strategies to increase your odds in selecting the correct answer. Educated selection sometimes is referred to as *educated guessing*; however, logical analysis goes beyond random guessing.

How can I use some logic to think this through?
Which answer is not feasible? Why?
What words in the question can help me use educated selection strategies?

CONCEPT CHECK 7.8
If you read a question and do not know the answer, what strategies are more effective than just guessing an answer?

See strategies 9, 14, 15, 23 and 27 in **Appendix A: Essential Test-Taking Skills** for educated selection strategies for objective test questions.

Learning from Your Tests

Do you sometimes receive your graded tests, look at the grade, and then stick the test into your notebook or backpack? A more effective approach involves using the tests for valuable feedback and then analyzing the effectiveness of your learning strategies. With the information you learn from analyzing your test, create a plan of action to adjust your study and learning strategies to bring even better results on your next test.

Examine the Questions You Answered Correctly

Understanding what processes you used to answer questions correctly helps you recognize what is working for you. Answer the following questions:

What strategies did I use to learn this information?
What was the original source of the information? Did I learn the information in class, through a homework assignment, from the textbook, or from a combination of sources?
Was the information new to me or did I already know this information at the time it was presented?

Look for Patterns of Errors

Repeat the process you used to examine the questions you correctly answered, but this time examine the processes, strategies, and sources of the information for the questions that you answered incorrectly. For example, perhaps the information that you missed the most frequently appeared mainly in the textbook or as information presented in class during lectures. Perhaps you skipped reciting or using review strategies for the topics in the questions you answered incorrectly. This feedback makes you more aware of the need to focus greater attention on your strategies for textbook reading or on your notetaking skills for class lectures.

CONCEPT CHECK 7.9

How can you use graded tests to improve performance? How can graded tests affect your attitude and mindset about tests?

Correct Your Errors

You want to override or erase incorrect information and replace it with accurate information. Create and practice new associations so the next time you need to retrieve that information from your schemas, you will recall accurate information. Frequently during the course of a term, previously learned information appears again on future tests or as knowledge upon which new information is built. Therefore, taking time to learn the correct information strengthens the memory schema with accurate details.

Textbook Case Studies

DIRECTIONS:

1. Read each case study carefully. Respond to the question at the end of each case study by using *specific* strategies discussed in this chapter. Answer in complete sentences.
2. Write your responses on paper or online in the College Success CourseMate, Textbook Case Studies. You will be able to print your online response or e-mail it to your instructor.

CASE STUDY 1: Adolpho has not been in school for fifteen years. He never learned how to study or take tests. He works hard, and he is able to respond in class and in study groups to questions that are related to the current assignment. However, when it is time to take tests that cover several chapters of information, he freezes and goes blank. What test-preparation and test-taking strategies would you recommend Adolpho start using?

CASE STUDY 2: Jenny does not study much for her communications class because she is taking the class for pass/no pass rather than a letter grade. As the end of the term approaches, she realizes that she may not have enough points to pass the class. She intends to deal with the situation the way she usually deals with tests—cramming in the day or two before the final exam. What test-preparation strategies would you suggest that Jenny use during the final two weeks of the term?

Access Chapter 7 Textbook Case Studies in your College Success CourseMate, accessed through *CengageBrain.com*.

Computerized Tests

Students who take online courses encounter online or computerized testing on a fairly regular basis. However, many students who attend classes on campus also encounter the use of computerized tests. In many cases, students must check into a computer lab to complete the assigned tests.

Computerized tests usually consist of multiple-choice questions. These tests may be written by the instructor, but more often they consist of questions from a test bank generated by the textbook author or publisher. Some of the test banks randomly assign test questions of varying levels of difficulty; other test banks allow the instructor to tag which questions to use on a test.

CONCEPT CHECK 7.10

Do you prefer computerized tests over paper-pencil tests? Why or why not?

One advantage of taking computerized tests is that students usually receive immediate feedback and a test score. If the response is immediately recorded as *correct*, the positive feedback increases students' confidence level. Another advantage is that the time limit to complete the test is less rigid than when students take the test in class. Students control the pace for answering questions, so they may feel less stress.

There are some disadvantages of taking computerized tests. Students may be anxious or uncomfortable taking computerized tests if they have limited experience or skills using computers. Students may also have increased stress or frustration if they receive any negative feedback that an answer is incorrect. Another disadvantage is that many computer tests do not allow students to go back to previous questions to change answers or use the test-taking strategy of assisted response. Finally, students do not have access to a printed copy of the test to view, correct answers, or use to study for a final exam.

If you have not already experienced computerized testing, chances are good that you will at some time during your college career. For practice taking computerized tests, go to the College Success CourseMate for this textbook to complete Practice Quizzes and Enhanced Quizzes for each chapter. **Figure 7.6** summarizes seven essential strategies for taking computerized tests. Following are details about these strategies.

Know the Rules for Computerized Testing

Prior to taking a computerized test, gather as much information as possible about the rules for computerized testing. Ask questions such as the following:

Is there a tutorial or practice test?
May I take the test more than once?

FIGURE 7.6 Essential Strategies for Taking Computerized Tests

- Know the rules for computerized testing.
- Allow yourself ample time to complete the test.
- Understand the computer and the testing software commands.
- Read and choose answers carefully.
- Learn from incorrect answers.
- Use relaxation techniques.
- Discuss your test-taking experience.

Is there a time limit for completing the test?
May I have blank scratch paper and pen to work out problems or to organize my thoughts?
Will I be able to get a printed version of the test to use for studying after the test is scored?

Allow Yourself Ample Time to Complete the Test

For many students, taking computerized tests requires more time than taking tests in the classroom. Select a time of day when you feel mentally sharp and are not rushed or pressed for time. When you enter the lab, choose a computer that is not in the line of a steady flow of traffic so you will experience fewer distractions. Finally, do not postpone taking the test or wait until close to the deadline to complete the test.

Understand the Computer and the Testing Software Commands

Ask for help if you are unfamiliar with the computer, need help logging on, or do not understand how to select or change answers. Ask for help if you do not know how to save your test results. Read all the directions carefully. Notice whether or not the software program allows you to return to previous questions or change previous answers.

Read and Choose Answers Carefully

The strategies for multiple-choice questions used for paper-pencil tests are the same as those used for computerized tests. See **Appendix A, Essential Test-Taking Strategies 10–15, pages A12–A19** for more test-taking strategies applicable to computerized tests.

Do not answer too quickly. Once you have decided on your answer, reread the opening part of the question with the option you believe completes the statement correctly. You can often avoid careless mistakes by double-checking an answer before selecting it as your final answer.

Learn from Incorrect Answers

Do *not* immediately move to the next question if you receive feedback that your answer is incorrect. Instead, use this feedback as a learning opportunity. Reread the question and if the correct answer is provided, study the correct answer. Similar information may appear in another question, so the feedback may help you answer later questions correctly. This strategy also keeps your mind focused on the materials and reduces the tendency to move too hastily to the next question.

Use Relaxation Techniques

Pause and use a short relaxation technique if you find yourself tensing up, feeling discouraged, or getting irritated. Working memory needs to remain free of mental clutter; stress or anxiety affects thinking processes. The breathing by threes technique, using positive self-talk, or stretching your arms, rolling your shoulders, or shaking out your hands help reduce stress.

Discuss Your Test-Taking Experience

Before you leave the test, jot down any questions that concerned or confused you. Discuss these questions with your instructor. Make a brief list of topics you need to review or study further. After taking several tests, if you remain uncomfortable with computerized tests, ask lab assistants or your instructor for additional test-taking strategies. Talk to other students to learn their strategies. Ask your instructor if there is an option to take a paper-pencil or written test.

EXERCISE 7.8

Practice Test-Taking Skills

DIRECTIONS: Go to Exercise 7.8: Practice Test-Taking Skills in Chapter 7 Topics In-Depth in your College Success CourseMate to practice answering objective and recall questions. After printing the exercise, you may work by yourself, with a partner, or in a small group to complete this exercise. If your instructor does not assign this exercise, you may complete the practice questions and use the exercise as a review tool for a midterm exam for this course.

Access Chapter 7 Topics In-Depth: Exercise 7.8 Practice Test-Taking Skills in your College Success CourseMate, accessed through *CengageBrain.com*.

CHECK POINT 7.3

Answers appear on page B3.

True or False? See Test-Taking Strategies 1–9 in Appendix A.

_____ 1. Looking for patterns of errors, using assisted response, and correcting errors are processes that students cannot do while taking computerized tests.

_____ 2. Once you mark an answer, you should never go back and change that answer.

_____ 3. The third level of response to answer test questions involves using other parts of the test to search for clues to answer a question.

_____ 4. When taking computerized tests, it is important to move through the test as quickly as possible to avoid forgetting information that appeared in earlier questions.

_____ 5. Educated selection is also referred to as educated guessing.

Access Chapter 7 Practice Quiz 3 in your College Success CourseMate, accessed through *CengageBrain.com*.

Test Anxiety Management Skills

4 *Identify the four main sources of test anxiety, and summarize strategies to reduce or eliminate test anxiety before and during the taking of tests.*

Stress is a reaction or response to events or situations that threaten to disrupt a person's normal patterns or routines.

Test anxiety is excessive stress that hinders a person's ability to perform well before or during a test.

Stress is defined as a reaction or response to events or situations that threaten to disrupt a person's normal patterns or routines. Stress specifically related to an upcoming test can be beneficial and motivate people to perform on higher levels; however, excessive stress that becomes *test anxiety* creates negative responses and consequences. **Test anxiety** is excessive stress that hinders a person's ability to perform well *before* or *during* a test. The following points are also important to understand:

- Students who experience bouts with test anxiety can learn strategies to reduce the effects, duration, and intensity of this form of anxiety.

FIGURE 7.7 Symptoms Related to Test Anxiety

Kinds of Symptoms	Examples of Symptoms of Test Anxiety		
Physical	Rapid heartbeat Upset stomach, nausea Abnormal nervousness Tight muscles, tension	Blurred vision Increased blood pressure Shakiness	Headaches Clammy palms More than normal sweating
Emotional	Fear, anger, frustration Irritable, short-tempered Fatigue	Feelings of hopelessness or lack of control of a situation	"Fight or flight" feelings Anxious, nervous, panicky Depressed
Cognitive	Mind filled with intrusive thoughts Poor concentration Inaccurate or limited recall Confusion, disorientation	Impulsive responses Negative self-talk Lack of clear thinking Misdirected attention "Going blank"	Fixating on one item too long Careless mistakes Overemphasis on negative thoughts
Behavioral	Crying, sobbing Strained facial expressions	Slumped posture Procrastination	Shaky voice Aggressive behavior

- Test anxiety before and during a test can exhibit its presence in physical, emotional, cognitive, and behavioral forms. **Figure 7.7** shows common symptoms related to test anxiety.
- Common signs of test anxiety include becoming ill or emotionally distraught, experiencing confused or disorganized thinking, or using avoidance strategies to procrastinate studying for a test.
- During a test, test anxiety affects cognitive processing and can immobilize thinking skills. A student may "go blank," make excessive careless mistakes, mark answers in the wrong place, or quit due to frustration.

EXERCISE 7.9

Test Anxiety Inventory

PURPOSE: Some students may experience test anxiety, which impacts their test performance; other students may experience test-related stress that actually motivates them to perform well. This inventory provides you with information about test anxiety indicators you may experience.

DIRECTIONS: Go to Exercise 7.9 in Appendix C, page C16, to complete the Test Anxiety Inventory.

Sources of Test Anxiety

Test anxiety is a *learned behavior.* As such, it can be unlearned. If you experience test anxiety, begin by analyzing the source of your anxiety. What triggers your test anxiety? Sometimes listening to the kinds of comments you make about tests will help you identify the source of your test anxiety. *Under-preparedness, past experiences, fear of failure,* and *poor test-taking skills* are four common sources of test anxiety.

Under-Preparedness

Students who do not apply study skills on a regular basis often need to resort to *cramming,* which is an attempt to learn large amounts of information in a short period of time. Cramming is a survival technique that often backfires. Frequently, students who cram become even more aware of how much *they do not know.* Feeling under-prepared can create test anxiety and lead to poor test performance. Following are student comments that indicate under-preparedness:

I am nervous about this test because I did not have enough time to study or review.
When I started reviewing, I realized how much I still needed to learn.
Everyone else seems to know more than I do. I should have studied more.
I can't keep up; there's too much information to learn in this class.

CONCEPT CHECK 7.11
For students who face a bout with test anxiety due to under-preparedness, what test-preparation strategies could they have used to avoid this excessive stress?

Return to pages 197–203 in this chapter to review strategies students can use to prepare for upcoming tests and not trigger test anxiety caused by under-preparedness.

Past Experiences

Low self-esteem is often the result of past experiences that left a person with a negative self-image or perception of his or her limited ability to perform well. Having experienced frustration, disappointment, or a sense of failure in past testing situations can create a cycle of negative self-talk, self-doubt, low self-esteem, and low self-confidence. Sometimes students who have experienced negative past experiences lay the blame for poor performance on other people instead of taking responsibility for their test results. Following are student comments that reflect test anxiety due to past experiences:

I never get decent grades on tests. I simply am not a good test taker.
I did not do well on the last test, so this test probably won't be any different.
Instructors write tricky tests that are not fair and are designed to flunk most students.
Tests make me feel stupid and embarrassed.

Students who encounter test anxiety due to beliefs, emotions, and attitudes based on previous experiences can try the following strategies to decrease or eliminate test anxiety:

- Use affirmations and positive self-talk to develop a stronger, positive self-image.
- Develop an internal locus of control.
- Focus on the present and not on the past.

Fear of Failure

CONCEPT CHECK 7.12
What strategies can students use to reduce or eliminate test anxiety based on fear of failure?

Another source of test anxiety is the fear of failure. Students with a fear of failure worry about the negative consequences of poor grades, which in turn increases stress levels which may trigger test anxiety. As discussed in Chapter 2, they also worry about disappointing other people.

Poor Test-Taking Skills

For many students, the source of test anxiety is linked directly to the lack of test-preparation skills and the lack of test-taking skills. Taking tests requires understanding various kinds of test questions as well as how to read and interpret questions accurately, conduct memory searches for answers, select answers carefully, and write appropriate answers. Following are student comments that reflect that poor test-taking skills are the source of test-anxiety:

I have never learned how to be a good test-taker. No one ever taught me.
I never know what to study or how to organize enough time to review.
I get nervous taking tests because I do not really know how to answer different kinds of questions.
I make a lot of mistakes because I have problems understanding the directions or the kind of answers that the instructor expects.
I never have enough time on tests to really show how much I know.

The majority of this chapter and all of **Appendix A: Essential Test-Taking Skills** focus on powerful and effective strategies for performing well on tests. Spend ample time understanding and applying the strategies to avoid test anxiety due to poor test-taking skills. Use the Practice Quizzes and Enhanced Quizzes in this textbook's College Success CourseMate to practice your test-taking skills. Practicing test-taking skills in a non-testing situation builds confidence and improves test-taking performance.

GROUP PROCESSING

A Collaborative Learning Activity

1. Form groups of three or four students. Your group will need to have a chart to record responses. Select one member of your group to be the group recorder.
2. Create the following chart. In the Strategies column, brainstorm and list strategies students could use to "unlearn" the behaviors and beliefs that cause test anxiety. Use your knowledge of memory strategies, self-regulation or self-management strategies, and strategies from this chapter to compile ways students can combat test anxiety.

Source	Strategies
Under-preparedness	
Past Experiences	
Fear of Failure	
Poor Test-Taking Skills	

Access Chapter 7 Topics In-Depth: Strategies to Reduce Test Anxiety in your College Success CourseMate, accessed through *CengageBrain.com*.

Strategies to Reduce Test Anxiety *Before* a Test

In the Group Processing Activity, you and members of your group listed an array of strategies from previous chapters to deal with test anxiety. Using strategies related to time management, goal setting, motivation, the twelve memory processes, and the Twelve Principles of Memory help you prepare for tests and create a positive mindset to perform well.

Systematic desensitization is an anxiety-reducing strategy that involves a series of activities designed to reduce strong negative emotional reactions to an upcoming situation.

A final strategy you can learn to use *before* a test to create a positive mindset and reduce or eliminate test anxiety is called *systematic desensitization*. **Systematic desensitization** is an anxiety-reducing strategy that involves a series of activities designed to reduce strong negative emotional reactions to an upcoming situation. You can use this strategy before the day of a test by replacing your fear-based thoughts with positive thoughts that emphasize the successes you have already experienced. Systematic desensitization stops the fear from accelerating and getting blown out of proportion. You can use systematic desensitization in the following ways:

1. **Reduce your emotional response to trigger words.** Make a list of specific situations or words that trigger your test anxiety. For example, "There will be a test next Monday" may trigger early test anxiety. After you have your list of *trigger situations or words,* visualize yourself reacting differently to those situations or words. See yourself responding in a more positive and constructive way. "Good. I have time to make a five-day plan, or I have stayed current with my work, so I can be ready for this test."
2. **Create a mock test situation to imitate the real test situation.** Predict and write practice test questions. Decide on an appropriate amount of time to answer the test questions. Create a test environment as close as possible to the real thing. If the classroom in which you will take a test is empty, be in that room when you take your practice test.
3. **Capture the feelings of the mock situation with less stress and anxiety.** Create an image of yourself in the mock situation taking the test in a relaxed, alert manner. Remind yourself that there is no need to be overly nervous about one test.

CONCEPT CHECK 7.13

Fears often become overexaggerated. How could you use systematic desensitization to deflate an overexaggerated fear? Give specific details.

Strategies to Reduce Test Anxiety *During* a Test

You can reduce or eliminate most test anxiety that occurs during a test by using the essential strategies for taking tests shown in **Figure 7.4**, page 213. The following strategies address specific symptoms that you might experience during a bout with anxiety during a test.

- **When you "go blank" and are unable to recall the needed information, do the following:**
  1. Use a quick relaxation technique to calm yourself down.
  2. Use positive self-talk. Become your own cheerleader.
  3. Reread the question in a whisper voice. Go into retrieval mode by conducting a new memory search. If necessary, place a check mark to return to the question later. Do not stay stuck on the question.
- **When your eyes start jumping from the printed line or skip over words when you read, do the following:**
  1. Use your arm, a blank index card, or a blank piece of paper to block off the rest of the test. Restricting your vision so you only see the question that you are contemplating helps your eyes stay focused on a line of information.
  2. Use your pencil to point to each word as you read silently. Doing this keeps your eyes from skipping words or jumping to other lines of print.
- **When you notice yourself making excessive careless mistakes in selecting or marking the correct answer, do the following:**
  1. Slow down the reading and answering process. Rush less and think more.

2. Activate your auditory channel by mouthing or quietly whispering the words as you read the directions, questions, and options for answers.
3. Highlight key words in the questions. Check to ensure that your answer relates to the key words.
4. Before moving to the next question, ask yourself: *Does this answer make sense?*

- **When your mind shifts away from the test and your concentration begins fading quickly, do the following:**

1. Become more active and interactive with the test. Circle direction words and highlight key words in directions and questions.
2. Use positive self-talk and force yourself to keep your eyes on the test. "*I can do this. My eyes and my mind stay focused on the paper. I can figure this out.*"

CHAPTER 7 REFLECTIVE WRITING 2

On separate paper, in a journal, or online in this textbook's College Success CourseMate, respond to the following questions.

1. For the majority of test-taking situations you encounter, what strategies do you use that help you enter the classroom feeling confident and well-prepared for the test?
2. Which specific skills in this chapter will help you the most in terms of preparing for tests, performing well on tests, and managing test anxiety? Discuss at least four skills and include specific strategies you intend to use.

Access Chapter 7 Reflective Writing 2 in your College Success CourseMate, accessed through *CengageBrain.com*.

CHECK POINT 7.4

Answers appear on page B3.

Definitions See Test-Taking Strategies 29–31 in Appendix A.

1. Define the term *test anxiety.*
2. Define the term *open-ended question.*

Essay Question See Test-Taking Strategies 45–51 in Appendix A.

DIRECTIONS: Choose one of the following essay questions to answer. Create an organizational plan for your answer. Use the five-paragraph format to write an essay answer. Proofread, revise, and print your answer.

Essay Question 1: Discuss ways students can avoid test-anxiety caused by under-preparedness. Include test-preparation strategies for any three of these areas: organizing materials, organizing time, creating review study tools, or using effective memory-boosting strategies.

Essay Question 2: Discuss how past experiences and fear of failure may trigger test anxiety. Then summarize strategies students could use to reduce or eliminate test anxiety caused by past experiences or fear of failure.

Access Chapter 7 Practice Quiz 4 in your College Success CourseMate, accessed through *CengageBrain.com*.

ACTIVITY

Chapter 7 Critical Thinking

DIRECTIONS:

1. To help prepare for a major upcoming test, predict and practice writing six review questions that cover the chapters and topics that will be included in the test. Write one question for each level of questions in Bloom's Taxonomy: remembering, understanding, applying, analyzing, evaluating, and creating.
2. Submit your questions to your instructor. Questions may be discussed in class, presented to the class for review activities, or used on the upcoming test.

Terms to Know

By yourself or with a partner, practice reciting or writing definitions for the following terms. You may also practice defining these terms by using the online flashcards or comparing your answers to the online glossary.

recency effect p. 199
five-day study plan p. 200
summary notes p. 201
true-false questions p. 204
multiple-choice questions p. 204
matching questions p. 205
closed questions p. 205
open-ended questions p. 205
direction words p. 205
fill-in-the-blanks questions p. 205
listing questions p. 207
definition questions p. 207
short-answer questions p. 207
problem-solving questions p. 208
essay questions p. 209
four levels of response p. 215
immediate response p. 216
delayed response p. 216
assisted response p. 216
educated selection p. 216

Learning Objectives Review

1 *Discuss effective strategies to organize materials and time, create a five-day study plan and summary notes, and use memory strategies to review for upcoming tests.*

- Appendix A: Essential Test-Taking Skills is a valuable resource with fifty-two detailed strategies for responding to all kinds of test questions.
- Organizing materials to prepare for a test involves jotting down tips from the instructor, gathering materials to review, and predicting test questions.
- Time-management strategies, a five-day study plan, and using the recency effect are strategies to organize time effectively to prepare for tests.
- Summary notes, special notes designed specifically for final reviews, help students be better prepared for upcoming tests.
- Memory strategies used to learn information and imprint information into memory are also used to review for upcoming tests.

2 *Identify the different kinds of objective, recall, math, and essay questions that appear on tests, and explain at least two strategies for answering each type of question.*

- Four kinds of questions that you will encounter on college tests include: objective questions, recall questions, math questions, and essay questions.
- Appendix A provides detailed strategies for responding to objective questions, which include true-false, multiple choice, and matching questions.
- Appendix A provides detailed strategies for recall questions, which include fill-in-the-blanks, listing, definition, and short-answer questions.
- Appendix A provides detailed strategies for responding to math questions, which often include problem-solving and word problems.

- Appendix A provides detailed strategies for organizing and writing answers for essay test questions.
- Different test-preparation strategies are used for essay tests which provide students with topics or questions in advance, in-class essays, open-book essays, and take-home essays.

3 ***Describe effective test-taking strategies to increase your performance on classroom, online, and computerized tests.***

- Jotting down information, surveying and budgeting time, deciding on a starting point, and using test time wisely are four strategies to use to create a plan of action to begin a test.
- Carefully reading directions and questions, answering all questions, changing answers carefully, and using four levels of response to answer questions are effective test-taking strategies.
- Using the following four levels of response for answering questions can improve your test results: immediate response, delayed response, assisted response, and educated selection (educated guessing).
- You can learn from your tests by examining correct answers, looking for patterns of errors in incorrect answers, and correcting errors.
- Computerized tests differ from paper-pencil tests. Seven essential strategies can boost your computerized test performance.

4 ***Identify the four main sources of test anxiety, and summarize strategies to reduce or eliminate test anxiety before and during the taking of tests.***

- Test anxiety is excessive stress that affects performance. Symptoms of test anxiety may be physical, emotional, cognitive, or behavioral.
- Four common sources of test anxiety include under-preparedness, past experiences, fear of failure, and poor test-taking skills.
- Test anxiety is a learned behavior that can be "unlearned" by using effective test-anxiety management strategies before and during a test.

Terms to Know

continued

stress p. 220

test anxiety p. 220

systematic desensitization p. 224

Access Chapter 7 Flashcards and Online Glossary in your College Success CourseMate, accessed through *CengageBrain.com*.

Chapter 7 Review Questions

Answers appear on page B3–B4.

True or False? See Test-Taking Strategies 1–9 in Appendix A.

_____ 1. A five-day study plan promotes spaced practice for test-preparation.

_____ 2. You can use the recency effect by doing a final review one or two hours before the time of a test.

_____ 3. Instructors usually announce or remind students about upcoming tests, but they never provide suggestions about what to study or what kinds of test questions to expect.

_____ 4. Recall questions include listing, multiple-choice, definition, and short-answer questions.

_____ 5. Summary notes are a detailed compilation of all of your textbook and lecture notes organized day by day and chapter by chapter.

_____ 6. Memory strategies to prepare for upcoming tests include using visualizations, associations, recitation, procrastination, stress, and test-anxiety.

Multiple Choice See Test-Taking Strategies 10–15 in Appendix A.

_____ 1. Effective test-preparation skills
 a. reduce the necessity to cram for tests and use rote memory techniques.
 b. include time-management and goal-setting techniques.
 c. involve making summary notes and predicting, writing, and answering practice test questions.
 d. include all of the above.

_____ 2. In a five-day study plan, you
 a. begin by listing the topics and materials you need to review.
 b. schedule review times on a calendar.
 c. may set aside more than one study block for each day in the plan.
 d. do all of the above.

_____ 3. Which of the following statements is *not* true about test anxiety?
 a. A person's self-esteem and locus of control may contribute to test anxiety.
 b. Test anxiety is productive and beneficial for many students.
 c. A person's lack of test-preparation and test-taking skills may trigger test anxiety.
 d. Test anxiety is a learned behavior that can be altered, eliminated, or "unlearned."

_____ 4. Cramming
 a. is a survival technique used for under-preparedness.
 b. is highly effective when used the day before a test.
 c. processes large amounts of information efficiently.
 d. involves all of the above.

_____ 5. Which of the following is *not* an effective test-taking strategy?
 a. Leave some questions temporarily unanswered when taking a test.
 b. Read directions and questions carefully to avoid unnecessary mistakes.
 c. Do not feel that you must work through the test questions in the order that they appear on the test.
 d. Your original answer is always the correct one, so avoid returning to questions to change the original answer.

Definitions See Test-Taking Strategies 29–31 in Appendix A.

Write a definition for the following terms. Each answer should include a three-part definition.

1. Systematic desensitization

2. Summary notes

3. Test anxiety

4. Closed questions

Short-Answer Questions See Test-Taking Strategies 32–36 in Appendix A.

On separate paper, answer any two of the following questions. Include details and chapter terminology in your answers.

1. True-false questions sometimes are considered by students to be "easy," yet students can answer incorrectly if they do not read questions carefully. Identify any three true-false strategies students can use to perform well on true-false tests.
2. Your instructor indicates that a section of matching questions will appear on the test. What kinds of information should you review to prepare for an upcoming test with matching questions?
3. Identify which one of the four levels of response cannot be used on computerized tests and explain why it cannot be used.
4. What strategies are effective for students who have difficulty organizing ideas to answer essay questions?

Take-Home Essay Question See Test-Taking Strategies 45–51 in Appendix A.

Question: Discuss strategies that you can use to prepare for tests, take tests, and learn from tests to improve your performance in your courses this term. Use the space below to draw your organizational plan for your essay.

Access Chapter 7 Enhanced Quiz and Chapter 7 Study Guide in your College Success CourseMate, accessed through *CengageBrain.com*.

Access all Chapter 7 Online Materials in your College Success CourseMate, accessed through *CengageBrain.com*.

8 Selecting a Reading System

© Stockbyte/Getty Images

Many college students have reading habits and use techniques that they have established over many years of reading, yet those habits and techniques may be inadequate to handle the demands of college-level reading and comprehension. In this chapter, you will begin the process of replacing old reading habits and techniques with more effective ones designed to strengthen your reading skills and improve comprehension of textbook materials.

CHAPTER OUTLINE

1 **FIRST STEPS OF THE READING PROCESS**
- *Developing Positive Attitudes and Behaviors*
- *Identifying Purposes for Reading*
- *Adjusting the Reading Rate*
- *Surveying a Textbook*
- *Surveying an Article or an Essay*

2 **ESSENTIAL TEXTBOOK READING PROCESSES**
- *Using a Reading System*
- *Surveying a Chapter*
- *Writing Focus Questions*
- *Reading Carefully*
- *Reviewing*

3 **THREE SPECIFIC READING SYSTEMS**
- *SQ4R*
- *The Outline Reading System*
- *A Customized Reading System*

4 **READING PROCESSES FOR ONLINE E-BOOKS**
- *Advantages of E-Textbooks*
- *E-Textbook Challenges*
- *Navigating the Essential Study Skills E-Textbook*
- *Effective Reading Strategies for E-Textbooks*

Access Chapter 8 Expanded Chapter Outline in your College Success CourseMate, accessed through *CengageBrain.com*.

YOUR CHAPTER MAPPING

After reading information under each heading, return to the chapter visual mapping below. Add key words to show subheadings and important details related to each heading.

Access Chapter 8 Visual Mapping in your College Success CourseMate, accessed through *CengageBrain.com*.

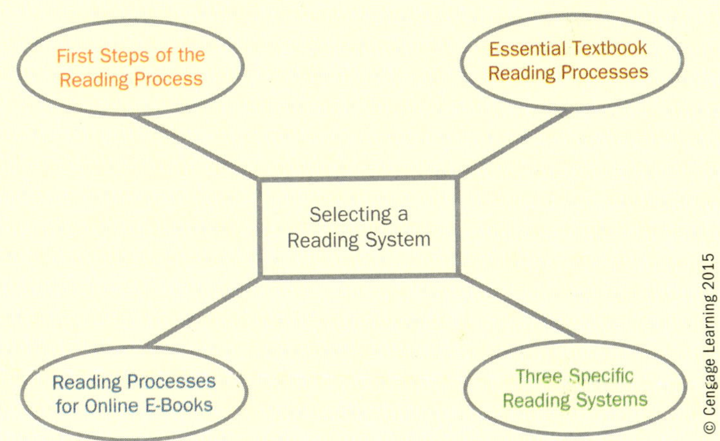

LEARNING OBJECTIVES

1. *Discuss the importance of attitude, purpose for reading, reading rate, and the process of surveying as first steps in the reading process.*
2. *Identify and explain the essential processes used in an effective textbook reading system.*
3. *Compare and contrast the steps used in three reading systems: SQ4R, the Outline Reading System, and a Customized Reading System.*
4. *Explain effective reading strategies to use for online e-textbooks.*

CHAPTER 8 PROFILE

Selecting a Reading System

ANSWER, SCORE, and **RECORD** your profile before you read this chapter. If you need to review the process, refer to the complete directions given in the profile for Chapter 1 on page 4.

Access Chapter 8 Profile in your College Success CourseMate, accessed through *CengageBrain.com.*

ONLINE: You can complete the profile and get your score online in this textbook's College Success CourseMate.

	YES	NO
1. I find that reading textbooks is difficult and confusing for me to do, so I read only enough to get by or to get a general understanding of the content.	______	______
2. I verbalize, visualize, and ask myself questions about content when I read textbook chapters.	______	______
3. I survey new textbooks and know how to use the sections in the front and the sections in the back of the textbook.	______	______
4. I use a textbook reading system that begins with surveying new chapters, involves some form of notetaking and reciting, and ends with a review of the chapter content.	______	______
5. I take notes and recite only when a textbook chapter is difficult for me to understand.	______	______
6. I take the time to create questions when I am reading and studying information from a textbook.	______	______
7. I have one textbook reading system and use that system to read all of my textbooks.	______	______
8. I read online e-textbook chapters more quickly and with fewer pauses than when I read traditional printed textbooks.	______	______
9. I use the read-record-recite cycle when I read online e-textbooks and printed textbooks.	______	______
10. I am confident in my ability to select effective processes and an effective reading system for my textbooks.	______	______

QUESTIONS LINKED TO THE CHAPTER LEARNING OBJECTIVES:

Questions 1–3: objective 1
Questions 4–6: objective 2
Question 7: objective 3
Questions 8–9: objective 4
Question 10: all objectives

First Steps of the Reading Process

1 *Discuss the importance of attitude, purpose for reading, reading rate, and the process of surveying as first steps in the reading process.*

As a college student, you will spend thousands of hours reading thousands of textbook pages filled with information you will be required to learn. You will also be required to comprehend information from other sources, such as Internet and online articles, excerpts, journal reviews, library books, and reference materials. You can save yourself time and increase your academic performance by developing and strengthening your college-level reading skills from basic skills to more advanced, critical reading skills.

Developing Positive Attitudes and Behaviors

The reading process begins as soon as you sit down with a textbook in front of you. *Do you look forward to reading and learning from your textbook, or does a negative attitude kick in? Do you value the reading process enough to set aside adequate time to read and work with textbook information without interruptions, or do you try to read quickly to get it done, or do you multitask during the reading process?* The attitude and choice of behaviors you bring to the reading process affect the quality of the reading experience.

Figure 8.1 shows important attitudes and behaviors that lay a strong foundation for the first steps of the reading process for college-level readers.

FIGURE 8.1 Attitudes and Behaviors for College-Level Readers

- **Begin with an attitude to learn**. A positive, inquisitive, receptive attitude signals to your working memory that the information is important to grasp and learn.
- **Create reading goals**. Know your intention or purpose for reading. Is it to get an overview, comprehend in-depth details, compare sources of information, or review?
- **Be patient and do not rush the reading process**. Thorough reading requires time for your mind to mull over, absorb, process, and integrate new information.
- **Be persistent**. You may need to reread difficult sections of material more slowly and multiple times. To comprehend, you may need to break paragraphs into smaller units, chunk information in new ways, and analyze details more carefully. Persistent readers do not skip a paragraph because it is difficult to understand, nor do they quit or give up when the content is more difficult than anticipated.
- **Use all available resources**. Take the time and show the effort to learn by being a resourceful reader. Use textbook resources, online supplementary materials, computer and lab resources, study guides, tutors, and study groups.
- **Adjust your reading rate**. Do not expect or attempt to use the same reading rate for all materials. Some materials can be read one page at a time, while other materials will require reading one paragraph, or even smaller sections of a paragraph, slowly and repeatedly in order to understand the information.
- **Take responsibility for your learning**. Attending class and listening to lectures is not sufficient to master course content. Creating a strong habit of scheduling adequate time to read and learn from textbooks reflects genuine goals to be an effective and successful college student.

FIGURE 8.2 Purposes for Reading

Purposes	Description
Recreational Reading	• Use to read newspapers, magazines, short stories, poetry, or fiction. • Read to be entertained, read for pleasure, or read to stay updated on current events.
Overview Reading	• Use for new material or difficult material. • Survey or skim to create a *big picture* or framework before reading thoroughly. • Read through difficult material uninterrupted and without stalling to become familiar with the topic before beginning thorough reading.
Thorough Reading	• Use for textbook or course-related materials. • Use reading flexibility to adjust to levels of difficulty. • Read slowly and systematically to allow your brain time to acquire and process new information and skills. • Read to understand paragraph structures, organizational patterns, and to identify important information to record in notes. • Use elaborative rehearsal strategies to practice new information.
Comparative Reading	• Use for two or more articles, excerpts, or books on the same subject. • Compare or contrast, organize, and analyze for similarities and differences in points of view, rationale, implications, interpretations, models, or approaches.

Identifying Purposes for Reading

Making sense of what you read does not occur automatically. With some reading materials, you are able to read and quickly grasp the meaning of new information without much effort or struggle, yet with other reading materials, you need to work to understand, process, store, retrieve, and use the information. **Figure 8.2** shows four different purposes for reading. ***Purposes for reading***—which include recreational, overview, thorough, and comparative—represent different reading skills and reading goals for different kinds of reading material.

Purposes for reading, which include recreational, overview, thorough, and comparative, represent different reading skills and reading goals for different kinds of reading material.

Recreational Reading

Recreational reading is the process of reading for the main purpose of being entertained or keeping up to date on current events. Television, the Internet, smartphones, digital tablets, laptops, and DVDs offer extensive access to news, current events, sports, games, movies, and other forms of entertainment. For many recreational readers, downloading newspapers, magazines, and books onto e-readers—such as a Kindle, a Nook, or an iPad tablet—has increased recreational reading. Despite the temptation to rely on digital media for information, traditional newspapers, books, and magazines remain important as sources for all types of reading material. Whether using traditional or digital e-reader materials, creating and strengthening the habit of reading has many benefits:

Recreational reading is the process of reading for the main purpose of being entertained or keeping up to date on current events.

- Reading for enjoyment does not require analysis or memory work.
- Recreational reading exposes the reader to new concepts and vocabulary.
- Reading for enjoyment lays a foundation for thorough reading, which focuses on comprehension, higher-level thinking skills, and memory work.
- Recreational reading reduces a dislike or negative attitude toward books.

CONCEPT CHECK 8.1

What kinds of recreational reading do you do on a regular basis? Do you read printed materials or electronic materials on an e-reader or tablet?

Overview Reading

Overview reading is the process of skimming or reading materials without interruption. Overview reading helps the reader form a big picture or a schema for the topic before engaging in more in-depth, thorough reading. You can use overview reading to:

- **Survey:** Scan the content of a new textbook, chapter, or a test.
- **Tune-in to the flow of action:** Get a sense of the flavor of a short story, essay, play, or excerpt by reading without stopping or pausing to analyze. This type of overview reading often stirs your imagination, creates an emotional connection with the words, immerses you in the material, and keeps the unity of the plot and the characters' actions moving steadily forward.
- **Gain background basics:** Get a sense of the material in a difficult or complex section or chapter of a textbook without focusing on immediately understanding the details. Reading *carefully but continuously* all the way through can provide you with basic background information, lay a foundation for more thorough reading, and alert you to sections that seem confusing or complicated.

Overview reading is the process of skimming or reading materials without interruption.

CONCEPT CHECK 8.2

What are effective uses for overview reading? How does overview reading affect comprehension?

Thorough Reading

Thorough reading is the process of reading slowly and systematically in order to comprehend and process printed or digital information. Reading is more than simply reading a string of words silently or out loud. Instead, reading is a complex process that involves many cognitive functions and processes designed to help the reader understand and use different levels of information. Following is a brief description of the process of reading to comprehend:

- As you read a chunk of information, your working memory retrieves related information from long-term memory to help you understand new information.
- Working memory then integrates the new information with retrieved information and returns the unit of information back into long-term memory and the appropriate schemas.
- The interaction and exchange of information between memory systems happens quickly and continually throughout the reading process.
- Integrated information is used on higher, critical reading levels to compare, contrast, question, challenge, prove, solve problems, or show other kinds of relationships.

Thorough reading is the process of reading slowly and systematically in order to comprehend and process printed or digital information.

CONCEPT CHECK 8.3

Why does thorough reading require a time commitment to do effectively? What reading actions are involved in thorough reading?

Learning college-level reading strategies saves you time and improves college-level comprehension. You cannot afford to spend your valuable time reading page after page in the *automatic pilot mode*. The **automatic pilot mode** is a state of mind in which you mechanically go through specific motions without registering information into your memory. As you work through this chapter and Chapter 9, you will strengthen your thorough reading and comprehension skills. **Figure 8.3** shows essential thorough reading skills that lay a strong foundation for comprehension.

Automatic pilot mode is a state of mind in which you mechanically go through specific motions without registering information into your memory.

Comparative Reading

Comparative reading is the process of using higher-level critical thinking and reading skills to compare and contrast two or more sources of printed or digital information.

Comparative reading is the process of using higher-level critical thinking and reading skills to compare and contrast two or more sources of printed or digital information.

FIGURE 8.3 Essential Strategies for Thorough Reading

- **Create a plan of action.** Use a systematic reading system to move you through the reading assignment and processes.
- **Use a warm-up activity.** Begin a study block by surveying or reviewing to create a mindset for careful, thorough reading.
- **Verbalize and visualize.** Reading out loud (verbalizing) activates auditory channels to memory. Visualizing activates visual memory.
- **Adjust your reading rate.** Slow down the intake process to give your mind sufficient time to attach meaning to words, process and integrate information, and create associations.
- **Relate new information to existing schemas in your long-term memory.** Thinking about associations and linking different chunks of information lead to greater comprehension. Ask questions such as *What do I already know about this topic? How is it similar and how is it different from previous learning or past experiences? What are the important points and details?*
- **Recognize different levels of information as you read.** Strive to become an analytical reader who can recognize major themes, large concepts (schemas), main ideas, and important supporting details.
- **Learn terminology and definitions.** Knowing definitions of key terms lays the foundation for more complex learning and provides you with tools to communicate subject matter effectively to others.
- **Use spaced practice or spaced studying.** Spreading the reading process and activities over several different time periods actually cuts down total learning time. Avoid *marathon studying*, or in this case, *marathon reading*, which can overload your working memory.
- **Use elaborative rehearsal and active learning techniques as you read.** Actions that engage you in the reading and learning process help you maintain attention and concentration, encode information in new ways, and make stronger impressions of the information for memory.
- **Include some form of feedback as you study.** Use self-quizzing, reciting, and Look-Away Techniques to check the thoroughness and accuracy of your comprehension and memory.

Assignments that involve comparative reading may involve contrasting two or more articles, essays, or reports about the same topic, model, or approach but with different points of views or different authors. After surveying the two different sources of information, use the following suggestions to compare or contrast the sources:

- What do the two sources have in common?
- What are the major differences in approaches, points of views, or outcomes?
- Do the authors or sources of each article carry the same level of authority or credibility?
- Does one provide more supporting details or prove the thesis statement better?
- Based on the assignment, what elements of the readings should be compared or contrasted?

Adjusting the Reading Rate

Thorough reading requires flexibility to adjust your reading approach to various levels of difficulty. Some textbooks are easy to read and understand; others require a considerable amount of attention and effort. In any given textbook, you may be able to read some sections more quickly, but then you may need to slow the reading process for more difficult sections. Following are important points about using flexibility during thorough reading:

- Selecting an appropriate amount of material to read before pausing to think about or work with information prevents overloading your working memory.
  - **Textbooks with relatively easy levels of difficulty:** Stop at the end of each *page* to think about the information, create visual images of the material, and associate it to other information in long-term memory.
  - **Textbooks with average levels of difficulty:** Use a *read-pause approach* after each paragraph for most textbooks. Stop at the end of *each paragraph* to think about and process the information. Identify main ideas, important details, and meanings of terminology.
  - **Textbooks with difficult reading levels and complex content:** Stop at the end of *each sentence* or *group of sentences* to check understanding and think about and process the information.
- ***Chunking*** information is a process of grouping information into meaningfully sized units of information to comprehend and process. Chunking gives working memory sufficient time to grasp, associate, and integrate information for understanding. It also helps you avoid going into automatic pilot mode, which results in little or no information registering in your memory.
  - When you *chunk up,* you look beyond the paragraph to determine how the paragraph fits into the bigger picture and in the context of surrounding material. Reread the previous paragraphs and read ahead to the following paragraph or paragraphs to find the natural flow or progression of information.
  - When you *chunk down,* you break the information into smaller units, perhaps as small as individual sentences or phrases, to identify the meanings of details.

Chunking information is a process of grouping information into meaningfully sized units of information to comprehend and process.

Surveying a Textbook

Surveying is the process of previewing or skimming information to get an overview. Surveying is one form of overview reading designed to help the reader get the big picture and set up schemas for all kinds of reading materials or for tests. Surveying a new textbook before you begin reading specific chapters acquaints you with the book's philosophy, organization, and special features; it also provides you with suggestions for using the book more effectively. Surveying a textbook is a process that usually requires less than 30 minutes of your time at the beginning of the term. Following are the sections of a textbook you should survey to familiarize yourself with the textbook and its features.

Surveying is the process of previewing or skimming information to get an overview.

CONCEPT CHECK 8.4

What is the value of surveying a textbook? Which sections of a textbook do you think you will use most frequently? Explain why.

1. The **table of contents** is the "roadmap" for the textbook. It provides you with an overview of the organization of the topics (chronological or thematic), chapter headings and subheadings, page numbers, and other textbook features.
2. The **introductory materials** include the *Preface, Introduction, To the Teacher,* and *To the Student.* The *Preface* or the *Introduction* provides insight into the philosophy, objectives, and structure of the book. The *To the Teacher* and *To the Student* sections feature valuable suggestions, study strategies, explanations, and ways to use textbook features.

The **appendix** is a section in the back of a book that contains supplementary materials that were not included within the chapters.

3. An ***appendix*** is a section in the back of a book that contains supplementary materials that were not included within the chapters. Answer keys, additional exercises, practice tests, supplementary readings, or important tables, graphs, charts, or maps are kinds of materials that may appear in an appendix.

The **glossary** is a minidictionary in the back of a book that contains definitions of course-specific terminology.

4. The ***glossary*** is a minidictionary in the back of a book that contains definitions of course-specific terminology. Definitions in a glossary are limited to the meanings of terms as used in the textbook. Bold, italic, or colored print within textbook chapters often indicate *key terms* that appear in the glossary. Use the following strategies with textbooks that do have a glossary.

   - Each time you see words in special print in a chapter, locate the terms in the glossary to see if the glossary provides more details or clarifies the definition.
   - As you encounter terminology while reading each chapter, place a star next to or highlight those terms in the glossary. Use the glossary as a review tool to prepare for tests.
   - Make separate definition cards or vocabulary sheets with the definitions of key terms to review to prepare for tests.

The **index** is an alphabetical listing of significant topics that appear in the book.

5. The ***index*** is an alphabetical listing of significant topics that appear in the book. The index is a valuable textbook section used to quickly locate pages for specific topics. Textbooks may have a *subject index,* an *author index,* or an *index of illustrations.* Topics are frequently cross-referenced so they appear in more than one place in the index. The following strategies will help you use the index effectively:

   - After a lecture or class discussion, locate an unfamiliar term in the index of your book to find the page number in your textbook that further explains the term or concept.
   - When you are assigned a specific topic for a research paper, an essay, a writing assignment, a project, or a test, use the index to locate pages in the textbook that discuss the topic. Turn to the page numbers provided to read or review the information.

EXERCISE 8.1

Surveying This Textbook

PURPOSE: Surveying a textbook, designed to familiarize you with the textbook structure and features, takes fifteen to thirty minutes. Surveying a chapter, designed to help you create a mindset for a new topic and get an overview or a big picture of upcoming information, usually takes less than twenty minutes.

DIRECTIONS:

Part I: Survey the front and the back section of this textbook. Then answer the following questions on separate paper.

1. What did you learn from reading the introductory information? How did it help familiarize you with this textbook?

Exercise 8.1 (continued)

2. What kind of information appears in the appendixes?
3. The glossary for this textbook is online. Explain how to access the online glossary.
4. Explain how you have already used the index this term.

Part II: After reading "Surveying a Chapter," survey a chapter in this textbook that you have not yet read. Then answer the following questions on separate paper.

1. Which features helped you begin to formulate a big picture of the chapter?
2. What benefits did you gain by examining visual materials?
3. What kinds of information in the margins helped you understand the new content?
4. What end-of-the-chapter features did you survey? What benefits did you gain by surveying these features?

Surveying an Article or an Essay

Surveying an article, an excerpt, an essay, or any other short reading requires a minimal amount of time but can provide you with valuable information. Following are six basic steps to use to survey an article or an essay:

1. **Think about the title**. Without reading the article or essay, what does the title mean to you? What do you predict that article will be about? What understanding or opinions do you already have about the subject?
2. **Identify the author**. Look in the byline or footnote for the author's name, affiliation with specific groups or organizations, additional publications, or other personal information. Think of ways the available information may relate to the subject matter and the author's point of view.
3. **Read and think about any introductory material**. Introductory material for short articles often provides necessary background information about the topic and the author.
4. **Read the first paragraph carefully**. The thesis statement, the main point or purpose of the entire article, often appears in this paragraph.
5. **Skim through the rest of the article**. Read the headings, subheadings, and side notes.
6. **Read the concluding paragraph**. The concluding paragraph often restates the thesis statement and summarizes the main ideas in the article.

To practice surveying articles, go to any of the excerpts in **Appendix D**. Use the above steps to survey and you will soon realize how much information you can obtain through the process of surveying before beginning thorough reading.

CHAPTER 8 REFLECTIVE WRITING 1

On separate paper, in a journal, or online in this textbook's College Success CourseMate, respond to the following questions.

1. What are your reading habits and interests? How often do you engage in recreational reading? What kinds of materials do you enjoy reading?
2. What type of reading is difficult or challenging for you? What specific difficulties do you encounter frequently?

Access Chapter 8 Reflective Writing 1 in your College Success CourseMate, accessed through *CengageBrain.com*.

CHECK POINT 8.1

Answers appear on page B4.

Multiple Choice See Test-Taking Strategies 10–15 in Appendix A.

d 1. Which of the following is *not* true about the reading process?
   - a. Reading is a complex process of recalling and creating associations.
   - b. You can use overview reading to become familiar with new material before reading and studying the details more thoroughly.
   - c. Chunking information into appropriate sizes gives your working memory time to process and integrate information.
   - d. When you have strong reading skills, your reading goal may be to use your *automatic pilot* to read many of your college textbooks.

d 2. Effective textbook reading strategies include
   - a. selecting meaningful and manageable sizes of information to process at one time.
   - b. identifying a purpose and a process to use for reading a textbook.
   - c. using spaced practice and including rehearsal techniques to reinforce concepts.
   - d. all of the above.

d 3. Surveying a textbook
   - a. does not require several hours to do correctly.
   - b. provides an opportunity to examine the index and glossary.
   - c. familiarizes the reader with the content of appendixes.
   - d. does all of the above.

a 4. Students with effective college-level reading skills
   - a. move into the reading process without feeling the need to create reading goals.
   - b. exhibit a positive attitude toward reading and a willingness to persist with difficult materials.
   - c. use their skills to read at a faster reading rate than they use for recreational reading.
   - d. exhibit all of the above characteristics.

Access Chapter 8 Practice Quiz 1 in your College Success CourseMate, accessed through *CengageBrain.com*.

Essential Textbook Reading Processes

2 *Identify and explain the essential processes used in an effective textbook reading system.*

Using a systematic approach for reading textbook chapters may take more time than you are used to spending for reading a chapter, but you will process and comprehend the information more thoroughly, eliminate the need to reread chapters multiple times to learn the content, and in the long run, save valuable study time.

Numerous reading systems are available for college students to use with college textbooks. No single textbook reading system is the most effective to use with all textbooks. As critical readers, a worthy reading goal is to familiarize yourself with individual textbooks, examine the kinds of information you will need to learn, pay attention to the level of complexity or difficulty of the content, and then select or create a textbook reading system that works most effectively for you and for each of your individual textbooks.

Using a Reading System

There are no shortcuts for reading and learning from college textbooks. Opening a chapter and surveying instead of reading or reading quickly from beginning to end does take less time than using a reading system, but it results in lower comprehension and ineffective use of your time. **Figure 8.4** shows you options and textbook reading processes to use to create a powerful reading system that strengthens your textbook reading skills. Note that *surveying* and *reviewing* are standard, essential steps to use in all reading systems. The following sections explain how to use the options in Figure 8.4.

Surveying a Chapter

Surveying is the process of previewing or skimming information to get an overview. Surveying a chapter is so important that most textbook reading systems begin with the process of surveying the chapter. You can survey a new chapter as a *warm-up* activity at the beginning of a study block before you begin thorough reading. Surveying a chapter is an effective part of the reading process because it does the following:

- Focuses your mind on the upcoming reading assignment
- Creates interest, enhances your motivation, and boosts confidence in mastering new material
- Reduces the tendency to procrastinate about starting to read a new chapter
- Forms a big picture or schema of the chapter and helps you connect new information to information you already know
- Familiarizes you with graphic and marginal materials used to explain concepts
- Provides you with a general idea about the length and difficulty level of the material
- Helps you set realistic reading and studying goals, manage your time, and select an appropriate reading process to use to work your way through the chapter

Surveying a chapter requires fewer than 20 minutes. For longer chapters, you can modify the process by surveying as many pages of the chapter as you think that you realistically can cover in one or two study blocks; survey the remaining pages at

CONCEPT CHECK 8.5
What may be some consequences of not *taking the time to survey a new chapter?*

FIGURE 8.4 Using a Reading System

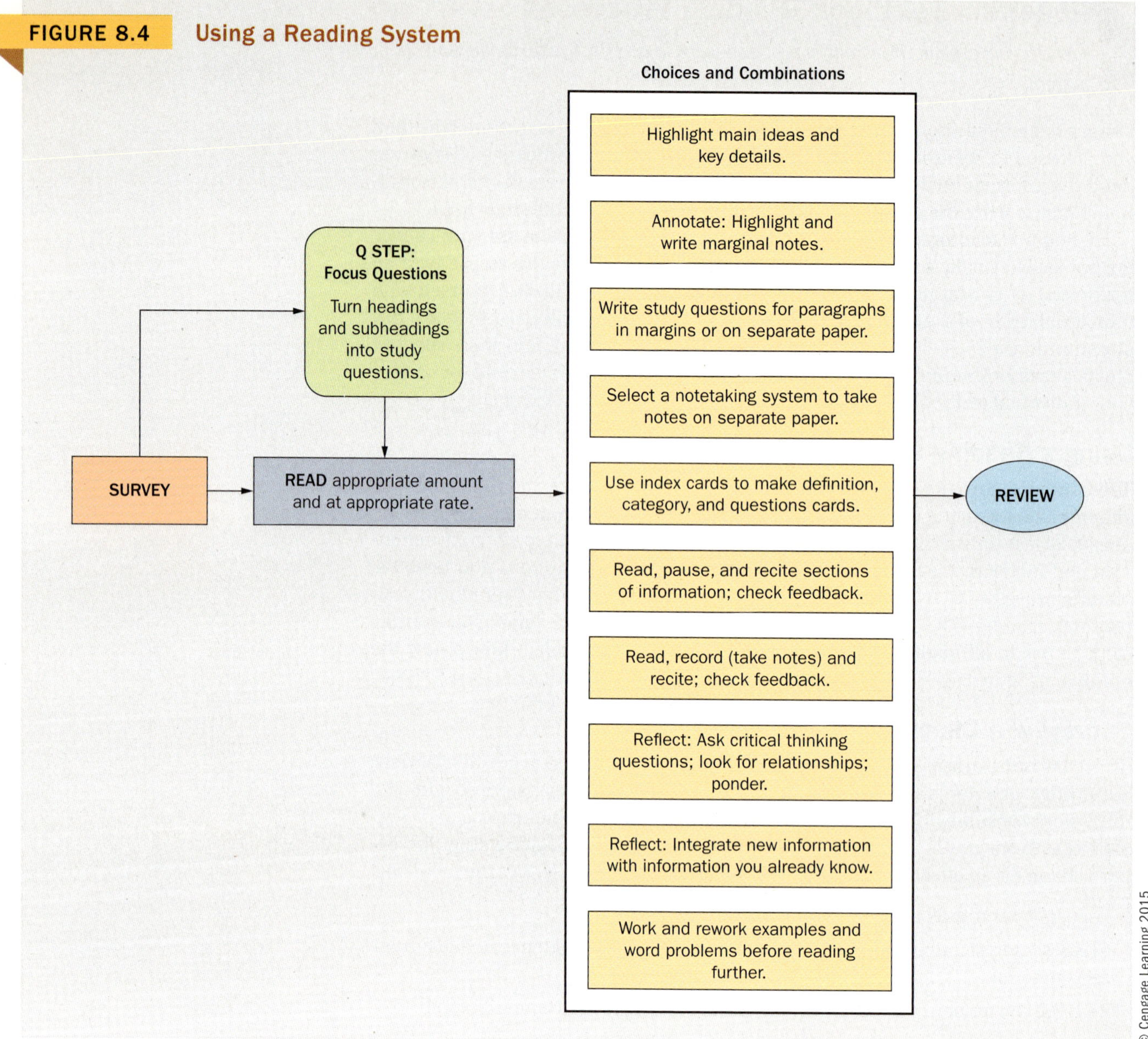

the beginning of a later study block. Following are the parts of a chapter to include in surveying:

- **Introductory materials:** Read the title of the chapter carefully; take a moment to think about the topic and relate the topic to information you already know. Read any lists, paragraphs, or visual materials that state the objectives for the chapter or introduce the chapter's content.
- **Headings and subheadings:** Different font colors and different formats or designs in a chapter differentiate headings from subheadings. Move through

the chapter by glancing over the headings and subheadings to see the skeletal structure of the chapter. Later, if you wish, you can use the headings and the subheadings to create a chapter outline.

- **Visual materials:** Examine visual materials, such as charts, graphs, diagrams, pictures, and photographs. Read the information and the captions that appear with the visual materials.
- **Marginal notes:** Marginal notes may be brief explanations, short definitions, lists of key points or objectives, or study questions that appear in the margins of the textbook pages. Marginal notes provide you with background details and emphasize important points to learn.
- **Terminology:** Skim over the terminology to get a general idea of terms you will need to learn. During surveying, do not spend time reading definitions for all the terminology.
- **End-of-the-chapter materials:** Read the chapter summary, list of key concepts, chapter review questions, or any other end-of-the-chapter materials. These materials highlight or summarize the important concepts and information you should learn in the chapter.

EXERCISE 8.2

Transfer These Skills: Surveying a Chapter

DIRECTIONS: Surveying before beginning the process of careful, thorough reading works effectively as a *warm-up activity* at the beginning of a study block. Select any textbook you are currently using. At the beginning of a study block, survey a new chapter. Then answer the following questions on your own paper.

1. Write the name of your textbook as well as the chapter number and title.
2. How did the introductory materials in the chapter help you focus your attention on the new chapter?
3. What was the value of reading all headings and subheadings in the chapter?
4. What other special features in the chapter did you examine during surveying?
5. What end-of-the-chapter materials appeared in this chapter? How did they help you obtain a big picture of the chapter?

Writing Focus Questions

The ***focus question step*** in the reading process involves turning the chapter title, each heading, and each subheading into questions. In Figure 8.4, notice that the *Q Step* or *focus questions step* is one step to use after surveying a chapter. Write the questions directly in your textbook next to the title, headings, or subheadings, or write them on notebook paper or index cards, leaving space to write the answers later. The 10 to 20 minutes it takes to write these focus questions is time well spent. You get one additional overview of the chapter, and you create a purpose for reading,

The **focus question step** in the reading process involves turning the chapter title, each heading, and each subheading into questions.

focus your attention on upcoming information, and activate working memory. Use the following suggestions when you write your questions:

- **Strive to use a variety of questions.** The wording of each question elicits a different kind of response. For example, answers to questions that begin with the following words elicit specific kinds of responses:

  What ... (Answer gives specific facts.)
  How ... (Answer gives steps/processes.)
  Which ... (Answer gives specific items.)
  Where ... (Answer gives specific locations.)
  Why ... (Answer gives reasons.)
  When ... (Answer gives time periods.)
  Who ... (Answer identifies specific people.)

- **Modify or delete some words in headings and subheadings** if necessary. Following are examples of questions for the beginning of this chapter. The italic print shows words added to the title, heading, and subheadings to create questions.

  Title: ***How should I*** Select~~ing~~ a Reading System?

  Heading: ***What are the*** First Steps of the Reading Process?

  Subheading: ***How do*** ~~Developing a~~ Positive Attitude and Behaviors ***affect reading?***

CONCEPT CHECK 8.6
Explain how to use headings and subheadings to create focus questions. Why do you think these questions are referred to as "focus" questions?

If you are reading an e-textbook, you may not be able to write questions directly across from the title, headings, or subheadings, but you can use the "notes" feature to create a list of questions or create a Word file for your questions. If you are using the printed textbook, you can write your questions in the book.

If you choose to use the Q Step in your reading process, you will have a set of questions to use to review after reading the chapter, as a warm-up activity at the beginning of a study block, or during a later review session to prepare for a test. After creating your focus questions, move to the next step: READ.

Reading Carefully

Some students feel that they should be able to "read fast" to get through chapters. Others read chapters without speeding through them—only to find at the end of the chapters that they must reread the chapter because they do not remember much of what they read the first time. The ***read step*** in the reading process involves reading *carefully and thoroughly*. The following suggestions promote effective, careful, thorough reading:

The **read step** in the reading process involves reading *carefully and thoroughly.*

- **Decide if overview reading of chapter contents would be beneficial.** Because overview reading involves reading straight through without pausing, use it sparingly. Do not take notes or highlight when your intention is to do overview reading. Overview reading is beneficial for difficult or unfamiliar content to help you begin to form schemas or to give you a "flavor" for the materials before beginning the process of thorough reading. Overview reading is not effective unless you commit to moving through the chapter a second time to examine, analyze, interpret, memorize, integrate, and comprehend what you are reading by using thorough reading strategies.
- **Begin thorough reading.** For most textbooks, you should read *one paragraph at a time* and then stop to dissect, analyze, and comprehend the content of the paragraph. Skilled readers of college textbooks are aware of the importance

of selecting the appropriate amount of information to read (*chunking*) before pausing and the appropriate *reading rate* to use that give their mind sufficient time to grasp the information.

- **Take the time to use effective reading strategies**. Figure 8.3 and other sections of this chapter, as well as Chapters 9 and 10, will provide you with a variety of strategies to use to unlock the meaning of difficult paragraphs, integrate concepts, and strengthen comprehension. Create the mindset of being open to trying new strategies and replacing some of your former strategies for reading textbooks which may not be as powerful or effective.

Choices and Combinations for Your Reading Process

As shown in Figure 8.4, after reading and pausing, you then have a variety of options to use to work with the information to increase comprehension and process the information into memory. For textbooks that are not very challenging, selecting one or two of the choices will suffice. For example, after reading, you may want to highlight and recite. For more complex or difficult textbooks, you may wish to use several of the choices to boost your comprehension and memory of the content: annotate, write study questions in margins, and reflect to integrate information.

Skillful readers do not use the same strategies for every textbook. Instead, they know how to use a variety of strategies and then select the strategies that work most effectively for the textbook and the content. **Figure 8.5** summarizes options to record (takes notes) and reflect. Regardless of which combination you choose, the steps should be clear in your mind and easy for you to recall and apply.

FIGURE 8.5 Combinations for a Reading System

		RECORD OPTIONS		**REFLECT** OPTIONS	
SURVEY	**READ** SLOWLY	Highlight textbook.	**RECITE**	Look for relationships.	**REVIEW** CHAPTER
		Annotate: Highlight and make marginal notes.		Integrate new and old information.	
		Make Cornell Notes.		Rearrange information in new meaningful ways.	
		Make 2- or 3-column notes.		Think critically about the topics.	
		Make outline.		Use critical thinking questions to think more deeply.	
		Make index cards.		Compare different sources of information.	
		Make visual mappings, hierarchies, or charts.		Formulate questions to pose in class.	

© Cengage Learning 2015

The **record step** in the reading process involves taking notes to capture important information encountered in textbooks.

The **recite step** in the reading process involves restating and explaining textbook information out loud and in your own words and without looking at the printed materials.

The **Read-Record-Recite Cycle** is a thorough reading strategy that involves reading a short section, taking notes, and then reciting without looking at the printed materials.

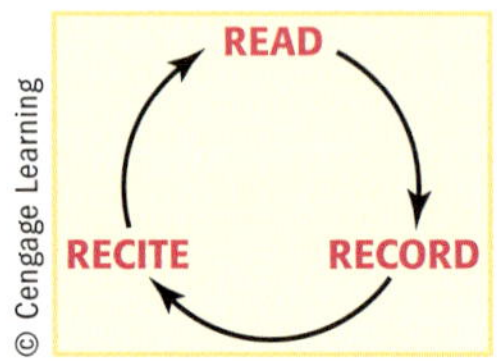

CONCEPT CHECK 8.7

Explain how to use the Read-Record-Recite Cycle throughout a chapter. How does this differ from the way you usually read a textbook chapter?

The **reflect step** in the reading process involves comprehending, elaborating, and using critical thinking skills to think seriously and deeply about the information you read.

CONCEPT CHECK 8.8

How could you use Bloom's Taxonomy in a reflect step of a reading system you create for a government or social science course?

The **review step** in the reading process involves using immediate and ongoing review to practice rehearsing and recalling information from long-term memory.

Record or Take Notes

The ***record step*** in the reading process involves taking notes to capture important information encountered in textbooks. After reading a paragraph or section of information, pause, and then identify the information you wish to record in notes. Taking time to record information (take notes) helps you stay actively involved in the learning process, which reduces the tendency of slipping into automatic pilot mode, or reading without clearly understanding or recalling. Taking notes holds information in working memory and provides more time for you to encode it clearly and accurately for your long-term memory. Comprehension improves when you actively strive to identify key concepts, important details, and relationships. Your notes become a valuable, time-saving, reduced or a condensed form of the information you need to study and learn.

After learning how to use all of the notetaking systems that appear in Figure 8.5, you will have the tools to personalize or tailor your approach to learning. You will possess the skills required for the third component of metacognition: strategies to use that are best matched to the task you are learning.

Recite Main Ideas and Details

The ***recite step*** in the reading process involves restating and explaining textbook information out loud and in your own words and without looking at the printed materials. If you are recording information or taking notes, you can recite after you take your notes. After reciting, look back at the textbook or your notes to check your accuracy.

The ***Read-Record-Recite Cycle*** is a thorough reading strategy that involves reading a short section, taking notes, and then reciting without looking at the printed materials. This three-part cycle works effectively for both traditional and e-textbooks. Using the Read-Record-Recite Cycle automatically slows down the reading process, promotes taking notes on key points, and provides feedback on the effectiveness of your strategies and your comprehension. You can use the Read-Record-Recite Cycle to move through any chapter efficiently and thoroughly.

Reflect and Think Critically

The ***reflect step*** in the reading process involves comprehending, elaborating, and using critical thinking skills to think seriously and deeply about information you read. Reflecting requires a willingness to set time aside to contemplate points of view, identify relationships, and integrate information from multiple sources. Adding a reflect step to your reading process promotes personalizing and internalizing the information you are studying.

Reviewing

The ***review step*** in the reading process involves using immediate and ongoing review to practice rehearsing and recalling information from long-term memory. Reviewing provides an opportunity to work with information before the process of inputting new information begins. Following are activities you can use to review the content in the chapter:

- Answer the chapter review questions that appear at the end of the chapter.
- Answer the questions you formulated during the *focus question step.*
- Study and recite from the notes that you took in the *record step.*

- Write a summary. In paragraph form, summarize the important concepts and details.
- Create additional study tools, such as flashcards, study tapes, or visual notes.
- Create a chapter outline. Use the outline to recite details for each section of the outline.
- Rework math problems from class or from your textbook. Compare the steps you used and your answers with those in the textbook. Check your answers for accuracy.
- For language courses, copy sentences or grammar exercises from the textbook. Rework the assignment, diagram the sentences, or identify parts of speech within sentences.

CONCEPT CHECK 8.9

The review step for different textbooks may vary. What different review activities would you use for your various textbooks this term?

EXERCISE 8.3

Reading Process Inventory

Go to Exercise 8.3 Appendix C, page C17, to complete the Reading Process Inventory to self-assess your awareness and skills of textbook reading processes.

CHECK POINT 8.2

Answers appear on page B4.

True or False? See Test-Taking Strategies 1–9 in Appendix A.

_____ 1. Not taking the time to survey reading materials may reduce motivation, reduce your ability to relate information quickly to a schema, and increase procrastination.

_____ 2. Surveying is a process that is used only to become familiar with the front and back sections of a new textbook.

_____ 3. Surveying a chapter involves overview reading.

_____ 4. Surveying a chapter involves reading headings, subheadings, visual materials, all the marginal notes, all the definitions, and all the review questions.

Listing Questions See Test-Taking Strategies 25–28 in Appendix A.

On separate paper, answer the following questions.

1. List six parts or features of a chapter that students should look at during the process of surveying the chapter.
2. List reasons that recording notes is an effective process to use during the reading process.

Access Chapter 8 Practice Quiz 2 in your College Success CourseMate, accessed through *CengageBrain.com*.

GROUP PROCESSING

A Collaborative Learning Activity

Form groups of three or four students. Then complete the following directions.

DIRECTIONS:

1. Each student brings two different textbooks to the group. These may be textbooks the students are using this term or textbooks used in previous terms.
2. Each student takes a few minutes to show how he or she would survey a chapter of one of the books and how surveying that chapter helps the student prepare to read the chapter.
3. Together, discuss what reading processes and system the group recommends for the individual textbooks.

Three Specific Reading Systems

Compare and contrast the steps used in three reading systems: SQ4R, the Outline Reading System, and a Customized Reading System.

You already know that you can create a reading system specifically designed by you for your textbooks. An effective reading system involves powerful processes proven to be effective: surveying, reading carefully and thoroughly, taking notes, reciting, thinking and reflecting, and reviewing. In the following sections, you will learn specific reading systems to use.

SQ4R

One of the first textbook reading systems, SQ3R, was developed by Francis E. Robinson in 1941. The letters represent a five-step process: *survey, question, read, recite,* and *review*. In other courses and textbooks, you may encounter different reading systems, but upon close examination, you will notice that other reading systems often use different labels for steps very similar to those in SQ3R. The reason is that the steps and activities used in the SQ3R are powerful and proven to increase comprehension and enhance learning.

SQ4R is a six-step system for reading and comprehending textbook chapters: **s**urvey, **q**uestion, **r**ead, **r**ecord, **r**ecite, and **r**eview. SQ4R adds a fourth "R" to remind students to record important information (take notes). To gain the most benefit from this system, use all six steps shown in **Figure 8.6** each time you use the SQ4R system to read a textbook chapter.

CONCEPT CHECK 8.10

What are the benefits of using all six steps of the SQ4R reading system? What would happen if you skip one or more of the steps?

SQ4R is a six-step system for reading and comprehending textbook chapters: survey, question, read, record, recite, and review.

EXERCISE 8.4

Transfer These Skills: SQ4R

PURPOSE: Learning to use a reading system, such as SQ4R, requires practice. With practice, the system becomes more comfortable and automatic.

DIRECTIONS: Use any textbook from one of your courses. Use all six steps of SQ4R for a new chapter. On separate paper, briefly summarize the activities you performed during each step.

FIGURE 8.6 **The Six Steps of SQ4R**

1. **Survey** the chapter to get an overview.
2. Write **Questions** for each heading and subheading.
3. **Read** the information, one paragraph at a time.
4. **Record** by selecting a form of notetaking to record information.
5. **Recite** the important information from the paragraph.
6. **Review** the information learned in the chapter.

Access Chapter 8 Topics In-Depth: Expanded SQ4R Visual Mapping in your College Success CourseMate, accessed through *CengageBrain.com*.

The Outline Reading System

The ***Outline Reading System*** is an active reading system that involves creating outline notes during the reading process and using the outline notes to review. After *surveying* the chapter, you can begin the process of reading and developing your chapter outline notes. The outline reading system is effective for the following reasons:

- Automatically triggers a reading goal that involves reading to understand, identify, and capture key concepts and phrases into notes
- Involves active learning as you use the cycle of read, pause, and take notes
- Requires slower, careful reading to identify information to write in the outline
- Promotes using Selectivity to identify what is important and what is not
- Results in chunking information into meaningful units that show different levels of information
- Promotes critical reading skills to think about, comprehend, and organize information
- Results in a set of notes that works as a study tool for immediate and ongoing review

The **Outline Reading System** is an active reading system that involves creating outline notes during the reading process and using the outline notes to review.

Outlines provide a *skeleton* or an overview of the basic structure of printed materials or, in this case, of a complete chapter. Some textbooks provide basic chapter outlines in the chapter introductory materials; however, chapter outlines often include only the chapter's headings and subheadings. You can use the textbook's chapter outline as a starting point, but the Outline Reading System requires the reader to add more details and to expand and personalize the outline during the reading process.

Formal Outlines

Formal outlines are highly structured, logically organized, detailed notes that show levels of information and relationships among larger concepts and smaller supporting details. You may already be familiar with formal outlines because

FIGURE 8.7 Formal and Informal Outlines

Formal Outline Format	Informal Outline Format
Chapter Title: I. First Main Heading (use Roman numeral) A. Subheading (use capital letter) 1. Supporting Detail (use Arabic numeral) 2. Supporting Detail B. Subheading 1. Supporting Detail a. Minor detail (use lowercase letter) b. Minor detail (1) Subidea of minor detail (use Arabic numeral in parentheses) (2) Subidea of minor detail 2. Supporting Detail II. Second Main Heading A. 1. 2. 3. *See graph, page XX.* B.	**Chapter Title:** I. First Main Heading (use Roman numeral) A. Subheading (use capital letter) 1. Supporting Detail (use Arabic numeral) 2. Supporting Detail B. Subheading 1. Supporting Detail — Minor detail - Can add subideas — Minor detail - Can add subideas 2. Supporting Detail II. Second Main Heading A. 1. 2. 3. *See graph, page XX.* B.

many composition instructors require formal outlines with your essays or papers. **Figure 8.7** shows the use of Roman numerals, capital letters, Arabic numerals, lowercase letters, and Arabic numerals inside parentheses. Following are the standard requirements or rules that you must follow when you develop a formal outline:

- **Roman numerals:** Use Roman numerals for main headings or main topics. Roman numerals from one to fifteen are written as I, II, III, IV, V, VI, VII, VIII, IX, X, XI, XII, XIII, XIV, and XV.
- **Alignment:** When you indent to show a lower level of information, place the new letter or the new number directly below the first letter of the first word that appears in the line above. For example, in Figure 8.7, notice how the "A" for the subheading appears directly below the "F" for the first main heading.
- **Two or more subheadings:** Each level in the formal outline must have *at least two subheading or subtopics* under each category. If you do not have two items [A, B; 1, 2; a, b; or (1), (2)], try renaming the larger category so you do not end up with only one item under that category.
- **Wording:** Most outlines consist of key words and short phrases; full sentences are seldom used.

Informal Outlines

For many students, the Outline Reading System works more effectively by using the *informal outline format*. Examine Figure 8.7 to note the differences between the formal and the informal outline format. Following are the benefits of using the informal outline format:

- Easier to organize by using the following format:
  - Use Roman numerals for headings; capital letters for subheadings; and Arabic numerals (1, 2, 3) for details.
  - Use dashes for all other levels of minor details.
- Less confusing and frustrating by simply using dashes for minor details
- Less cumbersome and more flexible as you can relax or modify the outline rules required by the formal outline format
- Can "mix and match" by using key words, phrases, or short sentences for any level of your outline

CONCEPT CHECK 8.11
Why would a student prefer to use the informal outline format when using the Outline Reading System?

Using a reading system that involves systematic steps helps you move through the chapter in an organized, meaningful way. When you use this system, you will engage yourself in the reading process and be less likely to slip into *automatic pilot mode*. Use the following steps and suggestions for using the Outline Reading System.

The Outline Reading System

1. Survey the chapter to get an overview. Pay special attention to headings and subheadings.
2. At the top of your notes, write the name of the chapter. Then create a heading that says *Introduction*. Read the introduction. Number important points.
3. Start your outline with the main heading. Use Roman numeral "I" for the first main heading in the chapter.
4. Use a capital "A" for the first subheading. Read the information, paragraph by paragraph. Use numbers 1, 2, 3, or more to list the important points under the subheading. If there are minor details you want to include, simply use dashes to jot down the details.
5. Make a note to return to the textbook to review any important charts or graphic materials.
6. Capture information in meaningful ways. You need to be able to understand your notes later, so do not be too brief or use only words or short phrases that lose meaning over time. Because this is an informal outline, you can regroup information, create new lists inside boxes, or add any other details that will help you capture the important points.

EXERCISE 8.5

Using the Outline Reading System

DIRECTIONS:

1. Unless your instructor assigns a different chapter in this textbook or in another textbook, use the Outline Reading System for this chapter.
2. Below is the beginning of the outline. As you read through the chapter, continue the outline on your own paper or on a computer.

Chapter 8

Introduction

1. Old reading habits may be inadequate for college texts
2. Replace old habits/techniques to strengthen reading skills & comprehension

I. **First Steps of the Reading Process**

A. Developing Positive Attitudes and Behaviors

1. Attitude & behaviors — affect reading experience
2. Review Figure 8.1, page 233

B. Identifying Purposes for Reading

1. 4 purposes: recreational, overview, thorough, comparative (Figure 8.2, page 234)
   — Recreational: entertained, updated, current events

Studying from Outline Notes

Outlines provide an excellent study tool to practice reciting and to give you immediate feedback about your level of understanding and recall of textbook information. Use the following tips to study from your outlines.

- **Read and explain line by line.** Read what appears on the first line with the Roman numeral. Recite what you know about the topic. Speak in complete sentences. Move to the next line of information. Recite what you know; strive to integrate and link ideas together and explain relationships. Recite as though you are teaching another person.
- **Check your accuracy and completeness of information.** As you recite, you will quickly become aware of your familiarity with the topic. Refer to your outline notes or your textbook to check your accuracy or to see what kinds of information you did not include in your reciting.
- **Branch off your outline to expand it by adding more clue words.** You can break away from the general structure of the outline at this point by jotting down key words or details that you did not initially include in your reciting. These clue words can guide you through the reciting process the next time you use your outline to review the contents of the chapter. Notice the clue words in the following example of an outline about stress responses.

B. Stress Responses
1. Physical Stress Responses: The GAS *general adaptation syndrome* — alarm, resistance, exhaustion
2. Emotional Stress Responses — fear, anger; diminish, persist, severe
3. Cognitive Stress Responses — ruminative thinking; catastrophizing
4. Behavioral Stress Responses

- **Use the outline to write a summary**. Many students learn and remember information more readily when they use their own words to explain and connect information in a logically sequenced manner and when they express themselves in writing. You can use the levels of information in your outline to organize and to write a summary. Include main ideas and briefly mention important supporting details.

A Customized Reading System

A ***Customized Reading System*** is an active reading system you design for a specific textbook based on the author's suggestions and the chapter features. Your goal with this system is to establish a consistent routine to use to read and study each chapter. Following are the steps to use.

A **Customized Reading System** is an active reading system you design for a specific textbook based on the author's suggestions and the chapter features.

CONCEPT CHECK 8.12

Which of your textbooks is well suited for you to use a Customized Reading System? What steps would you use for reading the chapters?

Step 1: Use the Author's Suggestions

Carefully read the *To the Student* or the *Preface* information in the front of the textbook. List the author's suggestions for reading and using the textbook.

Step 2: Use the Chapter Features

Examine the chapter features in the first few chapters. In some textbooks, such as composition and math textbooks, the chapter format and the chapter features "dictate" a reading process for you to use—work through each section and each feature in the order presented. For example, the textbook structure may begin with definitions of terminology, then move to an example or a prototype with explanations, and then provide problem sets to solve by applying the steps shown in the prototype or example.

Step 3: Create Your Customized System

Using the information learned by surveying, create a list of steps that you will use consistently and habitually to read and comprehend the information in each chapter. (See **Figure 8.8**.) To work successfully, your customized approach to reading the textbook should do the following:

- Utilize effective study skills strategies and memory processes
- Incorporate at least one form of notetaking to organize and record information
- Include reworking problem sets or portions of homework assignments
- End with review activities

FIGURE 8.8 A Customized Reading System for a Math Textbook

Step 1: **Read the introduction, goals, and objectives.**

Step 2: **Read the definitions.** Create a vocabulary sheet or definition flashcards each time you encounter new terminology, formulas, equations, and symbols.

Step 3: **Study examples until you understand the problem type and steps involved.** Choose one example to memorize as a *prototype*. Create meaningful notes.

Step 4: **Practice new skills.** Rework the example problems. Check your accuracy.

Step 5: **Do new problem sets.** These usually mirror the problem types shown by the examples. Pay attention to underlying patterns. Apply the steps; check work.

Step 6: **Do mixed problem sets.** Look for underlying patterns. Match problem types to prototypes you have memorized. Apply the steps; check answers.

Step 7: **Do the real-world story problems.** Look for familiar underlying patterns. Apply RSTUV steps (Appendix A, Strategy 41, page A34). Check work. Be sure to label units in the solution.

Step 8: **Review the chapter.** Read the chapter summary. Do review problems. Rework several examples and problems from the chapter. Recite and study the terminology, formulas, equations, and problem-solving steps.

CHAPTER 8 REFLECTIVE WRITING 2

On separate paper, in a journal, or online in this textbook's College Success CourseMate, respond to the following questions:

1. Which skills in this chapter provided you with valuable textbook reading skills or processes that you had not previously used? How will these skills or processes improve your textbook reading and learning performance? Explain with specific details.
2. Discuss your results from the Reading Process Inventory (Exercise 8.3). What did you learn about your current textbook reading habits and skills? What adjustments do you wish to make to modify your approach to textbook reading?

Access Chapter 8 Reflective Writing 2 in your College Success CourseMate, accessed through *CengageBrain.com*.

CHECK POINT 8.3

Answers appear on page B4.

Fill-in-the-Blanks See Test-Taking Strategies 21–24 in Appendix A.

1. In the SQ4R reading system, the "Rs" represent the following processes in sequential order: ____________, ____________, ____________, and ____________.
2. The process of ________________ a new chapter before beginning thorough reading is recommended for all reading systems.
3. In the Outline Reading System, Roman numerals, such as I, II, and III, are often used to show main ________________ used in the chapter.

Short Answers See Test-Taking Strategies 32–36 in Appendix A.

Question: What textbook reading system works most effectively for this textbook? Explain the specific steps or processes you use. Write your answers on separate paper.

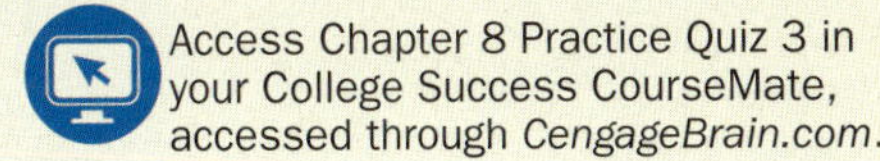

Reading Processes for Online E-Books

4 *Explain effective reading strategies to use for online e-textbooks.*

Digital e-books (electronic books) use technology to offer an alternative way to read textbooks and other materials. Digital reading can be at your fingertips by using various devices: a computer, a digital tablet, an electronic reader, or even a smartphone. Textbooks that have an e-book option provide you with alternative access to textbook information.

Advantages of E-Textbooks

As a student, you may have several options for using e-textbooks. If you enroll in an online course, an e-textbook may be a required part of the course and one of the main sources of course information; however, you may also have the option of using a printed version of the textbook to use side-by-side with the e-textbook. Some students find that certain reading and studying strategies work more effectively with printed materials, so having both printed and digital formats is advantageous. If you enroll in a course on campus that uses a printed version of the textbook, you may choose to access the e-textbook to take advantage of the digital format, features, and supplementary materials. Following are advantages for using e-textbooks with or without pairing with a printed version of a textbook.

- The digital format for many students is motivational. Some studies show that it is the digital format rather than the content that students favor. Many students use technology on a regular basis, so e-textbooks are simply another type of information to access via electronic devices.
- Digital books are readily accessible on electronic devices. Electronic devices, such as iPads, Kindle Fire, Nook, and other tablets are lightweight, hold multiple books, and are easier to carry around than multiple textbooks.
- Many digital textbooks are interactive. Students can click on links to complete online exercises and self-correcting quizzes that provide immediate feedback.

They can also view and enlarge colorful graphics, utilize online dictionaries and glossaries as they read, and download extensive apps (applications) related to course content. Students can also access high-resolution educational video and audio materials linked from the textbook website to other specific websites, or they can visit sites such as KhanAcademy.com for hundreds of videos demonstrating math problem-solving skills, or YouTube.com for videos demonstrating course-related processes or background information.

- Working with digital textbooks involves active learning as students use visual and kinesthetic skills to interact with the materials. With a few clicks, readers can highlight important text, type notes next to text, and print notes and sections of information.

E-Textbook Challenges

For many students, reading, comprehending, and remembering what they read occurs more consistently and smoothly when they read printed materials versus digital materials. As a result, for content that requires more thorough reading and studying, students may choose to download and print sections of the e-textbook pages or have a printed version available. To increase success using e-textbooks as the main source of course information, consider the following challenges and strive to adjust your reading habits to address the problems.

- **Distractions:** E-mails and social networking disrupt the reading process. If you find it difficult to refrain from responding to your e-mail, Facebook, or Twitter messages, use a program or app such as *Self-Control* to block access to your social media sites while you are reading.
- **More rereading required:** Digital text is processed differently by the brain. Until the brain is "trained" to process digital information more efficiently, reading digital information multiple times may be necessary to understand content more fully. Consider using active reading strategies and notetaking strategies to reduce the need to reread multiple times.
- **Shallow reading:** Students using digital devices may tend to do more "surface reading," or skimming. The result is less retention of online material compared to reading printed materials. Students may want to make a more concerted effort to force their eyes to use the traditional pattern for reading: left to right instead of roaming more quickly to the bottom of the screen.
- **Getting lost in a string of details:** As students read screen-by-screen, attention focuses on the details on the screen. Students may lose sight of the "big picture," the overall headings, and structure of the chapter. To connect details to the bigger pictures, use chapter outlines and notetaking systems to focus on the relationship between headings and details.
- **Losing sense of location:** Sometimes our brain recalls words or pictures based on the location in a chapter where the information was learned. For example, you might "see" or visually remember that specific information appeared in the upper corner of a textbook page. Digital books often lack such spatial landmarks or make visual images more difficult for the reader to form. In some digital books, readers see what percentage of a book or chapter they have read, but they are not given actual page numbers, so putting the screen information in context or in a specific location in the chapter is difficult. Comparing

the digital format to a printed version increases the sense of location of information in chapters.

- **Automatic pilot mode:** When reading e-textbooks, students may experience reading mechanically without grasping, comprehending, or registering information in memory. As soon as you feel yourself reading screen-by-screen without comprehending the content, change your strategy. Start highlighting, taking notes, or using active reading strategies.
- **Eye strain:** Eye strain reduces the ability to concentrate, create visual images of digital material, and comprehend the digital content. With many digital devices, you can change the font, the font size, and the brightness or the contrast on the screen. Change your position or location when there is a glare on your monitor or screen. Place the monitor or device at least 20 inches from your eyes. Take breaks by looking *away from the screen every 20–30 minutes.*

CONCEPT CHECK 8.13
What experiences have you had with using e-books for recreational and academic reading? What were the advantages and the challenges of digital reading?

Navigating the *Essential Study Skills* E-Textbook and CourseMate

To access this textbook's interactive e-textbook, you must purchase an access code that gives you permission to log on to this textbook's College Success CourseMate, accessible from *CengageBrain.com*. Once you have redeemed your code on CengageBrain and accessed the CourseMate, you have the following options:

- Click on "Chapter e-Book" in the left-hand navigation menu to access the entire student textbook online. You will be able to select specific chapters and sections of chapters to read and study.
- Use the same left-hand site navigation menu to access chapter features mentioned in the e-textbook such as the Expanded Chapter Outline, Visual Mapping, Profile, a list of Concept Checks, Case Studies, Topics In-Depth, Reflective Writing Assignments, Glossary, Flashcards, Enhanced and Practice Quizzes, and Chapter Study Guides.
- On the menu for Chapter 8, click on Topics-in-Depth: Navigating the Essential Study Skills E-Textbook for explanations and processes to use e-textbook features.

Access Chapter 8 Topics In-Depth in your College Success CourseMate, accessed through *CengageBrain.com*.

Effective Reading Strategies for E-Textbooks

Reading e-books or digital materials may require adjusting the reading strategies traditionally used for printed textbooks. However, many of the essential strategies that appear in Figure 8.1 and Figure 8.3 apply to both printed textbooks and digital e-textbooks. You can use the following strategies with any of your online textbooks.

CONCEPT CHECK 8.14
Explain how textbook reading processes for e-textbooks differ from reading processes for printed versions of the textbook. Be specific.

- **Survey a chapter:** Surveying printed textbooks involves moving page by page through a chapter. If your e-textbook has a PDF file, you can use traditional surveying strategies with the PDF file that reflects exact textbook pages with visual materials and other textbook features. If your e-textbook does not have a PDF file, you will need to change your strategy. E-textbooks organize information in levels and menus, so survey headings and topics by clicking on sections of the menu. You can also survey by using any available chapter outlines.
- **Write focus questions:** You can write focus questions by using the e-textbook's "Add Notes" feature, by opening a word processing program to write questions, or by writing questions on separate paper. If you are pairing a printed version

Olaf Speier/Alamy Limited

What are the advantages and disadvantages of digital and printed textbooks? Which do you prefer and why?

with an e-book version, you can write your focus questions in the printed version of the textbook.

- **Take notes:** Use the e-textbook's feature to highlight important information as a form of notetaking. For more detailed notes, open a word processing file to take separate notes or create notes on separate paper as you would with a printed version of the textbook.
- **Use the Read-Record-Recite Cycle:** For some students, the tendency may be to read digital textbooks screen after screen without pausing to think about information, take notes, recite, or reflect the content. With e-textbooks, make a concerted effort to pause after each paragraph or after the end of a page. Identify key points, and highlight or take some form of notes. Recite the information before continuing the reading process. Reciting slows down the reading intake process and provides valuable feedback.
- **Learn definitions:** Use terminology features included in your e-textbook. With some digital e-books, you can click on a word within the text to see the definition. For the greatest benefit of e-textbooks, use other online exercises or flashcards to practice defining course-specific terminology.

Learning from college textbooks involves tailoring or customizing the learning process to best understand the level and content of materials, as well as your learning style preferences. Reading and learning from e-books involves a willingness to explore strategies that produce positive results for you, build and strengthen comprehension, and boost memory. It also involves developing critical reading and critical thinking skills. The reading process for e-books differs from reading printed textbooks, so being flexible and willing to adjust your approach for each individual e-textbook is essential. It is important to remember that reading is a process that involves intentional effort and strategies to learn the information—whether the information is delivered in a digital format or a printed format.

EXERCISE 8.6

Textbook Case Studies

DIRECTIONS:

1. Read each case study carefully. Respond to the question at the end of each case study by using *specific* strategies discussed in this chapter. Answer in complete sentences.
2. Write your responses on paper or online in this textbook's College Success CourseMate, Textbook Case Studies. You will be able to print your online response or e-mail it to your instructor.

CASE STUDY 1: Justine reads all her textbooks the way that she reads paperback books. She starts at the beginning of the chapter and does not stop until she reaches the end of the chapter. She often finds that she needs to reread chapters two or three times before she can retain the information. What reading processes and strategies can Justine use to comprehend a textbook chapter better and spend less time rereading?

Exercise 8.6 (continued)

CASE STUDY 2: The instructor spent half the class time talking about a concept that was unfamiliar to Simon. Simon had not had a chance to read the last three chapters, so he thought perhaps the concept appeared in those chapters. When he sat down to work with a study partner, Simon started flipping through the chapters page by page and eventually located the section of information. What strategies would help Simon be a more efficient reader and student?

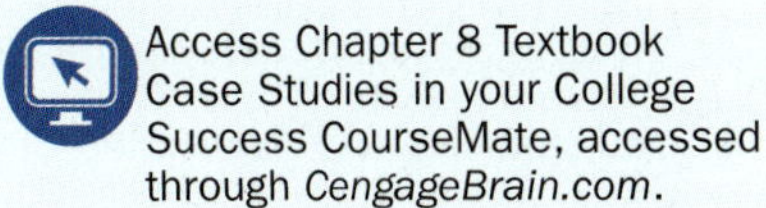

CHECK POINT 8.4

Answers appear on page B4.

Short Answers See Test-Taking Strategies 32–36 in Appendix A.

Go online to this textbook's e-book. Experiment and explore how to use *any four* of the following features. On separate paper, briefly explain the process you used to access the feature and the kind of information you discovered for each feature.

Table of contents	Glossary	Notes and highlights
Print	Appendixes	Topics In-Depth
Bookmarks	Add highlights	Practice quizzes
Index	Add notes	End-of-chapter materials

Access Chapter 8 Practice Quiz 4 in your College Success CourseMate, accessed through *CengageBrain.com*.

ACTIVITY

Chapter 8 Critical Thinking

PURPOSE: In this age of technology, for many people the computer is an integral part of daily personal and professional life. We use the Internet for e-mail, banking, travel plans, shopping, information searches, online courses, and reading e-books. Needless to say, many additional uses of computers occur in the work environment as most businesses and professions now rely heavily on computers for the majority of their operations and transactions. The more we integrate technology into our lives, the greater is the need to learn new skills to use the online sources of information cautiously and effectively. Critical thinking is an essential skill to use when accessing the Internet for information, some of which is reliable and some of which is not.

(continued)

Critical Thinking (continued)

DIRECTIONS:

1. Unless your instructor assigns you a specific website or topic, follow the directions below.
2. Go to a website to locate an online news article. Review the article for the following criterion related to reliability, quality, and usefulness.
3. Print a copy of the article. Be sure that the source of the article is provided.
4. Summarize your evaluation of the article in terms of reliability, quality, and usefulness.

Reliability	Quality	Usefulness
Contact information included	Avoids broad generalizations	Relates to your goals
Satisfactory author credentials	Up-to-date resources and references	Relates to your writing or research outline
Publication has a respectable reputation	Consistency of facts	Appropriate or similar audience
Sponsoring organization(s) of the author and/or publication are identified	Appropriate grammar and spelling	Appropriate level of detail for your goals
Blind peer-review process	From an online database	
Contacted author provided additional information	Avoids bias or one-sided perspectives	
	Comprehensive review	
	Citations and references are accurate and complete	
	Resource is original source	
	Support or corroboration of facts	

From Watkins/Corry, *E-Learning Companion*, 4e © 2014 Cengage Learning

Terms to Know

By yourself or with a partner, practice reciting or writing definitions for the following terms. You may also practice defining these terms by using the online flashcards or comparing your answers to the online glossary.

purposes for reading p. 234
recreational reading p. 234
overview reading p. 235
thorough reading p. 235
automatic pilot mode p. 235
comparative reading p. 235

Learning Objectives Review

1 *Discuss the importance of attitude, purpose for reading, reading rate, and the process of surveying as first steps in the reading process.*

- Creating reading goals, not rushing the reading process, being persistent, using resources, and taking responsibility for learning are several important attitudes and behaviors that affect the quality of the reading experience.
- Recreational, overview, thorough, and comparative are four purposes for reading; each has different reading goals and uses different reading strategies.
- Thorough reading, which is the type of reading used for textbooks, includes essential strategies of creating a plan of action, using a warm-up activity, verbalizing, visualizing, adjusting the reading rate, and relating information and concepts. Learning terminology, using spaced reading, elaborative rehearsal, and feedback are additional essential strategies to use during thorough reading.

- Adjusting the reading rate for different textbooks, levels of difficulty, and degree of complexity is important for reading textbooks. Adjusting the reading rate involves chunking information into meaningful, manageable units to read and comprehend.
- Surveying a textbook provides the reader with an overview of the important features in a textbook: table of contents, introductory materials, the appendixes, the glossary, and the index.
- Surveying an article or an essay provides the reader with valuable background information prior to reading carefully and thoroughly.

2 ***Identify and explain the essential processes used in an effective textbook reading system.***

- Even though a systematic reading approach takes more time than reading a chapter quickly, comprehension is better and rereading chapters multiple times is not necessary.
- A reader has several options for textbook reading systems to use, but surveying a chapter and reviewing are two processes that are a part of most effective systems.
- Surveying a chapter is an example of overview reading that involves looking at introductory materials, headings, subheadings, visual materials, marginal notes, terminology, and end-of-chapter materials.
- Writing focus questions, reading carefully, recording or taking notes, reciting, reflecting, and reviewing are essential processes to use in textbook reading systems.

3 ***Compare and contrast the steps used in three reading systems: SQ4R, the Outline Reading System, and a Customized Reading System.***

- SQ4R is a six-step reading system that involves surveying, questioning, reading, recording, reciting, and reviewing.
- The Outline Reading System involves creating formal or informal outline notes during the reading process. The outline notes created during the reading process work effectively as a study and review tool after the chapter has been read.
- A Customized Reading System is a system that includes essential processes tailored for a specific textbook. This system uses the author's suggestions and chapter features based on effective reading and memory processes.

4 ***Explain effective reading strategies to use for online e-textbooks.***

- Electronic books (e-books) are also referred to as digital books. E-books are portable, lightweight, and interactive.
- To get the full benefits of an e-textbook requires taking the time to learn to navigate the online textbook, its features, and its interactive resources. Instead of presenting information in a linear manner, digital textbooks are organized around levels of information presented as menus.
- Some reading strategies for printed textbooks are also effective for digital textbooks. Other strategies, such as surveying a chapter, may need to be modified or may be better suited for a printed version of the textbook.
- Writing focus questions, taking notes, using the Read-Record-Recite Cycle, and working with terminology are important skills to use with digital textbooks.

Terms to Know

continued

chunking p. 237
surveying p. 237
appendix p. 238
glossary p. 238
index p. 238
focus question step p. 243
read step p. 244
record step p. 246
recite step p. 246
Read-Record-Recite Cycle p. 246
reflect step p. 246
review step p. 246
SQ4R p. 249
Outline Reading System p. 249
Customized Reading System p. 253

Access Chapter 8 Flashcards and Online Glossary in your College Success CourseMate, accessed through *CengageBrain.com*.

Chapter 8 Review Questions

Answers appear on page B4.

True or False? See Test-Taking Strategies 1–9 in Appendix A.

_____ 1. For thorough reading of textbook chapters, the reading rate may vary for different sections in a chapter.

_____ 2. Formulating questions should only be done before you begin to survey a chapter.

_____ 3. Surveying a chapter or doing overview reading before you begin the process of thorough reading helps create a mindset and schemas for new information.

_____ 4. A positive attitude about reading and about a specific textbook affects the quality and effectiveness of the reading experience.

_____ 5. The final step in SQ4R is the same final step used in most reading systems.

_____ 6. In the Outline Reading System, outline notes are created after the student has read thoroughly the chapter at least one time.

_____ 7. A Customized Reading System allows students to create shortcuts to move through chapters quickly and focus only on the sections that are difficult for them.

_____ 8. Everyone finds that digital readers work most effectively for recreational reading but do not work well for academic or textbook reading.

Multiple Choice See Test-Taking Strategies 10–15 in Appendix A.

_____ 1. Which of the following statements is inaccurate?
   a. All e-textbooks have links to the textbook table of contents, glossary, index, and companion audio and video materials.
   b. Students have a variety of textbook reading systems to consider using to read, analyze, and comprehend textbook chapters.
   c. Students can survey, write questions, and take notes using special features that are available for many digital textbooks.
   d. Many textbook reading strategies work effectively for printed and digital formats.

_____ 2. Which of the following is *not* true about using an e-textbook?
   a. If an e-book is interactive, you may be able to access online activities by clicking on a specific icon or link.
   b. You can use the SQ4R reading system, or a modified version of it.
   c. The e-book pages may look the same as the traditional textbook pages.
   d. E-textbooks include only text and never graphic materials.

_____ 3. Which of the following processes appear in a variety of textbook reading systems?
   a. Reciting
   b. Reciting and taking notes
   c. Surveying and reviewing
   d. All of the above

_____ 4. Which of the following statements is *not* true or accurate?
   a. Chunking up refers to working with a larger section of material to understand a concept or clarify the meaning of information.
   b. Overview reading can be used to survey a chapter or read without pausing in order to get a big picture, develop a sense of the flow of action, or gain basic background information before conducting thorough reading.
   c. Recreational reading tends to use a slower reading rate than thorough and comparative reading.
   d. The process of reflecting involves taking time to think about relationships, ponder details, or make connections between concepts.

_____ 5. The process of surveying a new chapter

a. may be easier to do with printed textbooks than with digital textbooks.
b. may be easier to do with materials that are organized in a linear, sequential way rather than in a menu format that shows levels of information.
c. involves looking at headings, subheadings, marginal notes, graphics, bold print, and end-of-chapter materials.
d. involves all of the above.

Short-Answer Questions See Test-Taking Strategies 32–36 in Appendix A.

Write your answers on separate paper or in the space provided.

1. What are the benefits of surveying before reading?

2. How does the structure of a textbook chapter show the "skeleton" of the chapter and assist a student using the Outline Reading System?

Essay See Test-Taking Strategies 45–51 in Appendix A.

Question: Reading college-level textbooks involves using a variety of strategies to comprehend the material and boost memory. Summarize essential reading strategies college students should use to read and understand their textbooks.

Access Chapter 8 Enhanced Quiz and Chapter 8 Study Guide in your College Success CourseMate, accessed through *CengageBrain.com*.

Access all Chapter 8 Online Materials in your College Success CourseMate, accessed through *CengageBrain.com*.

9 Strengthening Reading and Notetaking Skills

Digital Vision/Getty Images

Textbooks are a focal point for learning and mastering course content. Sometimes students are fooled by the sense that they seem to understand and remember what they read, so they feel there is no need to analyze information as a critical reader or to capture key concepts and details in notes to study and review. Over time, however, information can fade, become inaccessible, or become confused with new information. Using active reading strategies to comprehend and record notes provides you with study tools to use to keep information active in your memory. In addition, research shows a high correlation between notetaking skills and test performance. The better students' comprehension skills, the better are their notes; better notes are linked to better grades.

CHAPTER OUTLINE

1 **ACTIVE READING**

2 **PARAGRAPH-LEVEL SKILLS**
Paragraph Elements
Terminology and Definitions
Definition Cards and Vocabulary Sheets

3 **ANNOTATING: HIGHLIGHTING AND MARKING PAGES**
Marking Paragraph Elements
Enumerating Steps or Lists of Information
Writing Marginal Notes
Studying from Annotations

4 **INDEX CARD NOTES**
A Comprehensive Set of Index Card Notes
Studying from Index Card Notes

5 **CORNELL NOTES**
The Five R's of Cornell Notetaking
Preparing to Take Notes
Step One: Record Notes
Step Two: Reduce
Step Three: Recite
Step Four: Reflect
Step Five: Review

Access Chapter 9 Expanded Chapter Outline in your College Success CourseMate, accessed through *CengageBrain.com*.

YOUR CHAPTER MAPPING

After reading information under each heading, return to the chapter visual mapping below. Add key words to show subheadings and important details related to each heading.

Access Chapter 9 Visual Mapping in your College Success CourseMate, accessed through *CengageBrain.com*.

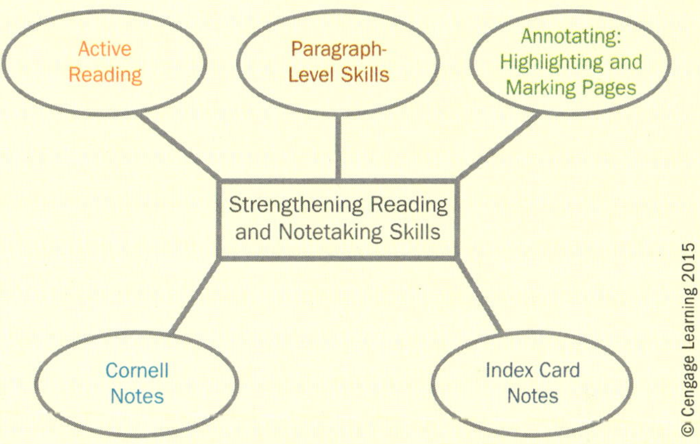

LEARNING OBJECTIVES

1 *Define active reading and describe its relationship to active learning and critical reading.*

2 *Summarize paragraph-level strategies to identify paragraph elements, learn terminology and definitions, and create definition cards and vocabulary sheets.*

3 *Explain the value of annotating textbooks and how to highlight, annotate, and study from annotations.*

4 *Describe the three kinds of cards used in a comprehensive set of index card notes; explain ways to study from index card notes.*

5 *Identify the Five R's of Cornell and describe the processes used for each of the five steps in the Cornell Notetaking System.*

CHAPTER 9 PROFILE

Strengthening Reading and Notetaking Skills

ANSWER, SCORE, and **RECORD** your profile before you read this chapter. If you need to review the process, refer to the complete directions given in the profile for Chapter 1 on page 4.

Access Chapter 9 Profile in your College Success CourseMate, accessed through *CengageBrain.com*.

ONLINE: You can complete the profile and get your score online in this textbook's College Success CourseMate.

	YES	NO
1. I tend to be more of a passive reader than an active reader.	______	______
2. I know how to identify, highlight, and mark main ideas and supporting details that are important to learn.	______	______
3. I use different kinds of clues in sentences to identify the definition or meaning of course terminology.	______	______
4. I make flashcards or vocabulary study sheets only for words that are new or difficult to remember.	______	______
5. When I highlight a textbook, I often over-mark or highlight too much information.	______	______
6. I work with chapter information by writing inside paragraphs or making brief notes in the textbook margins.	______	______
7. I create definition, category, and question flashcards to use as study tools.	______	______
8. I condense information by writing organized notes and recall columns with brief questions to answer and terms to define.	______	______
9. I recite my textbook notes, reflect and work with them in new ways, and review on a regular basis.	______	______
10. I am confident in my ability to read college textbooks and use different notetaking systems to take notes on textbook chapters.	______	______

QUESTIONS LINKED TO THE CHAPTER LEARNING OBJECTIVES:

Question 1: objective 1
Questions 2–4: objective 2
Questions 5–6: objective 3
Question 7: objective 4
Questions 8–9: objective 5
Question 10: all objectives

Active Reading

1 *Define active reading and describe its relationship to active learning and critical reading.*

Comprehending what you read is a complex process that involves active learning and active reading. ***Active reading*** is the process of using effective strategies to engage working memory to achieve specific reading goals. Active reading places heavy demands on your working memory, requires your undivided attention, and cannot be done quickly or effortlessly. Your working memory requires time to accomplish the following:

- Attach meaning to printed words
- Associate chunks of new information with previously learned information
- Move information rapidly back and forth through the different memory systems
- Analyze information by identifying its individual parts, characteristics, patterns, and relationships
- Integrate information to form generalizations

Active reading is the process of using effective strategies to engage working memory to achieve specific reading goals.

CONCEPT CHECK 9.1
What is active reading? What kinds of learning activities do active readers use to engage in the reading process?

Active readers are active learners. Active readers commit themselves to the reading process by creating a mindset that reflects their intention to engage actively in the reading process, comprehend content, process the information, and achieve reading goals. **Check the active reading strategies you use when you read textbooks.**

____Read with a pen in your hand so you are ready to work with the information, write notes in the margins of your textbooks, and use a variety of notetaking systems to record information on paper.

____Make flashcards for definitions, lists of key points, and study questions.

____Interact with the materials by copying diagrams, making study tools, writing practice test questions, and converting printed text into pictures.

____Identify and label organizational patterns used in paragraphs.

____Examine graphic materials and add notes to the materials.

Active readers are critical readers. College-level readers move beyond basic reading skills by acquiring and strengthening higher-level critical reading skills. **Check the critical reading skills you are aware of doing when you read college textbooks.**

____Evaluate the logic, accuracy, and structure of information.

____Question the content, accuracy, completeness, and relevance of information.

____Identify the author's purpose and point of view.

____Follow the author's development of ideas and details by understanding organizational patterns and the logical flow of ideas.

____Understand and interpret graphic or visual materials.

____Make inferences and assumptions; draw conclusions.

____Apply the information to new situations or to solve problems.

____Implement levels of Bloom's Taxonomy: *remembering, understanding, applying, analyzing, evaluating,* and *creating.*

EXERCISE 9.1

Active Reading Inventory

Acknowledging the complexity of reading and understanding textbook material supports the fact that reading is an active process that requires effort, attention, commitment, and effective reading skills. Go to Exercise 9.1 in Appendix C, page C18, to complete the Active Reading Inventory as a way to assess your familiarity and use of active reading strategies.

CHAPTER 9 REFLECTIVE WRITING 1

On separate paper, in a journal, or online in this textbook's College Success CourseMate, respond to the following questions:

1. Which of your textbooks is the most challenging for you this term? Explain the kinds of challenges that textbook presents and what you find to be difficult about the textbook.
2. After completing **Exercise 9.1 Active Reading Inventory**, discuss your total score. Do you agree with the results? Why or why not? Which active reading skills do you need to strengthen?

Access Chapter 9 Reflective Writing 1 in your College Success CourseMate, accessed through *CengageBrain.com.*

CHECK POINT 9.1

Answers appear on page B4.

True or False? See Test-Taking Strategies 1–9 in Appendix A.

_____ 1. Active reading strategies should be used only for complex, difficult textbooks.

_____ 2. Active reading engages your working memory to grasp concepts and process new information.

_____ 3. Active reading is defined as reading out loud.

_____ 4. Writing, which may include highlighting, taking notes, drawing diagrams, and writing questions, is a key process in active reading.

_____ 5. Active reading is not passive reading and does not use automatic pilot mode when reading.

Access Chapter 9 Practice Quiz 1 in your College Success CourseMate, accessed through *CengageBrain.com*

Paragraph-Level Skills

Summarize paragraph-level strategies to identify paragraph elements, learn terminology and definitions, and create definition cards and vocabulary sheets.

Active reading engages the reader in the thorough reading process. For most textbooks, *thorough reading* involves reading one paragraph at a time, and then stopping to understand, analyze, and digest the important information in each paragraph before moving on to the next paragraph. Working with paragraph elements and course terminology helps you understand the content of paragraphs more easily and improves overall comprehension.

Paragraph Elements

Each time you read and analyze a paragraph, focus your attention on the three basic paragraph elements in **Figure 9.1**. The topic, the main idea, and the supporting details represent three levels of information.

The Topic of a Paragraph

The ***topic*** of a paragraph is a word or a phrase that states the subject of a paragraph. Every paragraph has a topic that tells what the author is writing about in the paragraph. You can often identify the topic by asking yourself the following questions: *In one word or one phrase, what is this paragraph about? What word is repeated several times in the paragraph? Does that word work as the topic? What word or phrase do the details tell more about or explain?*

The **topic** of a paragraph is a word or a phrase that states the subject of a paragraph.

The Main Idea and the Topic Sentence

The ***main idea*** of a paragraph states the author's most important point about the topic of the paragraph. The ***topic sentence***, also called the *main idea sentence*, is the sentence in a paragraph that includes the topic and states the author's main idea for the paragraph. Actively search for the topic sentence as it is an essential key for understanding the information in a paragraph. Use the following tips to help you locate and work with the topic sentence:

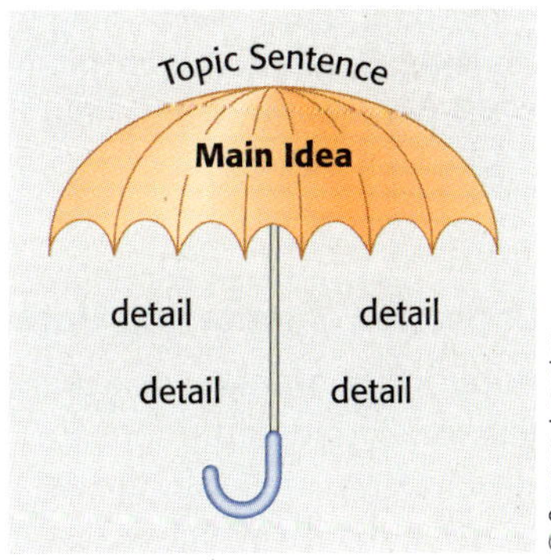

© Cengage Learning

- **The topic sentence is like an umbrella**. It needs to be broad enough for all of the other sentences and supporting details in the paragraph to "fit under it." In a well-written

The **main idea** of a paragraph states the author's most important point about the topic of the paragraph.

The **topic sentence**, also called the *main idea sentence*, is the sentence in a paragraph that includes the topic and states the author's main point or main idea for the paragraph.

FIGURE 9.1 Three Paragraph Elements

1. **The topic of the paragraph:** the subject
2. **The main idea of the paragraph:** the author's main point
3. **The important details of the paragraph:** details that support the main idea

© Cengage Learning

CONCEPT CHECK 9.2

What techniques can you use to identify the topic sentence of a paragraph? How will understanding the topic sentence help you comprehend the paragraph?

paragraph, each sentence relates to or supports the topic sentence. Ask yourself the following questions to help you identify the topic sentence:

- What is the topic (subject) of this paragraph?
- Is there a big picture or an "umbrella sentence" that contains this topic word?
- What is the main idea that the author wants to make about the topic? Which sentence states the main idea?
- Which sentence is broad enough to encompass the content of the paragraph?
- Do all the important details in the paragraph fit under this sentence?

- **Examine the first, the last, and then the sentences in the middle of the paragraph.**
    - *First Sentence*: Topic sentences appear most frequently as the first sentence of paragraphs. This is particularly true in textbooks.
    - *Last Sentence*: If the first sentence is not the "umbrella sentence," check the last sentence. Sometimes the last sentence summarizes the main point of the paragraph and thus states the main idea.
    - *Other Sentences*: If the first and the last sentences do not state the main idea, carefully examine each sentence in the body of the paragraph.

- **Highlight or underline the complete topic sentence.** Highlighting the topic sentence in each paragraph makes the author's most important point stand out in your mind and forms a clear impression of the significance of the paragraph. Strategies for effective highlighting appear in Figure 9.8.

- **Write implied main ideas in the margin.** On occasion, you will encounter a paragraph that has no stated main idea, which means you will not find a topic sentence in the paragraph. Instead, the main idea is *implied.* Use the details in the paragraph to draw your own conclusion about the main idea. Write the main idea in the margin.

Supporting details in a paragraph are facts, explanations, causes and effects, examples, and definitions that develop, support, or prove the main idea.

Important Supporting Details

Supporting details in a paragraph are facts, explanations, causes and effects, examples, and definitions that develop, support, or prove the main idea. In a well-developed paragraph, the details in each sentence must relate to the topic and the topic sentence, which states the main idea. Use the following tips to identify and work with important supporting details:

- Be selective. Decide which details are important to learn and which details provide understanding but are not essential to learn. You can ask yourself: *What details would I want to include in my explanation of the main idea to someone else?* Highlight only those details.
- Highlight or underline the key words or phrases that can serve as retrieval cues or associations to trigger recall of information later from your long-term memory. Strategies for effective highlighting appear in Figure 9.8.
- Carefully examine bulleted lists of information and marginal notes in your textbook. Highlight key supporting details that appear in these lists or notes.

CONCEPT CHECK 9.3

What kinds of information in a paragraph can function as supporting details? How do you know which details are important and which details you can ignore?

EXERCISE 9.2

Identifying Main Ideas

DIRECTIONS: Carefully read each paragraph from the textbook, *The Internet*. Identify the topic sentence with the main idea. Completely highlight the topic sentence.

1. "One of the most important tools you can use to assess the quality of information on the Web is the author's identity. On Wikipedia, contributors may post and edit articles anonymously, in which case the author is identified only by the IP address of his or her connection to the Internet. Even when the author or editor of an article chooses to be identified, it is through the Wikipedia account name, and the biographical information included on the user page is entered by the account holder. That information can be limited or incorrect if the account holder so chooses." (p. 177)
2. "Many people consult a weather forecast daily because they want to know the weather conditions before dressing and venturing out for the day. When planning a vacation, they can review weather patterns for their intended destination. Before packing for a trip, they can obtain detailed weather information to guide their clothing choices. Some people enjoy seeing the weather conditions for family and friends who live elsewhere. Many also want to follow current weather conditions when there is a major storm—whether snow, wind, rain, hurricane, etc. These weather forecasts, conditions, and other information are available on the Web." (p. 193)
3. "Periodicals—magazines, journals, and other articles—related to almost any industry, field, or topic abound. Originally periodicals were available only in printed format at libraries, but now thousands of periodicals are available on the Web. If you know what periodical you want to search, you could go directly to its Web site. If you are more interested in articles related to a particular topic, then you can use a periodical database to locate them." (p. 221)

From Schneider, Evans. *The Internet*, 9e. © 2013 Course Technology, Cengage Learning

For additional practice, go to any of the excerpts in Appendix D.

Terminology and Definitions

Course-specific vocabulary and definitions are other paragraph-level details you will encounter as you read college textbooks. Developing effective vocabulary skills lays a strong foundation for understanding the textbook concepts, participating in class discussions, writing effective essays, and using higher-level critical reading and thinking skills. Look for a list of course-specific terms to learn and words in bold or special print that often identify terminology. The definition for a term in bold or special print usually appears within the same sentence or in the following sentence. Following are basic strategies to use to work with terminology:

- **Circle terminology and highlight key words.** See the annotation strategies on page 279–283.
- **Use word clues, punctuation clues, word structure clues, and context clues** to find the definitions for terminology or unfamiliar words.
- **Use the textbook glossary** to verify and learn more about the terminology words.
- **Use the textbook's online glossary, flashcard drills, or vocabulary exercises.**
- **Make definition flashcards or vocabulary sheets** to recite, rehearse, and review definitions.

CONCEPT CHECK 9.4
Why is learning definitions of terminology important? What strategies help you find definitions in paragraphs?

As you read with an alert mind, you will notice many ways terminology and definitions appear in paragraphs. In Example 1, the entire paragraph defines one specific term (*galaxy*) by expanding the paragraph with details that further explain the term. However, another word that may be unfamiliar, *stellar nebulae*, appears in the paragraph and should be marked as a term to know.

Example 1

Galaxies

Portions of these clouds begin to collapse to form the millions of stars that together make up galaxies. A **galaxy** is a grouping of millions or billions of individual stars. Each one of these stars sprang up from the giant molecular clouds known as stellar nebulae. Galaxies appear as faint clouds of light when viewed through a telescope, unlike the bright points of light given off by stars. When viewed with powerful telescopes, galaxies are revealed to be amazing objects that contain billions of stars.

From Butz, *Science of Earth Systems*, 2e. © 2004 Cengage Learning

In Example 2, the paragraph introduces three terms (*meteoroids, meteors,* and *meteorites*), but you need to look further in the paragraph for definitions of each term.

Example 2

Meteoroids

Main Idea

Smaller chunks of rock that are located in the solar system are called **meteoroids, meteors,** and **meteorites.** Meteoroids are fast-moving chunks of rock that travel through space at high velocities. These rocks are the remains of the early solar system, comets, and fragments of our own Moon and nearby planets. These objects range in size from tiny grains of sand to large boulders. When a meteoroid's orbit crosses that of Earth, it may burn up in the atmosphere, creating a meteor, also known as shooting star. It is estimated that more than 1000 tons of meteoroid material rains down on the Earth every day! Meteors that make it all the way to the Earth's surface are called meteorites. Meteorites are grouped into three categories based on their composition. (1) Stony meteorites are composed of silicate rock material. (2) Iron meteorites are composed of an iron-nickel alloy and are very dense. (3) Stony-iron meteorites are composed of a mixture of silicate rock and iron.

From Butz, *Science of Earth Systems*, 2e. © 2004 Cengage Learning

Word clues are words that link the vocabulary word to its definition that appears in another part of the same sentence.

Word Clues to Identify Definitions

Word clues are words that link the vocabulary word to its definition that appears in another part of the same sentence. Familiarity with word clues—such as *defined as, is* or *are,* or *known as*—will help you locate definitions in paragraphs more quickly. **Figure 9.2** shows word clues that are used frequently in sentences to define terminology. Following are tips to use when you work with vocabulary terms and definitions:

- **Self-quizzing and feedback:** Use your definition cards frequently for self-quizzing and immediate feedback. Look at the front and then recite the information on the back. Turn the card over to check your accuracy.
- **Reflection:** You can sort the cards into two piles: ones you know and ones you need to review further. You can also sort the cards into different categories of information. Try writing a summary by using all of the cards placed in the same category.
- **Test-preparation:** If you anticipate fill-in-the-blank questions, read the back and then *name and spell* the word on the front. Check your accuracy.

Create Vocabulary Sheets

Vocabulary sheets are a form of *two-column notes* that show the term in the left column and a three-part definition in the right column. By creating vocabulary sheets, you create your own glossary of terms. **Figure 9.7** shows the beginning of a vocabulary sheet. To study from a vocabulary sheet, cover the right column with a piece of paper. Say the word and recite the definition. Remove the paper and check your accuracy. Reverse the order: cover the left column, read the right column, and then *say and spell* the term.

Vocabulary sheets are a form of *two-column notes* that show the term in the left column and a three-part definition in the right column.

FIGURE 9.7 Notetaking Options for Terminology and Definitions

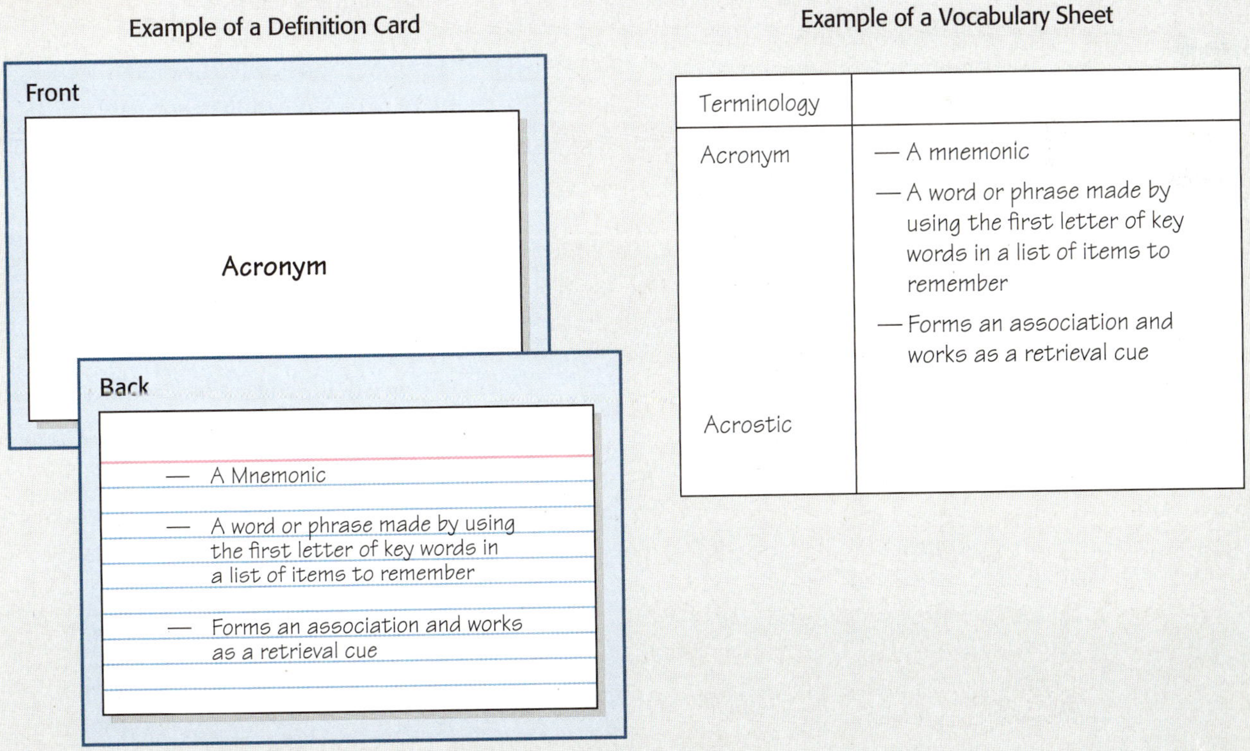

Example of a Definition Card

Front

Acronym

Back

— A Mnemonic

— A word or phrase made by using the first letter of key words in a list of items to remember

— Forms an association and works as a retrieval cue

Example of a Vocabulary Sheet

Terminology	
Acronym	— A mnemonic — A word or phrase made by using the first letter of key words in a list of items to remember — Forms an association and works as a retrieval cue
Acrostic	

EXERCISE 9.4

Transfer These Skills: Vocabulary

DIRECTIONS: Create one of the following vocabulary study tools: a set of definition cards or two-column vocabulary sheets.

1. Your instructor will assign one of the following, or will offer you a choice of options to use.
   a. Create vocabulary study tools for any chapter of this textbook. Include all the terminology used in the Terms to Know for the chapter.
   b. Create vocabulary study tools for any chapter of a textbook used in another course. Copy the list of terminology in the chapter and then use each term in your definition cards or your vocabulary sheets.
   c. Create definition cards for a specific excerpt in Appendix D.
2. Practice reciting the terminology and the definitions. You may be asked to demonstrate use of your definition cards or vocabulary sheets in class or in a small group.

CHECK POINT 9.2

Answers appear on page B4.

Multiple Choice See Test-Taking Strategies 10–15 in Appendix A.

a 1. Which of the following statements is inaccurate?
   a. The topic often is a word that appears several times within a paragraph.
   b. Details in a paragraph support or develop the main idea of the paragraph.
   c. Details in a paragraph support or develop multiple main ideas within the paragraph.
   d. The most common location of the topic sentence is the first sentence of a paragraph.

d 2. The topic sentence of a paragraph
   a. should be completely underlined so it stands out from the other sentences.
   b. expresses the author's main idea for the paragraph.
   c. may appear in any location of a paragraph.
   d. is characterized by all of the above.

b 3. Definition clues within sentences may involve using
   a. word clues, word structure clues, or punctuation clues.
   b. word clues, such as the words *defined as, are called*, or *means*.
   c. punctuation signals, such as the use of commas, dashes, and parentheses.
   d. the meaning of prefixes, suffixes, and roots.

c 4. Which statement about supporting details in a paragraph is not true?
   a. Supporting details may be facts, explanations, and examples.
   b. All supporting details in a paragraph are important and need to be memorized.
   c. Marginal notes sometimes organize or emphasize important supporting details in a paragraph.
   d. Course-specific terminology and definitions are important supporting details in paragraphs.

d 5. Which of the following is true about learning definitions for course terminology?
   a. Effective definition cards show three levels of information: the category, the formal definition, and an additional detail.
   b. Self-quizzing and feedback often involve reciting definitions.
   c. Vocabulary sheets and definition cards are effective study tools.
   d. All of the above statements are true.

Access Chapter 9 Practice Quiz 2 in your College Success CourseMate, accessed through *CengageBrain.com*

Annotating: Highlighting and Marking Pages

Explain the value of annotating textbooks and how to highlight, annotate, and study from annotations.

Annotating is the process of highlighting, underlining, making marginal notes, or marking specific information in printed materials. The term *marking* is a general term that includes *highlighting, underlining, circling,* or *writing* within the paragraph. Highlighting (using different colors of highlighter pens) is preferred by most students because it tends to make information stand out more than underlining. Annotating is an active learning process that holds information longer in working memory and reduces the risk of information fading or being displaced before it is processed into memory. **Figure 9.8** summarizes essential strategies for annotation.

Annotating is the process of highlighting, underlining, making marginal notes, or marking specific information in printed materials.

Marking Paragraph Elements

After you carefully read a paragraph, go back through the paragraph to search for the main idea, important supporting details, terminology, and definitions. Following are additional guidelines for marking paragraph elements effectively:

- **Highlight the topic sentence completely.** Completely highlight the topic sentence with the main idea. This is the only sentence in a paragraph that should be completely highlighted.
- **Mark only important supporting details.** Be selective. Only highlight key words or important short phrases to avoid over-marking.
- **Circle terminology and definitions.** Circle terminology that appears in special or bold print. Highlight key words that define the term.

FIGURE 9.8 Essential Strategies for Annotations

To Create Annotations:

- Highlight the **complete topic sentence**.
- Selectively highlight **key words or phrases** that support the topic sentence.
- **Circle terminology** and **highlight key words** in definitions.
- **Enumerate steps** or lists of information.
- Make **marginal notes** to emphasize important ideas and integrate information.

To Study Annotations:

- **Reread** out loud only the marked annotations.
- **Verbally string the ideas** together by adding your own words.
- **Recite** without looking. Check your accuracy.
- Decide if you want **additional study tools**: write a summary or create a set of notes using a different notetaking system
- Use **spaced practice, immediate review**, and **ongoing review**.

Highlighting and annotating textbooks helps identify important information and reduce the amount of information to study and review further. What effective strategies do you use to avoid over-marking and defeating the purpose of highlighting and annotating?

VisualField/iStockphoto.com

CONCEPT CHECK 9.8
How should you highlight and mark text? How can you avoid over-marking?

- **Avoid over-highlighting.** Over-highlighting defeats the purpose of highlighting, which is to reduce or condense the amount of information in paragraphs and chapters to study and review. Strive to be selective by limiting highlighting in paragraphs to no more than one-third of the paragraph.
- **Highlight examples sparingly.** You do not need to highlight every example, just a few specific examples that would work as memory cues.
- **Be selective.** Do not mark words such as *to, and, with, also,* and *in addition* because they are not key memory trigger words. Also, you do not need to mark a key word or a topic that appears multiple times.

Enumerating Steps or Lists of Information

Enumerating means "numbering."

Ordinals are words that signal a numbered sequence of items.

Enumerating means "numbering." A paragraph with a topic sentence that uses words such as *kinds of, reasons, advantages, causes, effects, ways,* or *steps* often has a list of supporting details that you should be able to identify. For example, if a topic sentence states there are "five reasons" for something, you should be able find those five reasons in the paragraph. The following points about enumerating are important:

- **Use ordinals and placeholders to signal steps or lists.** ***Ordinals*** are words that signal a numbered sequence of items. Ordinals, or "number words" such as *first, second,* or *third,* help you identify individual items. *Placeholders* are words such as *next, another,* and *finally* that substitute for ordinals and signal that additional items belong in the list of items you are enumerating.
- **Create easy-to-remember lists.** Enumerating or numbering serves as a memory device because it is easier to remember a fixed quantity of items than it is to recall an unknown quantity of items.

- **Write numerals.** To enumerate, simply write the numerals (1, 2, 3) above the individual items in the paragraph that appear by an ordinal or a placeholder word.
- **Make lists as marginal notes.** Often times, you will find that writing a brief list of the items in the margin, as a marginal note, is also helpful.
- **Use enumeration to clarify.** Notice how enumeration clearly identifies the six uses of podcasting in the following excerpt.

Podcasting's original use was to make it easy for people to create and broadcast their own radio shows, but many other uses soon followed. Podcasts are used by the (1) media to store and disseminate interviews with politicians and professors on specific subjects; by (2) colleges and universities to record lectures for distance learning classes; and by (3) movie studios to promote new movie releases. Some podcasts have different names that further identify the type of content they contain, such as a (ex.) Godcast to denote a (4) religious broadcast, a (ex.) vidcast to identify a (5) video feed, or a (ex.) learncast to identify content that is (6) educational in nature, such as a podcast produced by a university or other educational institution.

From Schneider, Evans. *The Internet*, 9e. © 2013 Course Technology, Cengage Learning

CONCEPT CHECK 9.9

How can enumeration in textbook paragraphs help your memory? What kind of information is appropriate for marginal notes?

Writing Marginal Notes

Marginal notes are brief notes written in the margins of textbook pages. Marginal notes give you a glimpse of the important points in a paragraph. To avoid cluttered or difficult-to-read marginal notes, be selective and brief. The following tips help you to create meaningful marginal notes:

Marginal notes are brief notes written in the margins of textbook pages.

- **Select meaningful information:** The following kinds of information work effectively as marginal notes:

numbered lists of key ideas	study questions
diagrams or pictures	definitions of unfamiliar terms
short comments or reactions	key words to define
definitions of terms	? for unclear information

- **Use brackets for large sections of information:** Rather than over-mark or clutter the margins with too many details, draw a bracket next to large sections of information or entire paragraphs that are densely written. You can add a note or abbreviation next to the bracket.
- **Use abbreviations to call attention to specific kinds of information:** You can use abbreviations next to brackets to draw your attention to sections you want to return to for further studying. The following are abbreviations you may want to use:

EX. = example or examples	Q. = question
DIFF. = differences	CE. = cause-effect
SUM. = summary	RE. = reasons why...?
F. = important fact	REL. = important relationship
IMP. = important to reread	FORM. = formula
DEF. = lengthy definition	H. = hypotheses

- **Use marginal notes to clarify information.** Notice how the marginal notes in the following excerpt organize and clarify the details in the paragraph.

Ecology

biotic
- plants
- animals
- bacteria
- fungi

INTERACT

abiotic
- air
- water
- rocks
- minerals
- light
- soil etc.

Two words that are important to the study of ecology are *biotic* and *abiotic*. The term biotic refers to any living organism, including plants, animals, bacteria, and fungi. Abiotic refers to the nonliving factors of the environment that interact with the biotic world. These include air, water, rocks, minerals, temperature, altitude, light, and soil. Scientists who study ecology are called ecologists. Ecologists study the interaction of the biotic and abiotic world in different levels of relationships on the Earth.

EXERCISE 9.5

Annotating Text

DIRECTIONS:

1. Your instructor will assign one of the following for you to use to practice annotating text:
   a. A specific excerpt located in Appendix D of this textbook
   b. A section from one of the chapters in your textbook
   c. A section or chapter from one of your textbooks for another course
2. Use the annotation strategies shown in Figure 9.8 and pages 279–283 to annotate the assigned material.
3. Go to Exercise 9.5 in Appendix C, page C19, to complete the Annotation Checklist. Use the checklist to assess the annotations created for this assignment. Note: You may use this checklist throughout the term to self-assess your annotating skills.

Studying from Annotations

To be truly effective, you need to practice using your annotations by personalizing, reciting, and working with the information in new ways. Simply rereading your highlighted notes tends to give a false sense that you "know" the information and have processed it into your long-term memory. Review Figure 9.8, Essential Strategies for Annotations, and use these strategies after you finish reading a paragraph, a group of paragraphs, or the end of a section in your textbook.

CONCEPT CHECK 9.10

What strategies for studying annotations are more effective than just rereading highlighted areas?

Reread Out Loud

When you reread or verbalize only the marked information, it will sound broken or fragmented; however, you will hear yourself stating only main ideas and important supporting details. Read slowly so that your working memory has time to absorb the key points and to make associations.

Verbally String Ideas Together

Stringing ideas together is the process of adding your own words to convert annotated text into full sentences and explanations. Use the following tips to string ideas together:

Stringing ideas together is the process of adding your own words to convert annotated text into full sentences and explanations.

- After reading fragmented annotated text, use the annotations as guides to help you string ideas together more coherently. Use your own words to form full sentences that use the highlighted words and phrases. Verbalizing in this manner personalizes information as you state it in less formal language.
- Use transition words, such as *therefore*, *however*, or *also*, and ordinals, such as *first*, *second*, or *next* to list details or items.
- If you wish to create an auditory study tool, tape yourself stringing ideas together.

Recite Without Looking

Take your eyes off the textbook and begin paraphrasing. Use complete sentences to recite and explain what you learned. Glance down at the annotated information and marginal notes to check your accuracy. If you omitted important points or stated some information incorrectly, redo the reciting process and correct your errors.

Write Summaries or Take Notes on Paper

By writing a summary or recording notes on paper, you may not need to return to the textbook to study the information further. Your summary or notes pull out the important information and organize it in a more concise format for studying. Your summary and your notes should include the same information that you stated when you verbally strung ideas together.

Use Spaced Practice and Review

Once you have annotated your textbook, taking time to rehearse (practice) the information is essential. To review annotations of the entire chapter, use *spaced practice*. Review sections of the chapter at one time, not the entire chapter without breaks. When you finish the chapter, do an *immediate review* and plan time to return to the information within the next week or two for *ongoing review*. You will find that the more frequently you return to review the information, the more thoroughly you will learn what is important to know.

EXERCISE 9.6

Practicing Annotating and Stringing Ideas Together

DIRECTIONS:

1. Go to Excerpt 5: Building Blocks of Medical Terminology in Appendix D.
2. Annotate this excerpt. Be selective. Use the strategies shown in Figure 9.8.
3. Return to your annotated excerpt. Use the strategies in Figure 9.8 to study your annotations. You may be asked to string ideas out loud in class, with a partner, or in small groups.

CHECK POINT 9.3

Answers appear on B4.

Listing and Short-Answer Questions See Test-Taking Strategies 25–28 and 32–36 in Appendix A.

Answer the following questions on separate paper.

_____ 1. List four different ways to "mark" textbook paragraphs.

_____ 2. List four strategies to use to avoid over-marking a paragraph.

_____ 3. Describe steps to use to study from chapter annotations.

Access Chapter 9 Practice Quiz 3 in your College Success CourseMate, accessed through *CengageBrain.com.*

Index Card Notes

4 *Describe the three kinds of cards used in a comprehensive set of index card notes; explain ways to study from index card notes.*

Index card notes involve creating three types of flashcards to use as study tools: definition cards, category cards, and question cards.

Index card notes involve creating three types of flashcards to use as study tools: *definition cards, category cards,* and *question cards.* Index card notes are effective study tools for learning definitions for terminology, lists of items under a specific category, steps in a process, or answers to questions that you predict will appear in one form or another on an upcoming test. Index card notes work effectively to study facts, dates, formulas, rules, and steps to perform a process.

A Comprehensive Set of Index Card Notes

Select a size of index card notes to use for notetaking. If you wish to use colored index cards, one color could be for definition cards, one for category cards, and one for question cards. On the top of the front side of the cards, write the chapter number, if you wish. To create stronger visual impressions of information on your index cards, use highlighters to emphasize key points and add pictures that you can use as retrieval cues. With practice, you can look up and to the left to picture the information on your cards. As you create each of the following kinds of cards, be selective. Limit each card to one topic to avoid cluttered, difficult-to-use cards. **Figure 9.9** shows examples of question, definition, and category index card notes. Following are the kinds of cards in a comprehensive set of index card notes:

Category cards are flashcards with a category or topic on the front and a list of items that belong to the category on the back.

Question cards are flashcards with a study question on the front and answers to the question on the back.

CONCEPT CHECK 9.11
Describe the different kinds of information that appear on each of the three kinds of index card notes.

- *Definition cards* are flashcards with the term on the front and a three-part definition on the back: the category, the formal definition, and then one more detail.
- **Category cards** are flashcards with a category or topic on the front and a list of items that belong to the category on the back. Do not clutter the back of the card with any additional details; you want to be able to visually memorize the list of items.
- **Question cards** are flashcards with a study question on the front and answers to the question on the back. Predicting and writing practice test questions on your index cards provides you with effective study tools to use by yourself, with a study partner, or in a study group for ongoing review or to prepare for an upcoming test.

FIGURE 9.9 Kinds of Index Card Notes

	Front	Back
QUESTION CARDS pose a study question on the front and the answer on the back.	Why is reciting important?	Reciting makes you explain information clearly in your own words. It also: • provides feedback • activates auditory channel • involves active learning • helps memory
DEFINITION CARDS give the vocabulary term on the front and a complete definition with additional details on the back.	Surveying	• Surveying is an overview reading process. • Surveying is the process of skimming or previewing material before you read. • It creates a "big picture."
CATEGORY CARDS give the category of information on the front and the list of items in the category on the back.	SQ4R	1. Survey 2. Question 3. Read 4. Record 5. Recite 6. Review
CATEGORY CARDS work effectively for math concepts and rules.	Three ways to define sets	1. Verbal description of the set 2. Roster method listing the elements of the set 3. Set-building notation

Studying from Index Card Notes

Index card notes are portable and convenient to use. You can carry them in a small plastic pouch or bag, hold them together with a rubber band, and punch a hole in the top of the cards and attach them to a large metal ring. Use the following suggestions to study your index card notes:

- **Use the cards for self-quizzing.** Look at one side of the card and recite the information on the reverse side. Check the reverse sides of the cards for immediate feedback on the accuracy and completeness of the information you recited.
- **Ask others to quiz you.** You can practice explaining information clearly by asking study partners, friends, or family members to use your cards to quiz you. Because all the information appears on the card, the person quizzing you does not necessarily need to know the information.

CONCEPT CHECK 9.12

What is a warm-up activity? Briefly discuss three or more ways you can use index card notes to study and review course content.

- **Sort the cards into two piles.** One pile contains the cards you know and can explain accurately. The other pile contains cards you need to study further. Continue rehearsing the pile of cards you need to study further.
- **Use your cards as a warm-up activity at the beginning of a study block.** Working with your cards before you begin a new assignment puts you in the mindset for the subject, activates previously learned information, and promotes ongoing review.

GROUP PROCESSING

A Collaborative Learning Activity

Form groups with three or four students. Then complete the following directions.

DIRECTIONS:

1. Have each student in your group choose a different chapter to review and to use for creating index card notes.
2. Each student creates a set of index card notes that includes three definition cards, three category cards, and three question cards for a total of nine cards.
3. Shuffle together all the cards created by members of your group. Take turns drawing a card and using the card to quiz another person in your group. Continue taking turns until all of the cards have been used for review.

CHECK POINT 9.4

Answers appear on B4.

Fill-in-the-Blanks See Test-Taking Strategies 21–24 in Appendix A.

1. ____________ card notes are effective study tools to use to learn facts, definitions, rules, and steps.
2. ____________ cards are flashcards that include the category, formal definition, and details about the vocabulary term.
3. ____________ cards show a topic on the front of the card and a list of details or items that belong under the topic on the back of the card.
4. ____________ cards, which work effectively to review for tests, pose a question on the front and answers on the back.

Access Chapter 9 Practice Quiz 4 in your College Success CourseMate, accessed through *CengageBrain.com*.

Cornell Notes

5 *Identify the Five R's of Cornell and describe the processes used for each of the five steps in the Cornell Notetaking System.*

The Cornell Notetaking System is one option to use to take textbook notes. In Chapter 8, you learned about *outline notes.* In this chapter you learned about *annotating* and *index card notes.* In Chapter 11, you will learn about other notetaking systems. The Essential Strategies for Textbook Notetaking in **Figure 9.10** apply to all notetaking systems.

Creating a goal to learn how to use a variety of notetaking systems provides you with the tools to select the most appropriate system or systems to use for your various textbooks. Textbook notes are important for the following reasons:

- Notetaking involves **condensing or reducing** large amounts of information into more manageable units that are easier to study and review.
- Notetaking requires you to **think carefully** about information, break it down, analyze it, and select what is important to learn. If you have difficulty understanding what you are reading, you will have difficulty taking notes.
- Notetaking processes involve **multisensory strategies.** Writing notes encodes visual images such as words, phrases, lists, or charts. Reciting encodes information linguistically. Writing encodes information kinesthetically.
- Studying from well-developed notes is **more time efficient** than reading and rereading chapters of information. Effective textbook notes save you time in the long run.

CONCEPT CHECK 9.13

What are the benefits of taking notes? What different notetaking systems have you learned to use?

FIGURE 9.10 Essential Strategies for Textbook Notetaking

- **Understand what you read before taking notes.** Read a paragraph or chunk of information, pause, think about the information, be sure that you understand it, and then take notes.
- **Be selective.** Your notes should be a *condensed* version of the textbook, not a word-for-word copy of the textbook pages. Capture only the important concepts, main ideas, and supporting details in your notes.
- **Paraphrase or reword.** Shorten textbook explanations or information by using your own words to state main ideas and important details as long as your wording presents the information accurately.
- **Include textbook reminders in your notes.** Instead of copying large charts or lengthy sections of important text, write a reminder in your notes to see page XX in the textbook.
- **Label your notes.** As you progress through the term, you will have many pages of notes. To avoid confusion, include textbook chapter numbers and number each page of your notes.
- **Use spaced practice.** Make several contacts with your notes over different periods of time. You can use them as a warm-up activity to put you in the mindset of the subject the next time you sit down to study, or you can schedule time each week to review your notes for the week.
- **Use feedback strategies.** Use the Look-Away Technique with reciting and visualizing to check the completeness and accuracy of your learning.
- **Review your notes.** Use immediate review to create a strong impression in memory. Use ongoing review to keep information active and accessible in working memory.

EXERCISE 9.7

Textbook Case Studies

DIRECTIONS:

1. Read each case study carefully. Respond to the question at the end of each case study by using *specific* strategies discussed in this chapter. Answer in complete sentences.
2. Write your responses on paper or online in this textbook's College Success CourseMate, Textbook Case Studies. You will be able to print your online response or e-mail it to your instructor.

CASE STUDY 1: Shauna learns by writing information and studying from handwritten information. However, when she creates outline notes or Cornell notes, she notices that her notes are longer than the textbook chapters. She copies everything and her notes become a steady stream of unorganized information. What notetaking strategies could Shauna use to produce more effective and useful notes?

CASE STUDY 2: With Cornell notes, Erick has learned to condense information effectively into the right column. However, in his recall column, Erick makes lists of important information, writes definitions for key terms, and writes study questions with their answers. He reads all the information out loud. What adjustments does Erick need to make in the way he uses his Cornell notes so he tests his memory more effectively?

Access Chapter 9 Textbook Case Studies in your College Success CourseMate, accessed through *CengageBrain.com*.

The Five R's of Cornell Notetaking

The **Cornell Notetaking System** is a five-step notetaking process used to take notes from textbooks and from lectures.

The **Five R's of Cornell** are record, reduce, recite, reflect, and review.

The ***Cornell Notetaking System*** is a five-step notetaking process used to take notes from textbooks and from lectures. This powerful notetaking system was designed by Dr. Walter Pauk at Cornell University more than forty-five years ago when he recognized students' need to learn how to take more effective notes. Many college and university instructors consider this the most effective notetaking system for college students.

The ***Five R's of Cornell*** are record, reduce, recite, reflect, and review. The goal of the Cornell Notetaking System is to take notes that are so accurate and detailed that you *may not need to go back to the book to study.* To avoid weakening this powerful system, use all five R's shown in **Figure 9.11** to record and study your notes.

2½" 6"

© Cengage Learning

Preparing to Take Notes

To prepare your notebook paper for Cornell notes, draw a two-and-one-half-inch margin down the left side of your notebook paper. (Check if your campus bookstore carries Cornell or "law notebook" paper with the wider left margin.) The following tips are important for the Cornell system:

- Only make columns on the front side of your notebook paper as you will *not* be taking notes on the back of these pages.
- Use the back of each page to list or summarize points when you do the fourth R: *reflect.*
- Label pages. On the top of the first page, write the course name, chapter number, and date. For all the following pages, just write the chapter number and the page number of your notes.

FIGURE 9.11 The Five R's of Cornell

1. **Record** your notes in the right column.
2. **Reduce** your notes into the recall column on the left.
3. **Recite** out loud from the recall column.
4. **Reflect** on the information that you are studying.
5. **Review** your notes immediately and regularly.

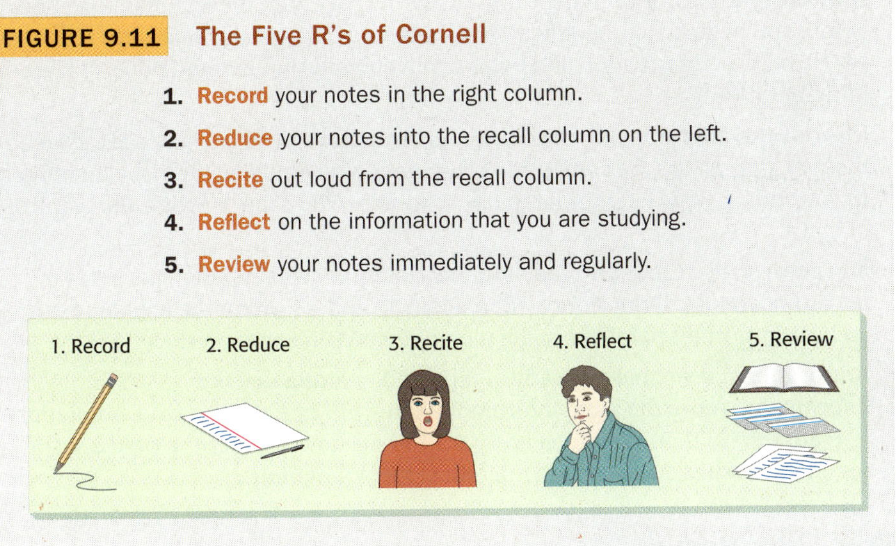

Step One: Record Notes

The ***record step*** in the Cornell system involves taking notes in the right column. Read each paragraph carefully, decide what information is important, and then record that information on your paper. Your notes should be a *reduced version* of the textbook. Be selective. Use the following suggestions for recording notes in the right column:

The **record step** in the Cornell system involves taking notes in the right column.

- **Skeleton of notes:** The headings and subheadings in the textbook are the *skeleton* or outline of the chapter. They serve as guides for identifying main categories of information.
- **Textbook headings and new headings:** Write a textbook heading on your paper. Underline it so it stands out and gives your notes structure. You do *not* need to number the headings. Reserve the use of numbers for details. If you wish to regroup or reorganize information into new headings or subheadings that are more helpful for understanding topics, you can add new headings or subheadings in your notes.
- **Details:** To separate details and avoid what appears to be an endless stream of random details, number the details. Numbering helps you create a stronger impression about the number of important points under each heading, and it breaks the information into smaller, more manageable units.
- **Minor supporting details:** Indent or use dashes to show minor supporting details under the main details that are numbered.
- **Sufficient information:** Your notes need to show the big picture and the little pictures (details), so be sure to record sufficient information to be meaningful later.
- **Meaningful phrases or short sentences:** Shorten or paraphrase information. Avoid using only individual words or short phrases that may lose their meaning when you return to them later. If phrases by themselves are not meaningful units of thought, convert them into short sentences.

- **Double-spacing between headings:** Leave a space after the end of one section before you begin a new heading. This double spacing visually separates sections or "chunks" of information and helps avoid crowded or cluttered notes that are difficult to study.
- **Charts and diagrams:** When you encounter important visual materials, sketch them or *summarize* the conclusions you make after studying the visual materials. In your notes, write a reminder to return to a specific page to review the graph or chart.
- **Marginal notes:** Carefully read marginal notes (or sidebars) that may appear in your textbooks. If this information does not appear within the regular text, include important points from the marginal notes in your notes.
- **Annotations:** If you have already highlighted or annotated the information, move the same information into your notes. Notice the annotations in **Figure 9.12**. Then examine **Figure 9.13** to see how a student created a set of the Cornell notes on a computer to reflect the annotations.

CONCEPT CHECK 9.14

Summarize strategies to use for each of the Five R's of Cornell notetaking.

The **reduce step** in the Cornell system involves condensing notes into the recall column.

The **recall column** is the left column in the Cornell notes that shows headings, key words, and study questions.

Step Two: Reduce

After you have finished taking notes for the chapter, you are ready to close the book and reduce your notes one step further. The ***reduce step*** in the Cornell system involves condensing notes into the recall column. The ***recall column*** is the left column in the Cornell notes that shows headings, key words, and study questions. Figure 9.13 shows the right notetaking column and the left recall column with the reduced notes. Use the following suggestions to create an effective recall column:

- **Copy headings.** To structure and organize your recall column, copy the headings from the right column into the left column and underline them. The headings should appear directly across from the headings in your notes.
- **Reread your notes.** Reread a section of your notes. If your notes seem vague or incomplete, go back to the book, reread, and add more details to your notes.
- **Create study questions.** Under the headings in your recall column, write brief study questions about the information in the right column. Your study questions can be in an abbreviated form such as *Why? Name the 6 ... Related to X how?*
- **Define key words.** In your recall column, across from your notes that define a key term, write "def." and the *key word* to cue you later to recite the definition for the word.
- **Do not write too much.** Do not clutter the recall column with too much information. Do *not write answers* to your study questions, definitions, or completed lists of information. You want to challenge yourself in the next step to see if you can recall the information from memory.

The **recite step** in the Cornell system involves using information in the recall column to explain information out loud in your own words without referring to detailed notes.

Step Three: Recite

The ***recite step*** in the Cornell system involves using information in the recall column to explain information out loud in your own words without referring to detailed notes. Use the following suggestions to recite from your recall column:

- **Cover up the right column.** To avoid the tendency to look at your notes as you recite, use a blank piece of paper to cover your notes on the right side of your paper. All you will see are the headings, your study questions, and key words in the left column.

FIGURE 9.12 Forgetting—Why We, Uh, Let's See; Why We, Uh ... Forget!

Why do we forget?

We don't expect sensory memories and short-term memories to remain with us for long. But when you deliberately encode and store information in long-term memory, you want it to stay there (after all, it's supposed to be *long*-term). For example, when you study for an exam, you count on your long-term memory to retain the information at least until you take your exam.

Why do we forget long-term memories? The more you know about how we "lose" memories, the better you will be able to hang on to them. Most forgetting tends to occur immediately after memorization. Herman Ebbinghaus (1885) famously tested his own memory at various intervals after learning. To be sure he would not be swayed by prior learning, he memorized *nonsense syllables*. These are meaningless three-letter words such as "cef," "wol," and "gex." The importance of using meaningless words is shown by the fact that "Vel," "Fab," and "Duz" are no longer used on memory tests. People who recognize these words as detergent names find them very easy to remember. This is another reminder that relating new information to what you already know can improve memory.

By waiting various lengths of time before testing himself. Ebbinghaus plotted a curve of forgetting. This graph shows the amount of information remembered after varying lengths of time (• Figure 7.8). Notice that forgetting is rapid at first and is then followed by a slow decline (Hintzman, 2005). The same applies to meaningful information, but the forgetting curve is stretched over a longer time. As you might expect, recent events are recalled more accurately than those from the remote past. Thus, you are more likely to remember that *The King's Speech* won the "Best Picture" Academy Award for 2010 than you are to remember that *Million Dollar Baby* was the 2004 winner.

As a student, you should note that a short delay between studying and taking a test minimizes forgetting. However, this is no reason for cramming. Most students make the error of *only* cramming. If you cram, you don't have to remember for very long, but you may not learn enough in the first place. If you use short, daily study sessions *and* review intensely before a test, you will get the benefit of good preparation and a minimum time lapse.

The Ebbinghaus curve shows less than 30 percent remembered after only 2 days have passed. Is forgetting really that rapid? No, not always. Meaningful information is not lost nearly as quickly as nonsense syllables. After 3 years, students who took a university psychology course had forgotten about 30 percent of the facts they learned. After that, little more forgetting occurred (Conway, Cohen, & Stanhope,1992.). Actually, as learning grows stronger, some knowledge may become nearly permanent (Berntsen & Thomsen, 2005).

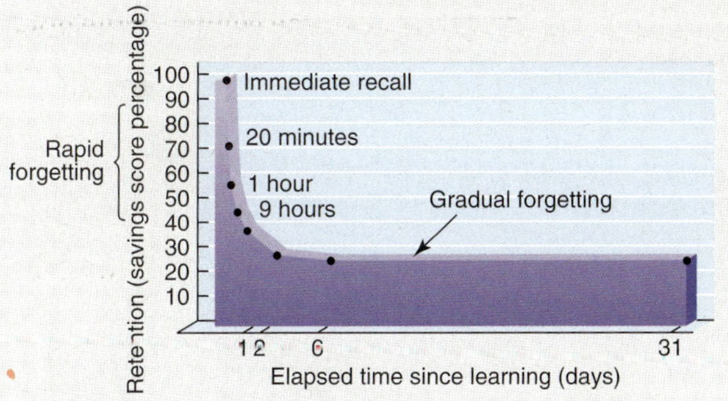

• **Figure 7.8 The curve of forgetting. This graph shows the amount remembered (measured by relearning) after varying lengths of time. Notice how rapidly forgetting occurs. The material learned was nonsense syllables. Forgetting curves for meaningful information also show early losses followed by a long gradual decline, but overall, forgetting occurs much more slowly. (After Ebbinghaus, 1885.)**

- **Begin reciting.** Begin reciting by looking at and then telling about the information in the recall column. Answer the questions, define terms, and tell what you remember about the key words. Talk out loud in complete, coherent sentences.
- **Use feedback.** After reciting a section of information, pull down the paper that covered the right column. Check your accuracy and the completeness of your recited information. If you have difficulty reciting, or if you "go blank," pull down the paper, reread your notes, cover them, and try reciting again.

CONCEPT CHECK 9.15

Explain how to use the recall column of Cornell notes. What kinds of adjustments might you need to make in the recall columns?

FIGURE 9.13 **Forgetting—Cornell Notes**

The following set of Cornell notes is based on the information in Figure 9.12, Since the excerpt did not have headings and subheadings, notice how headings were added to organize the information. This is an option you always can use to personalize and organize your notes.

<u>Forgetting – Why We...Forget</u>

<u>Intro</u>	<u>Intro</u>
Expect which memory to remain when study?	1. We don't expect sensory or short-term memories to remain for long 2. We do expect info we encode or study to be in LTM when needed for exam
<u>Forgetting</u>	<u>Forgetting – Why do we forget long-term memories?</u>
Most forgetting occurs when?	1. Most forgetting – immediately after memorization
Ebbinghaus – Did what?	2. Herman Ebbinghaus – • tested own memory – different intervals – memorized nonsense syllables • nonsense – not swayed by prior learning 3. Reminder: relate new info to what already know con improve memory
<u>Curve of Forgetting</u>	<u>Ebbinghaus Curve of Forgetting</u>
Def. curve	1. Curve of forgetting: graph that shows amount of info remembered after varying lengths of time 2. Curve shows:
Curve shows what?	• Forgetting most rapid at first • Forgetting followed by slower, gradual decline • applies same way to meaningful info over longer time • remember recent events more accurately than those from past Ex. Academy Award winners this year vs. 2010
Studying – reduce forgetting How?	3. For studying: • Short delay between studying and taking test minimizes forgetting • Cramming – don't have to remember long but may not learn enough • Better: short, daily study and review before a test
<30% explain	4. Curve shows: <30% remembered after 2 days (Nonsense syllables) = 70% forgotten! –Meaningful info not lost as quickly. –Ex. After 3 yrs, psych students forgot about 30% facts. Not much more forgetting then
Any knowledge permanent?	5. Imp.– Learning grows stronger ⟶ some knowledge almost permanent See Ebbinghaus Curve Figure in book.
Draw curve	

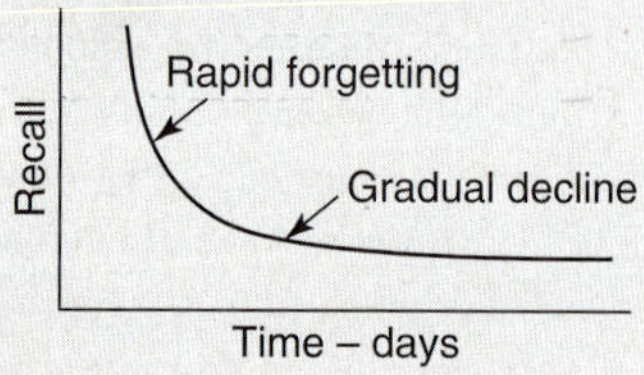

- **Adjust the recall column.** If the recall column lacks sufficient cues to direct your reciting or to focus you on the important points, add more key words or study questions to the recall column. If you find that the recall column provides you with too much information that results in simply reading with little information left to recite from memory, cross out (or whiteout) some of the details before you recite again.

Track your progress: If you wish, star items in the recall column that you recited with accuracy. Check or place an arrow next to information that you need to practice further.

EXERCISE 9.8

Practice Cornell Notetaking

DIRECTIONS:

1. Your instructor will provide directions for you to create a set of Cornell notes with recall columns for one of the following:
   a. A specific excerpt in Appendix D
   b. An excerpt from a new source that is provided by the instructor
   c. A specific section of information your textbook for this course or for another course
2. Read the assigned materials carefully. If you wish or if assigned, highlight main ideas and important supporting details and terminology. Make useful marginal notes.
3. Create Cornell notes that show a notetaking column and a developed recall column.
4. Go to Exercise 9.8: Cornell Notetaking Self-Assessment Checklist in Appendix C, page C20. Use the checklist to assess the quality of your Cornell notes. Note: The back of the checklist (page C21) shows an instructor assessment form that your instructor may use to evaluate your notes.

Step Four: Reflect

The ***reflect step*** in the Cornell system involves thinking seriously, comprehending, and using elaborative rehearsal strategies to work with information in new ways. The reflect step is a creative and highly individualized step, so no two students will create identical study tools or use the same rehearsal activities. Decide *what works best for you* and the materials you are studying. Use the following tips for reflecting on your notes:

- **Think and ponder.** Take time to think about the topic, relationships among details, and the importance of the information you are studying.
- **Line up your recall columns.** To see an informal outline and an overview of all the information in your set of notes, arrange the pages of your notes so you can see a lineup of all the recall columns.
- **Write a summary.** Look only at the information in the recall columns. Write a summary using full sentences and paragraphs to summarize the main ideas and important details.
- **Write on the back of your notes.** Use the back of your note paper to make lists of information, write study questions, add diagrams or charts, or jot down questions you want to ask in class.

The **reflect step** in the Cornell system involves thinking seriously, comprehending, and using elaborative rehearsal strategies to work with information in new ways.

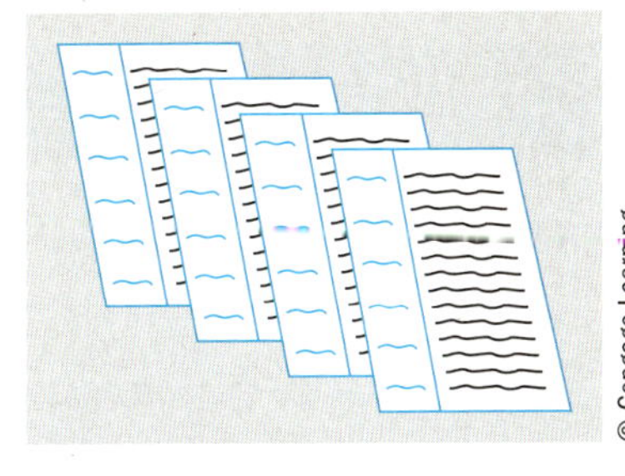
© Cengage Learning

Access Chapter 9 Topics In-Depth: Cornell with SQ4R in your College Success CourseMate, accessed through *CengageBrain.com*.

CONCEPT CHECK 9.16

What are effective reflect, immediate review, and ongoing review strategies to use by yourself? With a partner? In a study group?

- **Make study tools.** Reinforce your learning by creating study tools that you can use throughout the term: index card notes, visual mappings, charts, or mnemonics.

Step Five: Review

The **review step** in the Cornell system involves using immediate and ongoing review. **Immediate review** is the process of rehearsing information before you end a learning task. Use immediate review with your notes after you finish the reflect step. This review helps create a stronger impression of the information before you set it aside and move on to something new.

The **review step** in the Cornell system involves using immediate and ongoing review.

Immediate review is the process of rehearsing information before you end a learning task.

Ongoing review is the process of practicing previously learned information days and even weeks after the initial learning occurred.

Ongoing review is the process of practicing previously learned information days and even weeks after the initial learning occurred. Ongoing review keeps information active and accessible in your memory system. Ongoing review saves you time in the long run; when you prepare for tests or exams, you will not need to cram or spend excessive time "relearning" information.

CHAPTER 9 REFLECTIVE WRITING 2

On separate paper, in a journal, or online in this textbook's College Success CourseMate, respond to the following questions:

1. Which notetaking system or systems do you prefer to use to take notes from your textbooks? Explain your preference or preferences.
2. What is the value of taking textbook notes? How does notetaking help improve your academic performance?

Access Chapter 9 Reflective Writing 2 in your College Success CourseMate, accessed through *CengageBrain.com.*

CHECK POINT 9.5

Answers appear on B4.

True or False? See Test-Taking Strategies 1–9 in Appendix A.

_____ 1. You should always read the entire chapter before taking Cornell notes.

_____ 2. If you take Cornell notes, you never need to return to the textbook to reread sections.

_____ 3. The Five R's of Cornell are not *read, record, recite, reflect,* and *review.*

_____ 4. Headings are used to help organize information in both columns of Cornell notes.

_____ 5. An effective recall column includes questions without answers and terminology without the written definitions.

Matching See Test-Taking Strategies 16–20 in Appendix A.

_____ 1. Five R's of Cornell
_____ 2. the record step
_____ 3. reciting
_____ 4. reflecting
_____ 5. recall column
_____ 6. headings
_____ 7. content of recall column

a. questions, key words, headings
b. involves explaining in your own words
c. thinking, pondering, summarizing, questioning
d. record, reduce, recite, reflect, review
e. read, record, recite, reflect, review
f. involves taking notes
g. main topic or category of information
h. the left column of Cornell notes

Access Chapter 9 Practice Quiz 5 in your College Success CourseMate, accessed through *CengageBrain.com.*

ACTIVITY

Chapter 9 Critical Thinking

PURPOSE: Vocabulary study sheets are one form of "two-column notes." In some ways, this two-column notetaking format is a simplified version of Cornell notes. As you recall from Bloom's Taxonomy, critical thinking involves *applying* and *creating,* so this activity provides you with the opportunity to create new uses for two-column notes.

DIRECTIONS:

1. Use the format of two-column notes. Brainstorm a variety of ways you could use this two-column note format to take other kinds of notes. Jot down or list your ideas. What would the columns show? Which of your textbooks could you use for your two-column notetaking system?
2. Put your ideas to work! Create a set of two-column notes for some type of textbook content that does not involve terminology and definitions. You may be asked to share your system with the class or students in a small group.

Learning Objectives Review

1 ***Define active reading and describe its relationship to active learning and critical reading.***

- Active reading is a process of using effective strategies to engage working memory to achieve specific reading goals.
- Active readers use active learning strategies; active readers are also critical readers who move beyond basic reading skills to use higher-level reading skills.

Terms to Know

By yourself or with a partner, practice reciting or writing definitions for the following terms. You may also practice defining these terms by using the online flashcards or comparing your answers to the online glossary.

active reading p. 267
topic p. 269

Terms to Know

main idea p. 269
topic sentence p. 269
supporting details p. 270
word clues p. 272
punctuation clues p. 273
word structure clues p. 273
context clues p. 275
definition cards p. 276
vocabulary sheets p. 277
annotating p. 279
enumerating p. 280
ordinals p. 280
marginal notes p. 281
stringing ideas together p. 283
index card notes p. 284
category cards p. 284
question cards p. 284
Cornell Notetaking System p. 288
Five R's of Cornell p. 288
record step p. 289
reduce step p. 290
recall column p. 290
recite step p. 290
reflect step p. 293
review step p. 294
immediate review p. 294
ongoing review p. 294

Access Chapter 9 Flashcards and Online Glossary in your College Success CourseMate, accessed through *CengageBrain.com*.

Learning Objectives Review

2 ***Summarize paragraph-level strategies to use to identify paragraph elements, learn terminology and definitions, and create definition cards and vocabulary sheets.***

- Thorough reading involves reading, usually one paragraph at a time, to understand, analyze, and digest the information in the paragraph.
- The topic, the main idea, and the supporting details are the three paragraph elements active readers learn to identify.
- The main idea states the author's most important point about the topic. The main idea sentence is also called the topic sentence.
- Terminology and definitions are important supporting details in paragraphs. Circling terminology and highlighting key words in definitions separate the information from other kinds of supporting details.
- Word clues, punctuation clues, word structure clues, and context clues help identify definitions for course-specific terminology and unfamiliar words.
- Definition flashcards and vocabulary sheets are study tools to practice reciting definitions.

3 ***Explain the value of annotating textbooks and how to highlight, annotate, and study from annotations.***

- The process of annotating, which includes highlighting, underlining, marking, enumerating, and making marginal notes, holds information longer in working memory so it can be processed.
- Specific strategies guide students through the process of annotating textbooks selectively and in useful ways.
- Annotating is effective only when students take time to study the annotations. A process of stringing ideas together and reciting are review processes to use.

4 ***Describe the three kinds of cards used in a comprehensive set of index card notes; explain ways to study from index card notes.***

- A comprehensive set of index card notes includes definition cards, category cards, and question cards. Each type of card has a different purpose and kind of information.
- Studying from index card notes includes reciting, self-quizzing, and using the cards as review tools.

5 ***Identify the Five R's of Cornell and describe the processes used for each of the five steps in the Cornell Notetaking System.***

- Record, reduce (in the recall column), recite, reflect, and review are the five R's of the Cornell Notetaking System.
- Recording occurs in the right column; reciting from condensed notes occurs by using the left column, the recall column.
- Using a variety of strategies for recording and reducing notes results in organized, easy-to-use notes to practice and learn textbook content.

Chapter 9 Review Questions

Answers appear on page B4.

True or False? See Test-Taking Strategies 1–9 in Appendix A.

_____ 1. Active reading occurs naturally and automatically for all college students.

_____ 2. It is always best to read the whole chapter first and then go back to take notes.

_____ 3. All notetaking systems should result in a reduced version of textbook information.

_____ 4. The Cornell Notetaking System consists of six steps: read, reduce, record, recite, reflect, and review.

_____ 5. The main idea always appears as the first sentence in textbook paragraphs.

_____ 6. Annotating involves a variety of processes: marking main ideas, circling terminology, writing marginal notes, and possibly using abbreviations next to brackets.

_____ 7. Too much information in the Cornell recall column causes you to read and not do much reciting.

_____ 8. Word clues, which are also called word structure clues, are words that help you define terminology or unfamiliar words.

_____ 9. Definition cards usually provide more detailed definitions of terminology than appear on vocabulary sheets.

_____ 10. Index card notes include cards that provide definitions, cards that list items under categories, and cards that pose study questions with the answers on the back.

Multiple Choice See Test-Taking Strategies 10–15 in Appendix A.

_____ 1. Which of the following is *not* true about stringing ideas together from your annotated notes? Stringing ideas together

a. should occur after you have created written summaries.
b. involves connecting ideas by using transition words and informal language.
c. involves activating the auditory channel by verbalizing.
d. may occur after each paragraph or after sections of information.

_____ 2. Annotating a textbook includes

a. writing notes in the margins.
b. highlighting topic sentences and key words.
c. circling terminology and enumerating items in a list.
d. doing all of the above.

_____ 3. The five R's of the Cornell Notetaking System

a. involve developing and using two columns of information.
b. do not represent the processes of reading reciting, recalling, reviewing, and revising.
c. involve using active learning strategies of writing, reciting, and working with information in new ways.
d. are described by all of the above statements.

Access Chapter 9 Enhanced Quiz and Chapter 9 Study Guide in your College Success CourseMate, accessed through *CengageBrain.com*.

Access all Chapter 9 Online Materials in your College Success CourseMate, accessed through *CengageBrain.com*.

Appendix A

Contents for Essential Test-Taking Skills

Introduction

Throughout your college years, you will encounter many different kinds of tests and a variety of test-taking situations. This ***Essential Test-Taking Skills*** guide will help you recognize and understand different types of test questions and key elements in different test-question formats. Understanding how to read and respond to a variety of test questions will increase your test-taking performance and your grades.

Essential Test-Taking Skills provides you with **fifty-two** specific, easy-to-use strategies for understanding, interpreting, and answering the following kinds of test questions:

- **Objective test questions**, which include true-false, multiple-choice, and matching questions
- **Recall test questions**, which include fill-in-the-blanks, listing, definition, and short-answer questions
- **Math test questions**, which involve solving problems, applying equations, and answering word- or story-problem questions
- **Essay test questions**, which involve using a series of paragraphs to develop a thesis statement for an answer

For ***Essential Study Skills, 8th edition***, you can use the following resources to strengthen your test-preparation and test-taking skills:

- Chapter 7: Preparing for Upcoming Tests
- Exercise 7.5: Practice Test-Taking Skills in Chapter 7 Topics In-Depth in your College Success CourseMate.
- Practice Quizzes and Enhanced Quizzes in each chapter: Go to Quizzes in your College Success CourseMate, accessed through *CengageBrain.com*.
- Check Points throughout each chapter to practice answering test questions
- Chapter Review Questions in each chapter with self-correcting answer keys
- Online Chapter Study Guides

Remove this handy test-taking guide and place it in your notebook for quick reference.

Objective Test Questions

Objective test questions, also called recognition questions, require that you recognize whether information is correct or incorrect and then apply skills to identify the correct answer. The following easy-to-use strategies discuss each type of objective test question: true-false, multiple-choice, and matching. Applying these strategies will build your confidence for taking objective tests and improve your test performance.

Familiarize Yourself with Terminology for Objective Tests

To lay a foundation of understanding for objective test questions, read through the following glossary of terms. These terms are used throughout the sections for true-false, multiple-choice, and matching questions.

- **Modifiers:** Modifiers are words that tell to what degree or frequency something occurs. Absolute (100 percent) and in-between modifiers appear in objective test questions.

- **Definition clues:** Definition clues are words that signal that the question is testing your understanding of the meaning or the definition of terminology.
- **Relationship clues:** Relationship clues are words that signal that the question is testing your understanding of the relationship between two subjects.
- **Negatives:** Negatives are words or prefixes in words that carry the meaning of "no" or "not."
- **Stems:** Stems are the beginning part of a multiple-choice question that appears before the options for answers.
- **Options:** Options are the choices of answers to use to complete a multiple-choice question.
- **Distractors:** Distractors in multiple-choice questions are the incorrect answers or incorrect options.
- **Four levels of response:** The four levels of response are systematic steps to use to identify the best answer for an objective test question.

Four Levels of Response to Answer Test Questions

Do you move through tests by reading questions, answering them with certainty or hesitancy, and then moving on to the next question? Many students use this approach of plowing through tests—question after question—feeling confident about some answers and doubtful about others. Using the following four levels of response to answer test questions provides you with a structured, step-by-step process that leads to more correct answers and more self-confidence in your ability to perform well on tests.

- **Immediate response:** Read the question carefully. If you immediately know the answer, write the answer with confidence and move to the next question.
- **Delayed response:** If you do not immediately know the answer, reread the question carefully, and then conduct a memory search. Recall what you do know about the topic; strive to trigger an association that will link you to the answer. If you cannot answer with certainty, *leave the answer space empty.* Place a check mark next to the question and return to it after you have answered as many questions as possible on the remainder of the test.
- **Assisted response:** Return to the unanswered questions, the ones with the check mark reminder next to them. Identify one or two key words in the question. Scan through the other parts of the test for these key words and for other clues or associations that may help trigger recall of information to help you select an answer.
- **Educated selection:** Use an educated-selection strategy (educated guessing) to select an objective test-question answer if all else fails. Educated selection involves more than just guessing; it involves using logic and thinking skills to decide on the most reasonable answer. However, realize that educated selection is a last-resort strategy that may increase your odds for selecting the correct answer, but it does not guarantee that all answers will be correct. The following sections provide you with educated selection strategies to use with true-false, multiple-choice, and matching questions.

True-False Questions

True-false questions are the most basic kind of objective test question. Because they are usually one-sentence statements, students tend to read and respond too quickly without paying sufficient attention to key words in the true-false statement. Therefore, pay close attention to the following key elements or words in true-false questions:

- Items in a series
- Smaller words known as modifiers
- Definition and relationship clues
- Negative words that affect overall meaning

Nine Easy-to-Use Strategies for True-False Questions

Are you sometimes confused or unsure of how to read or interpret true-false questions? Do you later understand your incorrect answers when you review a graded test? Following are easy-to-use strategies that will help you understand and interpret true-false questions and select correct answers with more confidence and accuracy.

Understand How to Read and Respond to True-False Questions

STRATEGY 1

- **Read each statement carefully.** Pay attention to every word in the statement. If you tend to misread questions, point to each word as you read and circle the key words.
- **Be sure you completely understand the statement.** Read it a second time if necessary. For clarity, translate difficult words into more informal words. Create a visual picture of the information.
- **Be objective when you answer.** Do not personalize the question by interpreting it according to what you do or how you feel. Instead, answer according to the information presented by the textbook author or your instructor in class.
- **Do not add your reasoning or argument to the side of a question.** Frequently, the only information that the instructor will look at is the T or the F answer, so other notes, comments, or clarifications will be ignored during grading.
- **Make a strong distinction between the way you write a T and an F.** Trying to camouflage your answer so it can be interpreted as a T or an F will backfire. Unclear letters usually are marked as incorrect.
- **Mark a statement as TRUE only when the statement is completely true.** If any part of a statement is inaccurate or false, you must mark the entire statement as FALSE.

Carefully Check Each Item in a Series of Items

STRATEGY 2

- A true-false question is TRUE only when the entire statement is true.
- If one item in a series of items is false, the entire statement becomes a FALSE statement.
- Items in a series are separated by commas, so use the commas as signals to check each item carefully.

- The words in bold print in the following examples turn the statements into false statements.

> __F__ 1. Effective lecture notes show ***details of all examples***, *main ideas, important details,* and *sketches of visual materials* used by the instructor.
>
> __F__ 2. *Active listening, critical listening,* ***informal listening***, and *appreciative listening* are the four kinds of listening, each with different purposes.

STRATEGY 3 Understand and Identify Modifiers

- **Modifiers** are words that tell to what degree or frequency something occurs. There is a huge difference between saying that something *always* happens and saying that something *sometimes, often,* or *seldom* happens.
- **Figure 1** shows two kinds of modifiers to watch for in true-false statements: 100 percent modifiers and in-between modifiers.
- Pay close attention to modifiers, for a single modifier alters the meaning and the accuracy of the statement.
- As you read questions, actively look for and circle 100 percent and in-between modifiers in statements.

FIGURE 1 Learn to Recognize These Modifiers

100 percent	In-Between	100 percent
all, every, only	some, most, a few	none
always, absolutely	sometimes, often, usually	never
everyone	may, seldom, frequently	no one
everybody	some, few, most	nobody
best	average, better	worst
		least, fewest
Any adjective that ends in *est*, which means "the most," such as largest, smallest ...	Any adjective that ends in *er*, which means "more," such as larger, smaller ...	
Absolute phrases: is/are, definitely, with certainty, beyond a doubt, without exceptions	Non-absolute words: perhaps, possibly, maybe, tend to	

STRATEGY 4 Pay Close Attention to 100 Percent Modifiers

- **100 percent modifiers**, also called *absolute modifiers*, are words that indicate absolutes or a total degree without any exceptions. In Figure 1, the 100 percent modifiers appear in the first and the third columns. Words such as *best* or *worst* show the extremes and indicate that there is *nothing* that is better or worse; they are absolutes.

- When you identify a 100 percent modifier, ask yourself: *Is this accurate? Does this happen or occur all the time without any exceptions?* If you answer "yes," then the statement is TRUE. If you answer "no," then the statement is FALSE.
- In the following examples, the 100 percent modifiers appear in boldface print. Notice how statements with 100 percent modifiers may be true, or they may be false.

__F__ 1. Sentences with absolute modifiers are **always** false.

__F__ 2. Sentences with absolute modifiers are **never** false.

__T__ 3. Well-written true-false statements have **only** one correct answer.

Pay Close Attention to In-Between Modifiers

STRATEGY 5

- **In-between modifiers** are words that indicate something occurs in varying degrees or frequency. The in-between modifiers appear in the middle column of Figure 1.
- In-between modifiers allow for more flexibility, variance, or exceptions because they indicate that a middle ground exists where situations or conditions do not occur as absolutes (100 percent of the time).
- When you identify an in-between modifier, ask yourself: *Is this accurate? Does this happen or occur this frequently or to this degree?*
- In the following examples, the in-between modifiers appear in boldface print. Notice how statements with in-between modifiers may be true, or they may be false.

__T__ 1. Spaced practice is **usually more** effective than massed practice for studying textbook information.

__T__ 2. **Sometimes** students can reduce stress by changing their sleeping or their eating habits.

__F__ 3. The Look-Away Technique **seldom** provides students with effective feedback.

Watch for Definition Clues

STRATEGY 6

- **Definition clues** are words that signal that the question is testing your understanding of the meaning or the definition of terminology.
- Word phrases such as *defined as*, *states that*, or *also known as* may be working as clues for definitions.
- **Figure 2** shows common definition clues and the sentence pattern often used in statements that test your understanding of definitions.
- Circle definition clues when you see them in true-false statements.
- Then underline the terminology word and ask yourself: *What is the definition I learned for this word?*
- Compare your definition to the definition that appears in the statement. If your definition matches the test question definition, answer TRUE.

FIGURE 2 Learn to Recognize These Definition Clues

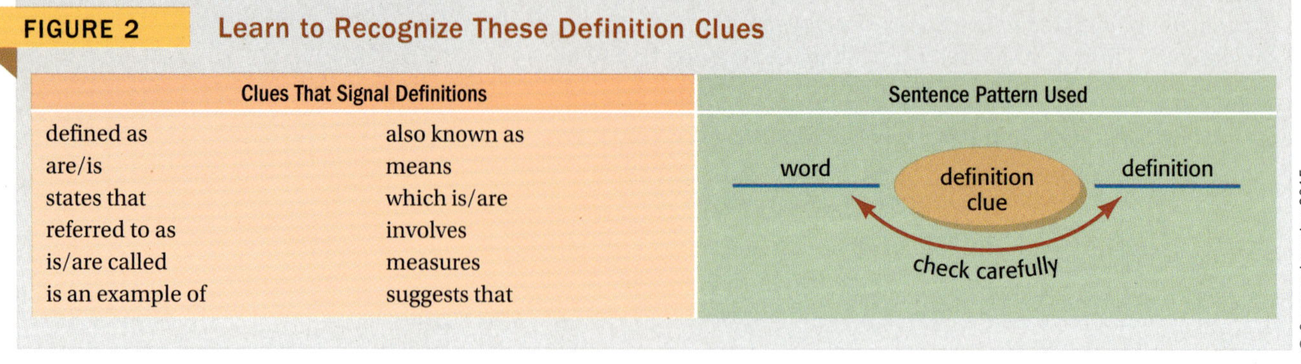

Clues That Signal Definitions	
defined as	also known as
are/is	means
states that	which is/are
referred to as	involves
is/are called	measures
is an example of	suggests that

- If there is a discrepancy, analyze the test question definition carefully because it may be saying the same thing but simply using different words. If your definition and the definition in the statement are not the same, answer FALSE.
- In the following sample test questions, the definition clue appears in boldface print. Notice that the definition clue appears between the terminology word and the definition.

__T__ 1. Annotating **is** the active learning process of marking textbooks to show main ideas and supporting details.

__F__ 2. Marathon studying **is also known as** distributed practice.

__T__ 3. A traditional IQ test **measures** intellectual abilities in the areas of verbal, visual-spatial, and logical mathematics.

STRATEGY 7 Look for Relationship Clues

- **Relationship clues** are words that signal that the question is testing your understanding of the relationship between two subjects.
- Relationships often show cause and effect—one item causes another item to occur.
- Relationships may also show other organizational patterns: chronological, process, comparison-contrast, and whole-and-parts.
- **Figure 3** shows common relationship clue words and a sentence pattern often used in statements that show relationships.
- Circle relationship clues when you see them in true-false statements.
- Then underline the key words for the two subjects involved in the relationship.
- Ask yourself: *What do I know about how these two subjects are related to each other?*
- Compare your relationship idea with the relationship presented in the question.
- If the relationship in the statement is logical, answer TRUE.
- If the relationship statement varies considerably from your thoughts about the relationship, analyze the accuracy and logic of the statement more carefully. If the statement shows a faulty relationship, answer FALSE.

FIGURE 3 Learn to Recognize These Relationship Clues

Clues That Signal Relationships		Sentence Pattern Used
increases	result	
produces	since	
reason	so, so that	
affects	creates	
because	decreases	
causes	effects	
before/after	differs	
consists of	leads to	

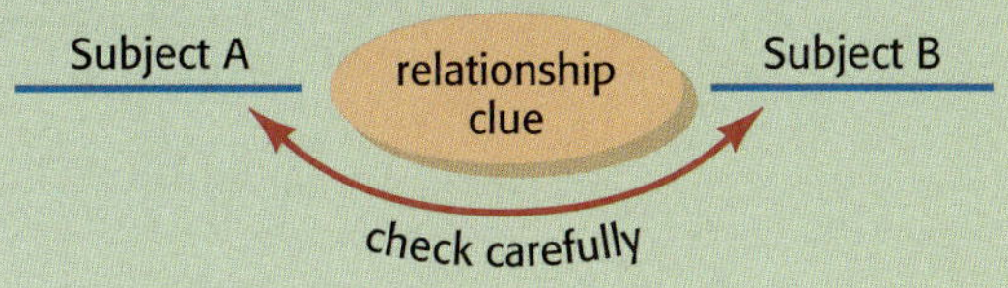

- In the following examples, the relationship clue appears in boldface print. Notice that the relationship clue appears between the two subjects in all but the last example, which shows a second sentence pattern that places the relationship clue in the front of the sentence.

__T__ 1. Linking a picture to a word **creates** an association that you can use as a retrieval cue.

__F__ 2. Rote memory is effective for learning textbook information **because** it promotes deep comprehension and memorization of important facts.

__F__ 3. **Because** rote memory promotes deep comprehension and memorization of important facts, it is effective for learning textbook information.

Watch for the Use of Negatives

STRATEGY 8

- **Negatives** are words or prefixes in words that carry the meaning of "no" or "not."
- Negatives affect the meaning of the sentence; if you ignore or miss them, the meaning of the sentence is the opposite of the correct meaning.
- For example, if you skip over and ignore the negative in the following statement, *The ABC Method is **not** a goal-setting technique*, then your mind reads the statement as *The ABC Method is a goal-setting technique.*
- **Figure 4** shows words and common prefixes often used as negatives in true-false statements.
- Negatives can cause some confusion in understanding or interpreting a statement accurately. If a question with a negative word or prefix confuses you, use the *Negative Cover-Up Technique*:
  - *Cover up the negative* and reread the statement without the negative.
  - If the sentence has two negatives, cover up *only one* negative.
  - If the statement without the negative makes a *true* statement, the answer to the original question will be the opposite: FALSE.

FIGURE 4 Learn to Recognize These Common Negatives

Negative Words	Negative Prefixes
no	dis (disorganized)
not	im (imbalanced)
but	non (nonproductive)
except	il (illogical)
	in (incomplete)
	ir (irresponsible)
	un (unimportant)

- If the statement with the negative removed is a false statement, the answer to the original question will be the opposite: TRUE.

- In the following examples, the negatives appear in boldface print. If the negatives confuse you, use the Negative Cover-Up Technique to better understand the question before answering.

__F__ 1. A **dis**organized desk is **not** an external distractor.

__F__ 2. The principle of Selectivity is **not** used during the fourth step of SQ4R.

__T__ 3. Using chained associations is **not im**practical during a test when you need to conduct a memory search to find an answer to a question.

STRATEGY 9 Use Educated Selection as a Last Resort

- **Educated selection**, sometimes referred to as *educated guessing*, is the fourth level of response for answering objective test questions.
- Educated selection is more than random guessing because it often involves using common sense, basic logic, critical thinking skills, and specific test-taking strategies to improve your odds for supplying the correct answers for objective test questions.
- Even though educated-selection strategies may help you gain a few additional points on a test, the strategies do not always result in correct answers, so do not become overly confident about taking tests simply because you know how to use educated-selection strategies.
- **Figure 5** summarizes five educated-selection strategies that apply to true-false questions.

Select True: In-Between Modifiers

- **In-between modifiers** allow for exceptions or for the statement sometimes to apply and sometimes not to apply.
- If you are using educated selection, and you see an in-between modifier in a true-false question, or in an option in a multiple-choice question, select TRUE.

FIGURE 5 **Educated-Selection Strategies for True-False Questions**

1. Select *true* if there is an in-between modifier.
2. Select *true*, the "wild-shot guess," if there are no other clues in the true-false statement.
3. Select *false* if there is a 100 percent modifier.
4. Select *false* if there is a relationship clue.
5. Select *false* if the statement is obviously incorrect, silly, or ridiculous.

- Notice how the in-between modifiers work in the following true-false questions. Also notice how you use a variety of thinking skills other than random guessing to select answers.

__T__ 1. **Sometimes** reviewing notes from a previous paragraph can help you understand a difficult paragraph.

__T__ 2. People **often** use empathic listening to try to understand another person's feelings.

Select True: The "Wild-Shot Guess"

- For true-false questions, if there are no modifiers to use, and no relationship is shown, you may need to use TRUE, the "wild-shot guess."
- If you run out of time on a test and simply must guess, select TRUE. There is a logical reason for this. When instructors write tests, they often prefer to leave the correct, accurate information in your mind. Therefore, they tend to write more true statements than false statements.

Select False: 100 Percent Modifiers

- The **100 percent modifiers** are the *absolutes*, meaning that they are the extremes; no exceptions are allowed.
- Few things happen or exist without exceptions, so the odds are in your favor that true-false questions, or options in multiple-choice questions, with 100 percent modifiers will be false. Select FALSE.
- Notice how the 100 percent modifiers work in the following true-false questions.

__F__ 1. Classroom attendance in college is required for **every** class.

__F__ 2. **Always** begin by studying your favorite subject first.

Select False: Relationship Clues

- If you cannot determine the correct answer for a cause-effect or relationship question, select FALSE. Why? Relationship questions often involve higher-level thinking skills, and test writers can easily write questions that show false relationships.

- Notice how the following true-false questions do not show a true or accurate relationship.

F 1. Lack of motivation is the **reason** unsuccessful students avoid using time management.

F 2. Cramming is ineffective **because** it uses only ten of the Twelve Principles of Memory.

Select False: Obviously Incorrect Answers

- If you read statements that are ridiculous, foolish, or insulting, mark them FALSE in true-false statements or eliminate them as answers (options) for multiple-choice questions.
- If you read statements that have unfamiliar terms, mark them FALSE. If you have attended class regularly and have done all the reading assignments, odds are in your favor that statements with unfamiliar terms are false.
- Notice how this works in the following examples.

F 1. Howard Gardner's Multiple Intelligences Theory applies only to people with IQs over 175. *Ridiculous*

F 2. Howard Gardner added an eighth intelligence called psychic/intuitive to his Multiple Intelligence Theory. *Unfamiliar term*

Multiple-Choice Questions

Multiple-choice questions may be the most frequently used type of question that appears on both paper-pencil and computerized tests. As a form of objective test questions, unless directions indicate otherwise, only one answer is correct. Students must carefully read and analyze answer options before selecting the best one for each question. When answering multiple-choice questions, pay attention to the following parts or elements of the question:

- The **stem**, which is the beginning of the question
- The **options**, which are the choices of answers
- The **distractors**, which are the options that are *not* the correct answer

Six Easy-to-Use Strategies for Multiple-Choice Questions

Do you sometimes answer multiple-choice questions incorrectly because you select the first possible answer without reading the other options? Do you have difficulty selecting the best answer from the list of options? The following six easy-to-use strategies provide you with step-by-step processes to use to analyze multiple-choice questions and select the best option to answer the questions.

STRATEGY 10 Understand How to Read and Respond to Multiple-Choice Questions

- **Read the directions carefully.** Unless indicated otherwise, select only one answer. Realize, however, that some directions may state that you should mark all the correct answers.

- **Use the three-step approach** for answering multiple-choice questions. Identify which options form true statements when used with the stem and which options form false statements when used with the stem. (See Strategy 11.)
- **Read all of the options** before you select your answer. Do not stop reading and analyzing as soon as you find an acceptable answer. A later option may be more comprehensive or a better answer.
- **Pay attention to modifiers, definition clues, relationship clues, and negatives.** After you combine the stem with each option to create true-false statements, use the same strategies you use for answering true-false questions.
- **Choose the *best* answer.** One or more of the answers may be correct, but only the most inclusive (with the broadest information), most accurate, or most complete is the best answer.
- **Select "All of the Above"** only when every option is accurate and forms a true statement when combined with the stem. If any one option forms a false statement, you cannot select "All of the above" as your answer.
- **Expect different formats.** Some tests may have a blank line within the stem. Your task is to select an answer from a list of answers that fits on the blank line to form an accurate statement. On some computerized tests, you may find a drop-down box on the blank line within the stem. The options appear in the drop-down box. You simply click on the option that best completes the statement.
- **Avoid careless mistakes.** To avoid writing the wrong letter on the line, circle the letter of the best answer and then write the letter on the line. You may not need to use this strategy all the time, but it is effective when you get nervous, tend to respond too quickly, or your eyes skip around because of test anxiety.
- **Use the four levels of response.** If you do not immediately know the answer, conduct a memory search. Cross off options you know are distractors. If you cannot confidently select an answer, use assisted response later to look through the test for assistance. As a last resort, use educated selection to write an answer to a multiple-choice question.

Use the Three-Step Approach for Answering Multiple-Choice Questions

STRATEGY 11

Step One: Finish the Stem in Your Mind

- Read the stem carefully and, without looking at the options, quickly finish the stem in your mind. This step puts you in retrieval mode and into a long-term memory schema related to the statement.
- Then glance down to see if any of the options are similar to what you had in mind.
- For practice, how would you complete each of the following stems in your mind?

1. A mnemonic is ______________.
2. When you ______________ time on your weekly schedule, you exchange time blocks of a social activity and a study block.
3. Metacognition is ______________.

Step Two: Create True-False Statements

- Create a true-false statement by reading the stem of a multiple-choice question with the "a" option in the list of options.
- Continue by creating true-false statements by reading the stem with each of the remaining options. If you have four options, you will have four true-false questions to examine.
- Following is an example of creating three true-false statements for a question with three options:

_____ 1. Schemas in long-term memory are
a. small details attached to larger impressions.
b. clusters of related information or concepts.
c. visually encoded impulses.

By combining the stem and the options, you create three true-false statements:

1. Schemas in long-term memory are small details attached to larger impressions.
2. Schemas in long-term memory are clusters of related information or concepts.
3. Schemas in long-term memory are visually encoded impulses.

Step Three: Identify the Distractors and Select the Answers

- Examine each of the true-false statements you create by combining the stem with each option. Use the true-false test-taking strategies you have learned.
- Cross off the *distractors*, the options that you know are false.
- Examine the remaining statements and select the *best* answer from those options. The following example shows how to use *step three* of this process.

~~1.~~ Schemas in long-term memory are small details attached to larger impressions. *This is false, so cross off this option.*

2. Schemas in long-term memory are clusters of related information or concepts. *This forms a true statement.*

~~3.~~ Schemas in long-term memory are visually encoded impulses. *This is false, so cross off this option.*

STRATEGY 12 Choose the Most Inclusive or Comprehensive TRUE Statement

- When you combine a stem with the options, the result may be some *true* and some *false* statements.
- In such situations, you must then carefully examine the *true statements* to decide which statement is the *most inclusive, most comprehensive,* or *most accurate* and thus is the correct answer.

- The following example shows how two of the true-false statements created by adding the options to the stem form true statements (*b* and *d*), and two form false statements (*a* and *c*). However, *b* is the *best* option because it is more comprehensive and includes the information stated in option *d*.

__b__ 1. The Incentive Theory of Motivation suggests that

a. a person must receive monetary rewards in order to be motivated. *False*

b. both positive rewards and negative consequences may activate specific behaviors and increase motivation. *True*

c. unobtainable rewards are the greatest motivators to push for higher goals. *False*

d. positive rewards activate specific behaviors and kinds of motivation. *True*

Carefully Examine "Not" or Exclusion Questions

STRATEGY 13

- One type of multiple-choice question you may encounter is a "*not*" or an exclusion question. This kind of question asks you which of the options is *not true* or does *not belong* in the same category as the other options.
- When the options are complete sentences, read each option as a true-false statement by itself. Then carefully examine the statement or statements marked *false* because these statements will reflect what is *not true* or what *does not belong* in a given category. One of these statements will be the correct answer.
- In the following example, you are looking for the *false* statement, the "not true" statement. Systematic desensitization *is* a strategy to decrease test anxiety; it *does* replace negative emotional responses with positive ones, and it *does* involve visualizing different responses to words that trigger anxiety. The statement that is *not true*, and thus is the correct answer, is option *c*.

__c__ 1. Which of the following statements is ***not*** true about systematic desensitization?

~~a.~~ It is a strategy to use to decrease test anxiety. *True*

~~b.~~ It replaces negative emotional responses with positive ones. *True*

c. It involves a four-step process to use during a test to reduce procrastination. *False*

~~d.~~ It may involve visualizing a different response to words that trigger anxiety. *True*

Use True-False Educated-Selection Strategies

STRATEGY 14

- The educated-selection strategies you use for true-false questions (Figure 5) also work for multiple-choice questions when you combine the stem with the options to form your own true-false statements.
- Select TRUE for options with in-between modifiers and FALSE for statements that have 100 percent modifiers, relationship clues, or options that obviously are incorrect answers.

- Remember to cross off and then ignore all the distractors.
- In the first example that follows, both *b* and *c* have in-between modifiers. However, before randomly guessing between these two options, think carefully. Option *c* does not show accurate information; option *b* makes sense and is the correct answer.
- In the second example, notice the key words that you can use to analyze the question and select the best answer.

__b__ 1. Intrapersonal intelligence is an intelligence that
~~a.~~ **always** shows leadership and group charisma. *False*
b. **often** involves a special interest in personal growth and insights. *True?*
c. **seldom** is combined with linguistic or interpersonal intelligence. *True?*
~~d.~~ is **never** taught in schools. *False*

__d__ 2. Systematic desensitization
~~a.~~ **causes** a person to react more mildly to criticism from authorities. *False*
~~b.~~ works **because** the immune system is strengthened. *False*
~~c.~~ should **never** be used to avoid undesirable situations. *False*
d. **helps** a person change his or her negative reaction to specific events. *True*

STRATEGY 15 Use Educated-Selection Strategies for Multiple-Choice Questions

In addition to the educated-selection strategies in Figure 5 that also apply to multiple-choice questions, **Figure 6** shows five additional educated-selection strategies for multiple-choice questions. Even though these strategies help you analyze questions more carefully and guide you to selecting an answer, do not feel overly confident or rely on these strategies, except as a last resort, because they will not always produce a correct answer.

Select a Middle Number

- When the options in a multiple-choice question are numbers, chances are better that the correct answer is one of the numbers in the middle range.

FIGURE 6 Educated-Selection Strategies for Multiple-Choice Questions

1. Select one of the **middle numbers** when numbers are the options.
2. Select one of the "**look-alikes**" when two options are almost identical.
3. Select the **longest** or the **most inclusive** option.
4. Select c, the **wild-shot guess** if there are no other clues.
5. Select "**All of the above**" in specific situations.

- Therefore, treat the highest and the lowest numbers as distractors; eliminate them.
- That leaves you with two options. Try to reason through to make the better choice from the remaining two options.
- If any one of the other educated-selection strategies applies (such as choose *c*), consider that strategy as well to choose your answer.

c 1. An average rate of thinking speed is
~~a.~~ 800 words per minute. *Eliminate the highest.*
b. 600 words per minute. *Choose between these*
c. 400 words per minute. *two options.*
~~d.~~ 200 words per minute. *Eliminate the lowest.*

Select One of the "Look-Alikes"

- Some questions have two options that look almost identical except for one or two words. Chances are good that the correct answer is one of these two options.
- Eliminate the other options and focus on these two "look-alikes."
- Carefully think through and associate the information with what you have learned. If you cannot decide, choose either one. You have a fifty-fifty chance of being correct.
- In the following example, focus on *c* and *d* because they are "look-alikes." Now try to reason your way through this. You have already eliminated *a*, which deals with language. Because *c* also relates to language, it, too, must be incorrect. This leaves you with *d* as the correct answer, which it is. (Notice in this case how the guessing strategy to use *c* does not work—there are no guarantees!)

d 1. Compared to the left hemisphere of the brain, the right hemisphere of the brain
~~a.~~ understands spoken language better.
~~b.~~ has better logical abilities.
c. perceives words better.
d. perceives emotions better.

Select the Longest or Most Inclusive Option

- Look at the *length* of the options. If one option is much longer than the others, choose it. Sometimes more words are needed to give complete information, so selecting the longest option may result in a correct answer.
- Also look at the *content* of the options. An option that covers a wider range of possibilities is more likely to be correct.
- Sometimes two or three options may be correct to some degree, but one option contains more information or is a broader idea. This answer is the most inclusive, so choose it.
- Notice in the following example how all of the options are correct to some degree. However, *d* is the longest and includes a wider range of information.

The answers *a*, *b*, and *c* fit under the information given in *d*. Therefore, *d* is the best option.

__d__ 1. You can reduce test anxiety by focusing on
   a. the test and not on other students. *True*
   b. conducting careful memory searches. *True*
   c. positive statements and affirmations. *True*
   d. effective test-taking skills related to both your actions and your thoughts. *True*

Select C: The "Wild-Shot Guess"

- For multiple-choice questions, many instructors favor the *c* answer for the correct answer. If you try writing some of your own multiple-choice questions, you may find that you, too, tend to put more correct answers in the *c* position than in any other position.
- The position of *c* seems to hide the answer best and force the reader to read through more of the options.

Select "All of the Above" in Specific Situations

- If you know for certain that two options are correct, but you are not sure about the third option, and the fourth option is "All of the above," choose "All of the above."
- If you do not know for certain that two are correct, and you have found no other clues to help you, you can choose "All of the above." However, be aware that this strategy is not very reliable, especially if the option "All of the above" is used throughout the test.
- Apply this strategy to options that are variations of "All of the above." Examples of these variations are *doing all of the above, involves all options,* and *includes all of the strategies.*

Matching Questions

Matching questions consist of two columns of information. The left column often consists of key words or terminology. The right column contains definitions, descriptions, events, examples, or other factual information that matches with the items in the left column. Matching questions are created through the use of *paired associations.* The following are examples of paired associations you may encounter on matching tests:

- Words and their definitions
- Dates and events
- Problems and their solutions
- People and what they did
- Terms and their function or purpose
- Causes and effects

Five Easy-to-Use Strategies for Matching Questions

Do you tend to get confused and frustrated with the process of matching items from two columns? Do you sometimes use answers more than once or almost finish the matching tests only to find that the remaining items do not belong together or match? If so, the following five strategies will provide you with a systematic method to use to avoid confusion, frustration, and incorrect matches.

Examine the Matching Format Carefully

STRATEGY 16

- Read the directions carefully. Usually you can use each item on the right only once. If you can use an item on the right more than once, the directions usually indicate this.
- Count the number of items in each column. If both columns show an equal number of items, each item will be used once. If the right column contains *more* items than the column on the left, some items on the right will be extra and will not be used.

Work Systematically

STRATEGY 17

- Use a systematic approach for matching items on the two lists. If you *incorrectly* match an item on the right with an item on the left, the result will be two or more incorrect answers rather than one.
- Read through the list with the shortest entries to familiarize yourself with the topics and the kinds of paired associations in the matching test. If the items in each column are about equal length, read the left column.
- Start with *a*, the first item at the top of the right column. Scan the items in the left column to find a match.
- Once you see a definite match, write the letter on the line and *cross off the letter you used so you do not reuse it.* Crossing off used letters also helps avoid confusion.
- Do *not* make a match unless you are confident that the item on the right matches the item on the left. When in doubt, leave the item unmatched and move to the next letter in the column to look for its match.
- After you have matched as many items as possible by using immediate and delayed response, return to the unmatched items. Use assisted response by looking through other parts of the test for related information that may help you match up the remaining items.
- **Figure 7** shows the systematic approach to matching items on a matching test.

Look for Word Clues and Grammar Clues

STRATEGY 18

- Word clues (helper words) can help you find correct matches. For example, if you see a word such as *system, technique, process,* or *rule* in the right column, narrow your focus by searching for choices in the left column that deal specifically with a *system, technique, process,* or *rule.*
- Grammar clues can help you find correct matches. If an item in the right column is a *plural,* the match in the left column will also refer to a *plural.* Similarly, *singular* items in the right column are matched with *singular* items in the left column.

- In the following example, notice how the word clues in bold print in the right column help you match to the items in the left column. The words in italics in the left column match up to the boldface words in the right column.

c	1. core *abilities* (plural)	a. **two kinds** of locus of control (2)
e	2. assisted *response*	b. a cognitive learning **style** (singular)
e	3. relaxation *technique*	c. **subintelligences** (plural)
a	4. *internal* and *external* (2)	d. soothing mask **technique** (1 technique)
b	5. visual *learner* (singular)	e. third level of **response** for test questions (response)

FIGURE 7 Steps for Answering Matching Questions

1 Directions say to use each answer once.

2 Two answers are extra and won't be used.

5 Use delayed response. Use helper words to try to connect the items that you do not know well.

6 Use assisted response. Use the rest of the test for assistance in finding more answers.

7 Use educated guessing. Fill in any remaining blanks with letters you did not already use.

Matching

Match the items on the left to the items on the right. Write the letter of each answer on the line. Each item on the right may be used only one time.

3 Read the shorter list.

4 Start with "a." Do only the ones you know.

h	1. working memory	a. permanent storage center
___	2. motivation	b. associating items together
a	3. long-term memory	c. short-term memory and feedback loop
j	4. affirmations	d. feeling, emotion, or desire that elicits an action
f	5. chunking	e. feedback
___	6. sensory stimuli	f. group into bigger units or break into smaller units
b	7. linking	g. procedural memory
i	8. primacy-recency effect	h. conscious mind
___	9. self-efficacy	i. items easiest to recall in a list
___	10. result of self-quizzing	j. positive statements written in present tense
		k. belief in one's own abilities
		l. words, sounds, pictures

Connect Items in Each Column by Making Logical Sentences

STRATEGY 19

- As you look at an item in the right column, ask yourself questions to find logical matches. For example, in Figure 7, item *k*, ask yourself, "What item on the left has something to do with belief in one's abilities?"
- When you think you have found a match, connect the two items by forming a sentence. For example, for *k* in Figure 7, you could say, "Self-efficacy is the belief in one's own abilities."
- When the items in the matching example in Strategy 18 are matched up, you can check the logic of your answers by forming sentences that make sense:

  Core abilities are subintelligences.

  Assisted response is the third level of response for test questions.

  A relaxation technique is the soothing mask technique.

  Internal and external are two kinds of locus of control.

  Visual learner is a cognitive learning style.
- If you cannot form a logical sentence by connecting an item on the right with an item on the left, chances are that the two items are not a match.

Write an Answer in Every Space

STRATEGY 20

- If you have not been able to match all the items after using the above strategies, fill in the missing blanks with the remaining letters. Refrain from the urge to start changing answers that you previously marked with certainty.
- An empty answer line obviously will be wrong, so filling in the remaining answers with "leftover" letters may result in one or more correct answers, but this strategy is risky and should only be used as a last resort.

Recall Test Questions

Recall questions are questions that require you to conduct memory searches to retrieve (recall) information from your memory to respond with an answer. Unlike objective test questions, recall questions do not provide you with direct clues or answers to recognize as accurate or not. Recall questions require higher levels of thinking and processing information.

By using effective study strategies that include creating associations that link two or more items in memory, you will be able to recall correct answers for the following kinds of questions:

- Fill-in-the-blanks to complete sentences
- List items or steps in a process
- Define specific terminology
- Write a short paragraph or short answer
- Solve a word problem or an equation (See math tests.)

Familiarize Yourself with Terminology for Recall Tests

In strategies for recall questions, you will encounter terms that are specific to recall questions. Read through the following glossary of terms before proceeding to the strategies for recall tests.

- **Closed questions:** Closed questions are questions that require specific answers. Sometimes the answers must appear in a specific order, such as giving the steps of a process. Other times the answers are limited to course-specific concepts, topics, or details that may appear in any order.
- **Open-ended questions:** Open-ended questions are questions that have many possible answers. A variety of answers may be correct if they reflect course content, show logical connections to course material, or reflect understanding of concepts, topics, or details.
- **Direction words:** Direction words are words in test questions that signal a specific kind of answer that is required. *List, define, discuss, tell, describe, explain why,* and *when* are a few examples of direction words.

Fill-in-the-Blanks Questions

Fill-in-the-blanks questions are recall questions in the form of sentences that have one or more missing words. The words used to "fill in the blanks," or to complete the statement, usually are key terms that appear in your textbook, course materials, or lectures.

- In most cases, fill-in-the-blanks questions are *closed questions,* which means you must use specific words rather than a variety of possible words for a correct answer.
- Spelling is important. Usually your instructors require you to spell words correctly to receive full points. On computerized tests, misspelled words will be marked as incorrect answers.

Four Easy-to-Use Strategies for Fill-in-the-Blanks Questions

Do you sometimes go blank and have difficulty thinking of the exact word needed to complete fill-in-the blanks questions? When you receive your graded test and see the correct answer, do you recognize the word? Using the following three strategies will help you recall the words needed to complete this type of question.

STRATEGY 21 Understand How to Read and Respond to Fill-in-the-Blanks Questions

- **Identify the number of words required to complete the statement.** You can write only one word per blank space. (See Strategy 22.)
- **Identify the kind of word needed for each blank space.** Based on the position of the word in the sentence, you often can recognize that the missing word is a noun (naming an object, concept, step, process, or person) or a verb stating some type of action.
- **Conduct memory searches for answers.** Use key words in the statement to trigger associations. Ask yourself the following kinds of questions: *What do we call .... Who .... Where did I learn this? What is this related to?* This type of memory search and questioning works well during the delayed response to answering a question.
- **Form complete sentences.** When you read the completed sentence with the filled-in words, the sentence must make sense and be grammatically correct.

Determine the Number of Words Required in the Sentence

STRATEGY 22

- You can write only one word on each blank line. If there is only one blank line, you will write only one word. Trying to write a two-word phrase on a single line will result in an incorrect answer.
- In the following examples, only one word completes each statement. Remember, you must spell answers correctly.

1. An __________ personality preference describes a person who tends to focus attention on the inner world of ideas, thoughts, and reflection. *Introversion*
2. __________ motivation is the driving force that comes from within you to take action. *Intrinsic*

- When you see two or more blank lines, a comma between each blank line signals that your response will require a series of separate items.
- If no commas separate the blank lines, your response is a two- or a three-word term, expression, or phrase.
- The following examples show both types of statements that require more than one-word answers:

1. ______ ______ is also known as your conscious mind. *Two-word answer: Working memory*
2. You can use the Increase-Decrease Method to adjust the time you plan to spend in the three main areas of your Pie of Life: ______, ______, and ______. *Answers in any order: school, work, leisure*
3. The five R's of Cornell in order are ______, ______, ______, ______, and ______. *Answers in order: record, reduce, recite, reflect, review*

Modify the Four Levels of Response to Provide Answers

STRATEGY 23

- **Write the correct word for a blank if you immediately know the answer.**
- **Use delayed response.** Conduct a memory search. Try to recall an association to help you recall the term. If you cannot recall the correct word to fill in the blank, leave the question unanswered. Place a check mark next to the question. Return to it later.
- **Use assisted response to fill in the blanks.** If you cannot recall the necessary word, identify other key words in the statement, skim through the rest of the test to look for those key words. Try inserting a possible word into the statement, then read the statement, remembering that the completed sentence must be grammatically correct, make sense, and be logical.
- **Write a substitute word, a synonym, or even a phrase to complete the sentence.** A *synonym* is a word with a similar meaning. Even though a substitute word, a synonym, or a short phrase is not the exact answer for the fill-in-the-blanks statement, you may receive partial points for your effort.

STRATEGY 24 Study Course Terminology to Prepare for a Test

- Many key words used to answer fill-in-the-blanks questions will be course vocabulary.
- Use flashcards to study. Read the definition side of your flashcards. *Recite* the key term and *spell* it. Turn the card over to check your answer and the spelling of the key word.
- If your textbook provides a list of terms, use the terms to write your own practice fill-in-the-blanks test questions. Practice completing your own questions. Check your spelling.
- Use any textbook or online exercises that include practice filling in missing words and spelling key terms correctly.

Listing Questions

Listing questions are recall questions that ask for a specific list of ideas, items, or steps that belong together in a specific category. Unless the directions say otherwise, answers on listing questions are words or phrases, not complete sentences.

Four Easy-to-Use Strategies for Listing Questions

Do you have problems providing the number of items required to complete a listing question? Do you tend to include items in your list that do not answer the question? The following four easy-to-use strategies will help you complete listing questions with appropriate answers.

STRATEGY 25 Understand How to Read and Respond to Listing Questions

- **Underline the key words in the question.** This helps you focus on what kind of information you need to include in your answer.
- **Pay attention to the number of items required in your answer.** If the question asks you to "List five kinds of …," number your answer one to five. Begin listing the five different answers. If the question does not indicate how many items to include in your list, list as many items as possible. Avoid duplicating or restating items.
- **Identify the question as a closed or an open-ended question.** (See Strategy 26.)
- **Use words or phrases for your answers.** Unless the directions say differently, you do not need to answer by using complete sentences.

STRATEGY 26 Identify Questions as Closed or Open-Ended Questions

- **Closed questions** are questions that require specific answers. Some closed questions, such as questions about the steps used in a specific process, require that you list the items in their proper order.

- The following are examples of *closed* listing questions:

1. What are the Four Levels of Response to use for answering objective questions? *Specific order required: immediate, delayed, assisted, educated selection*
2. List the four most common ways to encode information to process into memory. *Nonspecific order: linguistic, visual, kinesthetic, semantic*

- **Open-ended questions** are questions that have a variety of possible answers.
- To answer open-ended questions, you can list a variety of answers as long as the items in your answers relate to or belong in the category of the question. Items in your list may come from different chapters and different parts of the course.
- Often answers to open-ended questions were not studied as a specific list of information. Therefore, you must pull together information that relates to the question. For this reason, students who rely on rote memory often find open-ended questions challenging.
- The following are examples of open-ended questions that have a variety of possible correct answers:

1. List any four subintelligences of Gardner's musical intelligence.
2. List five *reflect activities* a student could use during the fourth step of the Cornell Notetaking System.
3. List three statements a student with an external locus of control might make after performing poorly on a test.

Modify the Four Levels of Response to Provide Answers

STRATEGY 27

- **Write immediate responses to develop your list.** List as many items as possible to answer the question.
- **Use delayed response.** Conduct memory searches for answers. Use the key words you underlined in the question to trigger associations and answers to expand your list. Ask yourself questions: *What else belongs here? What other things are related to the answers I already listed?* Place a check mark next to the list if you were not able to complete it.
- **Use assisted response.** Return to the listing questions that are not complete. Use other parts of the test to locate items to complete your list.
- **Write a substitute word, synonym, or phrase to complete the list.** An empty space brings only one result: no points for your answer—so attempt to complete the list. Avoid restating an item already listed as duplicate answers will not receive points.

Predict Listing Questions When You Study

STRATEGY 28

- As you read and take notes, watch for items that appear in lists or steps in a process.
- Create study tools, such as flashcards, for these lists. Practice reciting these lists from memory.

- Predict listing questions when you use self-quizzing strategies to prepare for an upcoming test. Write your own test questions that require you to list specific items or steps in a process.
- Use chapter objectives and chapter summaries as additional sources for lists of information to learn.

Definition Questions

Definition questions are recall questions that ask you to define and expand upon a word or terminology. For definition questions, a one-sentence answer that simply provides a formal definition of a term often is insufficient and does not earn you the maximum points for the question.

Three Easy-to-Use Strategies for Definition Questions

Do you tend to have problems recalling definitions for course-specific terminology? Do you tend to receive only partial points for short answers to definition questions? The following three easy-to-use strategies provide you with a step-by-step process to write strong answers that define terminology.

STRATEGY 29 Understand How to Read and Respond to Definition Questions

- **Read the question carefully; underline the word you need to define.**
- **Use paired associations.** When you studied the term, you paired it with the definition. Say the word to yourself; conduct a memory search for the definition. Try to recall hearing yourself reciting or reading the definition on your flashcard or vocabulary sheet. Try to visualize the information in your notes.
- **Include three or more sentences in your answer.** Simply defining the term is usually insufficient and results in an underdeveloped answer. By using the category-definition-expanded detail format, you demonstrate greater understanding of the meaning of the term. (See Strategy 30.)
- **Use assisted response.** If you are not able to define the word after conducting a memory search, place a check mark next to the question, and move to another question. Later, use other parts of the test for clues you can use to complete your answer.

STRATEGY 30 Practice Writing Definitions with Three Levels of Information

1. **Name the category associated with the term.** To identify the category, ask yourself: *In what group or category of information does this belong? In what chapter (topic) did this appear? What is the "big picture" word or schema for this word?*
2. **Give the formal definition.** Give the course-specific definition you learned from your textbook or from class lectures.
3. **Expand the definition with one more detail. Figure 8** shows seven methods and examples for expanding an answer for a definition question.

FIGURE 8 **Methods to Expand a Definition Answer**

Method	Example
Add one more fact.	Distributed practice often occurs when the 2:1 ratio is used.
Give a synonym.	Distributed practice is the same as spaced practice.
Give an antonym, a contrast, or a negation.	Distributed practice is the opposite of marathon studying or massed practice.
Give a comparison or an analogy.	Distributed practice is like working on a goal a little every day instead of trying to complete all the steps in one block of time.
Define the structure of the word.	The root of neuron is neuro, which means nervous system.
Give the etymology.	The term locus comes from the Latin loci, which means place, so locus of control refers to a place that is the source of the control.
Give an application.	Surveying can be used to become familiar with a new textbook, chapter, article, or test.

Predict and Study for Definition Questions

STRATEGY 31

- Use key words in boldface print or lists of important terms in each chapter to predict definition questions.
- Spend ample time reciting definitions and explaining what terms mean and how they are used. With a strong understanding of course-specific terminology, you will have a solid foundation for other concepts and skills in the course.
- Create flashcards or vocabulary study sheets for vocabulary terms you need to know. Use your textbook and glossary to clarify definitions.
- Work with a partner or in a study group to practice reciting and explaining terminology out loud. Use the three levels of information in your response.
- Use self-quizzing and practice writing definitions as you prepare for tests. Use feedback throughout the process to evaluate your understanding.
- Examine and study other students' answers for definition questions. Notice the category, definition, and the expanded detail other students use in their answers. Following is an example of weak and strong answers.

Question: Define the term *distributed practice*.
Weak Answer: It means you practice at different times.
Strong Answer: Distributed practice is a time-management strategy. Distributed practice means that a task or study blocks are spread or distributed over time. Distributed practice, also known as spaced practice, is the opposite of marathon studying or massed practice.

Short-Answer Questions

Short-answer questions are recall questions that require a short paragraph for an answer. After carefully reading the question, you must conduct memory searches to locate or recall relevant information in long-term memory to answer the question. Unlike listing questions, your answer will consist of five or more sentences written in paragraph form. Writing information in lists instead of full sentences usually does not suffice or earn you full points.

Five Easy-to-Use Strategies for Short-Answer Questions

Do you tend to have difficulty expressing your ideas in a clear, well-organized way? Do you sometimes write answers that do not directly answer the short-answer question? The following five strategies show how to organize and develop answers for short-answer questions.

STRATEGY 32 Understand How to Read and Respond to Short-Answer Questions

- **Read the question carefully to determine if the question is closed or open-ended.** Doing this directs your memory searches for the kind of information needed to answer the question. Are you looking for specific details that perhaps were a part of a list or set of steps, or are you searching for a variety of possible answers related to the topic?
- **Underline key words in the question.** Key words focus your attention on the subject or topics that must appear in your answer. As you work on developing your answer, check back to the underlined key words to check that you are focusing on the topic and including important details. This also helps you avoid wandering off course with nonessential information.
- **In your response, include key words that appear in the question.**
- **Answer in complete sentences.** Answers to short-answer questions often are graded not only on the content, but also on your writing skills. Use correct grammar, punctuation, and spelling. If time permits, proofread to correct grammar, punctuation, and spelling errors.
- **Answer in paragraph form.** (See Strategies 35 and 36.)
- **Write legibly.**
- **Use assisted response if necessary.** Scan through other parts of the test to identify additional details to include or to strengthen your answer.

STRATEGY 33 Pay Attention to and Circle Direction Words

- **Direction words** are words in test questions that signal a specific kind of answer is required.
- To get full points for your answer, your response must reflect the expectation associated with the question word.
- As soon as you identify a direction word in a question, *circle it.* Review in your mind what is required by this direction word.

FIGURE 9 Direction Words for Short-Answer Questions

Direction Word	What Is Required
Discuss/Tell	Tell about a particular topic.
Identify/What are?	Identify specific points. (This is similar to a listing except that you are required to answer in full sentences.)
Describe	Give more specific details or descriptions than are required by "discuss."
Explain/Why?	Give reasons. Answer the question "Why?"
Explain how/How?	Describe a process or a set of steps. Give the steps in chronological (time sequence) order.
When?	Describe a time or a specific condition needed for something to happen, occur, or be used.

- **Figure 9** shows common direction words used for short-answer questions.
- Notice in the following examples how each of the test questions has the same subject: *visual mappings*. However, think how answers will vary slightly because of the different direction words used.

Why is recitation important to use while studying a visual mapping?

Explain how to create a visual mapping.

How should you study from a visual mapping?

When should you use visual mappings?

Make a Mental Plan or a Short List of Key Ideas — STRATEGY 34

- **Conduct a memory search.** Use your memory search to identify appropriate details related to the key words and the direction word in the question.
- **Create a mental plan or a short list of ideas to use as a guide to write your answer.** This helps you save valuable test time as your answer stays focused and you avoid wandering off the topic. If for some reason you run out of time to write a paragraph answer, turn in your list of ideas for possibly partial points for your answer.
- **Refer to your mental plan or list of ideas to write your answer.** Develop the list into full sentences and a well-planned paragraph.

Start Your Paragraph with a Strong, Focused Opening Sentence — STRATEGY 35

- Begin your answer with a sentence that is direct and to the point. Do not beat around the bush or save your best information for last. The first sentence of your answer should clearly state the main idea of your answer and include the key words from the question.

FIGURE 10 **Examples of Opening Sentences**

Question:	Why is recitation important in the learning process?
Weak:	Recitation is important because it helps a person learn better.
Strong:	Recitation, one of the Twelve Principles of Memory, is important in the learning process for three reasons.
Strong:	Recitation is important in the learning process because it involves the auditory channel, feedback, and practice expressing ideas.

- The first sentence, when well written, lets your instructor know right away that you are familiar with the subject, your answer is "on target," and you are responding appropriately to the direction word and providing the required kind of information.
- Your opening sentence may indicate the number of items that you will discuss or even possibly list the series of items you will explain further.
- **Figure 10** shows differences in quality in three opening sentences. The first one does not get to the point. The second and third examples are direct, focused, and show confidence.

STRATEGY 36 Expand Your Answer with Details

- Support your opening sentence by expanding into a paragraph with details.
- For a strong answer, use course-related terminology or examples used in class or in your textbook.
- Stick to the point. Do not pad the answer with unrelated information or attempt to write too much or to write an essay.
- **Figure 11** shows a weak answer and a strong answer to the question, "Why is recitation important in the learning process?"

FIGURE 11 **Weak and Strong Answers**

Weak:	Recitation is important because it helps a person learn. Everyone wants to do the very best possible, and recitation helps make that happen. When you recite, you talk out loud. You practice information out loud before a test.
Strong:	Recitation is important in the learning process because it involves the auditory channel, gives feedback, and provides practice expressing ideas. When a person states information out loud and in complete sentences, he/she encodes information linguistically and keeps information active in working memory. Reciting also gives feedback so that a person knows immediately whether or not the information is understood accurately and on the level that can be explained to someone else. Taking time to recite also provides the opportunity to practice organizing and expressing ideas clearly.

Math Test Questions

Performing well on math tests requires an alert mind ready to manage a variety of thinking processes and tasks that result in an exact, correct answer. Because math tests require you to apply a sequential set of skills and concepts to solve new problems, memorizing specific answers is not possible. To prepare for math tests, spend ample time using repetition to rework problems multiple times, checking your understanding of each step of the process, and checking your answers for accuracy. Your learning goal during studying and test preparation is to increase your accuracy and your problem-solving speed so you can work new problems and move through the test without wasting time or running out of time to complete the test.

Familiarize Yourself with Math Terminology

Your math textbooks include a wide range of special terminology required to understand, explain, and use mathematical operations and formulas. Study the meanings of all key terms in your textbook that appear in boldface print. Practice reciting definitions, giving examples of concepts, rules, formulas, or equations. Creating and using a glossary of terms helps you understand and communicate mathematical concepts. Following are examples of key terms and their definitions.

- **Algebraic expressions:** statements that show values by using letters, symbols, and numerals. Examples include: $x - 5$ (means a number decreased by 5) and $x + 8$ (means eight more than x).
- **Algebraic symbols:** marks or signs used in mathematical expressions and equations to represent specific processes or functions. For example, the symbol "/" may mean: divide, quotient, or per.
- **Algorithms:** sequences of steps and operations used to solve problems.
- **Equations:** mathematical sentences or linear arrangements of mathematical symbols used to show equalities on each side of an equal sign.
- **Prototypes:** original formulas or examples of problems that serve as models to use to solve new problems with similar characteristics.
- **Word problems or story problems:** a series of sentences that presents a variety of facts that are needed to solve a problem.

Eight Easy-to-Use Strategies for Math Tests

Do you tend to make specific kinds of errors on math tests? Do you forget to show all your work, omit mathematical signs, use incorrect steps to solve problems, or make careless errors? Do you use specific strategies to answer word problems or to check your work before you turn in a test for grading? Do you run out of time to complete math tests? The following eight strategies will help you increase your performance on math tests.

Understand How to Read and Respond to Math Test Questions — STRATEGY 37

- **Jot down important information to refer to during the test.** Before you survey or begin the test, jot down information you do not want to forget and believe you will need to have ready to use. This may include specific formulas, equations, problem-solving steps (algorithms), or prototypes.

- **Survey the test.** Skim through the test to familiarize yourself with the types of questions, different test question point values, and the length of the test.
- **Create a quick plan for budgeting your time.** Ideally, you will have time to complete the easier problems, adequate time to tackle more difficult problems, and time available at the end of the test to check your answers.
- **Circle direction words and underline key words.** These two actions help you maintain a focus on what is required and what is essential for a complete answer. Pay special attention to directions or questions that ask you to provide two-part answers.
- **Begin with familiar or the easiest problems.** You do *not* need to work problems in the order that they appear in the test. By starting with familiar problems or the easiest problems, you create a mindset for the material, and you build self-confidence.
- **Show all the steps to solve a problem.** Skipping steps or not showing all your work may reduce the points you earn for the test question. Showing all the steps that lead to the solution also helps you or your instructor identify errors if answers are incorrect.
- **Do not spend too much time on one problem.** If you struggle completing a specific problem, work as many steps as possible and then move on to another problem. (See Strategy 42.)
- **Do not change answers without a valid reason.** During bouts of test anxiety, students sometimes start changing answers quickly at the last minute. If you carefully worked through a problem and felt confident about your answer, do not change the answer unless you find an error during the process of carefully checking your work.

STRATEGY 38 Use Prototypes to Solve New Problems

- A **prototype** is a model of a specific type of math problem that can be used to solve new problems with similar characteristics. By memorizing and understanding a prototype, you can use this model to solve new problems more quickly and more confidently.
- Prototypes often appear in textbooks when you are introduced to a new type of math problem or equation. Explanations and examples accompany the prototype.
- Study prototypes carefully. Memorize them. Practice explaining the steps in the prototype. Your goal is to be able to recognize when to use or apply the prototype and its steps to new problems on tests.
- **Figure 12** shows examples of prototypes.

STRATEGY 39 Identify and Think about the Pattern of the Problem

- Read the problem carefully. Ask yourself:

  What do I already know about this kind of problem?

  What problems did I study that are similar?

FIGURE 12 Examples of Prototypes

Prototype: Convert Centigrade to Fahrenheit

Fraction Formula	Decimal Formula
$(°C \times \frac{9}{5}) + 32 = °F$	$(°C \times 1.8) + 32 = °F$

Prototype: Exponential Notation

6^4 "Six to the fourth power" means $6 \times 6 \times 6 \times 6$

Prototype: Add Fractions with Different Denominators

Find the total of $\frac{1}{2} + \frac{1}{3}$

1. Find the common denominator: $\frac{1}{2} = \frac{3}{6}$ $\frac{1}{3} = \frac{2}{6}$
2. Add the fractions: $\frac{3}{6} + \frac{2}{6} = \frac{5}{6}$

What steps did I use to solve similar problems?

What prototypes did I memorize that I can use to solve this problem?

- Conduct a memory search or use associations to recall the prototype (model) problem you memorized for this pattern and the steps or formula you used to solve that problem.
- Focus your attention on the specific steps used in the prototype and then apply those steps to the new math test problem.

Use Basic Strategies to Solve Word Problems

STRATEGY 40

- **Read carefully.** Carefully examine all the details, including any tables or charts related to the word problem. Reread until you understand what the question requires you to do.
- **Focus first on the problem-solving details and not on the operations you will need to use.** Understanding the relationship between relevant facts and identifying the unknown details should occur before shifting your focus to the mathematical operations needed to solve the problem.
- **Restate the problem in your own words.** If you have problems understanding the question after rereading it several times, try restating the same problem in your own words. Sometimes using your own words without distorting the question adds clarity.
- **Underline key words.** This includes information that is needed to solve the problem. Making a list of the facts given to solve the problem may be helpful.
- **Cross out nonessential details.** Some details in word problems are not needed to solve the problems. Ignore these details, which are distractors.
- **Draw a simple picture of the problem.** Putting the information into a picture form may provide a clearer understanding of the information and help you see what you will need to do to solve the problem.

- **Visualize the story.** Visualizing the story and its details is a "mental drawing." Visualizing the details may help you identify the processes needed to solve the problem. Visualizing may also help you estimate reasonable answers before performing the precise calculations. Try visualizing the following word problem.

Word Problem: After playing tennis for 2 hours, Ruben ate a banana split containing 650 calories and a fudge brownie containing 250 calories. Playing tennis uses 720 calories per hour. Did the banana split and the fudge brownie contain more or fewer calories than Ruben burned off playing tennis?

- **Translate the information in the word problem to an algebraic equation.** Remember that the unknown will appear on one side of the equation. Examine the equation and conduct a memory search to see if the equation is similar to other equations or prototypes you have studied.
- **Mentally talk or explain to yourself the steps you will use to solve the problem.** Shift your focus to the mathematical operations you need to use to solve the problem.
- **Apply the steps to solve the problem.** Show your work for each problem-solving step.
- **Use strategies to check the accuracy of your answer.** (See Strategy 44.)

STRATEGY 41 Use RSTUV to Read and Solve Problems

The **RSTUV Problem-Solving Method** is a five-step approach to solve math word problems. Each letter of RSTUV represents one step of this problem-solving approach.

- **R = READ** the problem, not once or twice, but until you understand it. Pay attention to key words or instructions such as *compute, draw, write, construct, make, show, identify, state, simplify, solve,* and *graph.*
- **S = SELECT** the unknown; that is, find out what the problem asks for. One good way to look for the unknown is to look for the question mark (?) and carefully read the material preceding it. Try to determine what information is given and what is missing.
- **T = THINK** of a plan to solve the problem. Problem solving requires many skills and strategies. Some of them are *look for a pattern; examine a related problem; make tables, pictures, and diagrams; write an equation; work backward;* and *make a guess.*
- **U = USE** the techniques you are studying to carry out the plan. Look for procedures that can be used to solve specific problems. Then carry out the plan. Check each step.
- **V = VERIFY** the answer. Look back and check the results of the original problem. *Is the answer reasonable? Can you find it some other way?*

Source: Bello and Britton, *Topics in Contemporary Mathematics,* 6th ed.

Avoid Getting Stuck on One Problem

STRATEGY 42

- When you feel stuck and unsure how to solve a problem, shake your head a few times, look away from the problem, take a few deep breaths, and ask yourself a few questions to help change your thought processes.

  Why does this problem look familiar?

  What prototype do I know that looks similar?

  What processes are we studying that apply here?

- To solve math problems often requires your mind to shift back and forth rapidly and multiple times between the problem and the information in your long-term memory. Reread the problem, shift your eyes away a few seconds, do a memory search to scan memory for possible ways to solve a specific problem, and then look back at the problem.
- If you have tried a variety of strategies without success, or if you have spent too much time on one individual problem, place a check mark next to the question and move on.
- After completing as many questions on the test as possible, return to the questions with the check marks. Sometimes working on other problems will trigger associations that will make it possible for you to see the problem differently and recall a strategy to use to complete the problem-solving steps.

Check Accuracy of Steps and Answers

STRATEGY 43

Checking the accuracy of your work leads to getting the most points possible on your test. Rather than hurry to exit the classroom after a test, use all of the test time to check your work and your accuracy. Following are four methods for checking your work.

- **Logical Method:** Ask yourself, *Is this answer reasonable? Does it make sense?* Sometimes when you look back at an answer, you realize it does not make sense. Perhaps the number in the answer is too large because you misplaced the decimal point. Perhaps you forgot to complete a final step to reach a reasonable answer. Reexamine your processes and steps if the answer is not logical.
- **Estimation Method:** Use the given facts to estimate a reasonable answer. Round whole numbers. Use the mathematic operation (addition, subtraction, multiplication, or division) with the whole numbers to estimate a reasonable answer. Compare the estimate with your original answer. If there is a large discrepancy, return to the problem to identify errors.
- **Substitution Method:** Place the answer or the solution back in the original equation. Verify that each side of the equation equals the other side. If one side of the equation does not equal the other side, you need to rework the problem to find the correct solution.
- **Algorithm Method:** Use sequential math steps to rework the problem. Compare your original answer with the answer for the reworked problem. If you do not end up with the same answer, find the discrepancy. Use one of the previous methods to check the answers for both the first and the reworked problem.

STRATEGY 44 Analyze Your Errors on Graded Tests

Math is a sequential set of skills, so understanding concepts and processes on one level is essential in order to understand and solve problems on the next higher levels. As soon as you receive a graded test, examine the questions you answered correctly as well as the ones you answered incorrectly. Reworking and correcting your thinking and processes for the incorrect answers are important and should be done as soon as the graded test is returned to you. Your goal is to eliminate common errors or error patterns on future tests. Learn from your tests and strengthen your test-taking skills by asking the following kinds of questions:

- *Did I use incorrect mathematical operations to solve problems?*
- *Did I forget the proper equation to use to solve the problem?*
- *Did I forget to label answers in word questions?*
- *Did I misunderstand the necessary processes to use in application questions?*
- *Did I apply an incorrect prototype to a question that did not have the same characteristics as the prototype?*
- *Did I forget to show all the steps to reach the solution?*
- *Did I stop before completing the final step to solve the problem?*
- *Did I make careless mistakes that I easily identified when reviewing the graded test?*
- *Did I forget to align numbers in place value columns when calculating?*
- *Did I experience test anxiety that reduced my ability to stay focused and think logically?*
- *Did I leave the test early instead of using the extra time to check my work?*

Essay Test Questions

Essay questions require an organized composition that develops several main ideas that are related to one thesis sentence. The thesis sentence directly states the main point of the entire essay. Following are additional points about essay test questions.

- Answering essay questions is demanding because it requires you to know information thoroughly, to be able to pull the information from your memory, and to know how to integrate facts to show relationships.
- The way you express the information and the relationships you show need to follow a logical line of thinking and include sufficient details to develop an effective essay answer.
- Essays also require a sound grasp of writing skills (grammar, syntax, and spelling) and a well-developed, expressive vocabulary.
- Review Chapter 7 for different kinds of essay questions and additional strategies.

Familiarize Yourself with Terminology for Essay Test Questions

The structure of essays involves key concepts that you will also encounter in composition classes. Carefully read through the following terms before focusing your attention on the specific strategies.

- **Thesis statement:** A thesis statement is a strong, focused sentence that states the main point of an entire essay. The thesis statement often appears as the first sentence of the essay, but it may appear other places in the introductory paragraph.
- **Direction words:** Direction words are words in test questions that signal a specific kind of answer that is required. *List, define, discuss, tell, describe, explain why,* and *when* are a few examples of direction words.
- **Organizational plan:** An organizational plan is an outline, a hierarchy, a visual mapping, or a list of main ideas the writer intends to use in an essay to develop the thesis of the essay.
- **Five-paragraph format:** The five-paragraph essay format consists of an introductory paragraph, three paragraphs in the body of the essay to develop three separate main ideas, and a concluding paragraph.
- **Main idea:** A main idea is the most important point in a paragraph that the writer wishes to make about a topic. Each paragraph has only one main idea. The main idea supports or helps develop the thesis statement.
- **Supporting details:** Supporting details are facts, examples, or definitions that are related to the subject of a paragraph. A paragraph has adequate development when sufficient details appear in the paragraph to support the main idea.

Eight Easy-to-Use Strategies for Essay Test Questions

Do your essay answers tend to be underdeveloped and lack sufficient supporting details? Do your essays wander off course by including irrelevant information? Do you have difficulty clearly organizing information and expressing your ideas? The following eight easy-to-use strategies will guide you through the process of developing strong answers for essay test questions.

Understand How to Read and Respond to Essay Test Questions

STRATEGY 45

- **Budget your time carefully**. Allow sufficient time to answer all questions or to at least write some information for each question. If you run short on time, turn in your outline or organizational plan to show the main points you intended to discuss.
- **Weigh the value of different questions.** If one question is worth more points, take more time to develop that answer or to return to that answer later and add more information to strengthen your answer.
- **Carefully select which questions to answer when you have a choice.** Examine the questions carefully. Do not automatically choose the questions that look the shortest or the easiest. They are usually more general and more difficult

to answer than longer questions that tend to be more specific. Also, select the questions that contain the topics that you are most familiar with and topics for which you can recall specific and sufficient supporting details.

- **Begin with the most familiar question.** Developing an answer for the most familiar question first tends to boost your confidence level and puts you in the "essay writing mode."
- **Use complete sentences to express your ideas.** Short phrases, charts, or lists of information are not appropriate for an essay.
- **Include supporting details so your essay will not be underdeveloped.** Include facts such as names, dates, events, and statistics; include definitions, examples, or appropriate applications of the information you are presenting. Do not make the mistake of assuming that information is obvious or that your instructor knows what you are thinking or clearly sees the connection.
- **Include quotations for details.** For some courses, you may want to memorize important quotations that appear in your textbook and that you predict you may be able to use to develop an essay test answer. Remember to place quotation marks around the quoted material and cite the source.
- **Use key words in the question and course-specific terminology in your answers as much as possible.**
- **Strive to write as neatly as possible.** Illegible handwriting will hurt your grade. If you need to delete some of the information, delete it by crossing it out with one neat line or by using correction fluid.

STRATEGY 46 Understand the Questions and the Direction Words

- Read each question carefully and identify the question as a closed or an open-ended question.
- Underline key words in the question as a reminder to include these key words in your introductory paragraph and to emphasize these words throughout your essay.
- Be sure you understand the direction word as it signals the type of response required. Circle the direction word to maintain a focus on the direction of your answer.
- **Figure 13** shows direction words frequently used for essay questions.

STRATEGY 47 Write a Strong, Focused Thesis Sentence

A **thesis sentence** is a strong, focused sentence that states the main point of an entire essay. The thesis sentence for an essay test answer usually appears as the first sentence on your paper. The following points about your thesis statement are important to remember:

- Clearly state the topic of the essay. Include key words that are a part of the question. If you wish, you may indicate the number of points you plan to develop.
- Show that you understand the direction word and plan to focus your answer in the direction indicated by the direction word.

FIGURE 13 Direction Words for Essay Questions

Direction Word	What Is Required
Compare	Show the similarities and differences between two or more items.
Contrast	Present only the differences between two or more items.
Define	Give the definition and expand it with more examples and greater details.
Trace/Outline	Discuss the sequence of events in chronological order.
Summarize	Identify and discuss the main points or the highlights of a subject. Omit in-depth details.
Evaluate/Critique	Offer your opinion or judgment and then back it up with specific facts, details, or reasons.
Analyze	Identify the different parts of something. Discuss each part individually.
Describe	Give a detailed description of different aspects, qualities, characteristics, parts, or points of view.
Discuss/Tell	Tell about the parts or the main points. Expand with specific details.
Explain/Explain why	Give reasons. Tell why. Show logical relationships or cause-effect.
Explain how	Give the process, steps, stages, or procedures involved. Explain each.
Illustrate	Give examples. Explain each example with details.
Identify/What are	Identify specific points. Discuss each point individually. Include sufficient details.
When	Describe a time or a specific condition needed for something to happen, occur, or be used. Provide details and any relevant background information.

- Your thesis statement serves as a guide for developing the rest of your essay. It suggests the basic outline of main ideas to develop with important supporting details.
- Your thesis statement serves as an immediate indicator for your instructor that you understand the question and know the answer.
- Because of the significance of the thesis statement, take time to create a strong, direct, confident opening sentence.
- **Figure 14** shows examples of two essay test questions, the meaning of the direction words, and examples of strong thesis statements.

FIGURE 14 Thesis Sentences

Question	Direction Words	Possible Thesis Statement
Discuss the characteristics of each of Howard Gardner's multiple intelligences.	**Discuss = tell about** What are the eight intelligences?	Each of Howard Gardner's eight intelligences has clearly recognizable characteristics.
Explain why elaborative rehearsal is more effective for college learning than rote memory strategies.	**Explain why = give reasons** What are the reasons? How many reasons?	Elaborative rehearsal is more effective than rote memory because more Memory Principles are used and information in memory is in a more usable form.

STRATEGY 48 Develop an Organizational Plan

- After you have developed a strong thesis statement, take the time to develop an organizational plan.
- Your organizational plan provides an overview of the main ideas you plan to include in your essay. Once you conceptualize and develop your plan, you will be able to write your response faster and avoid wandering off course or becoming confused about the next point to write in your answer.
- Your organizational plan becomes your step-by-step outline that guides the writing process.
- Your plan may be an outline, a visual mapping, a hierarchy, or a basic list of main ideas.
- **Figure 15** shows the four basic kinds of organizational plans you can use.

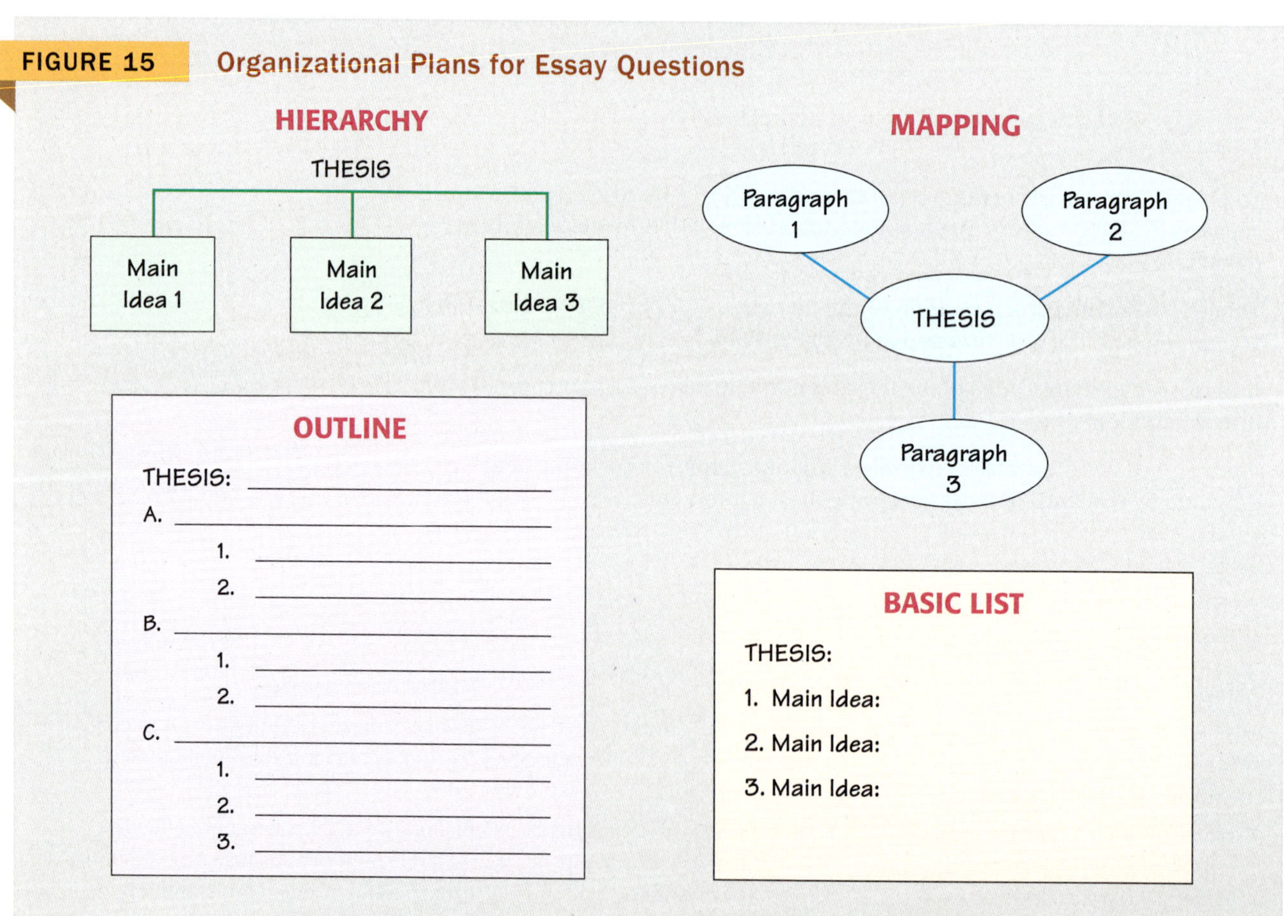

FIGURE 16 Key Elements in a Five-Paragraph Essay

Paragraph	Details
Introductory Paragraph (one paragraph)	• Includes the thesis statement • Indicates that you understand the direction word • Repeats key words from the essay test question
Body of the Essay (three paragraphs with three different main ideas)	• Expands *each category or section* of information in your organization plan into separate *paragraphs* • States a main idea in each paragraph and develops the main idea with details, such as facts, examples, reasons, or definitions • Limits one main idea per paragraph
Concluding Paragraph (one paragraph)	• Briefly summarizes your essay or draws a conclusion • Leaves a clear picture in your reader's mind of the main points • Repeats key words from the essay test question

Use the Five-Paragraph Format

STRATEGY 49

- For many essay test questions, the five-paragraph essay is an effective format to use to write your essay answers.
- The five-paragraph essay format consists of an introductory paragraph, three paragraphs in the body of the essay to develop three separate main ideas, and a concluding paragraph.
- If you have more than three main ideas to develop, you can expand this format by adding additional paragraphs to the body of the essay.
- **Figure 16** shows the key elements of each part of the five-paragraph essay.

Create a Pre-Writing Chart to Guide Your Writing

STRATEGY 50

Many students waste too much precious test-taking time trying to "get started" on an essay. A systematic approach helps you gather your thoughts and move into action. Use the following steps to organize yourself and your thoughts before writing the actual essay.

- Circle the direction word. Underline key words in the question to use in your essay answer.
- Use this information to write a strong thesis sentence that will appear in the introductory paragraph. Quickly sketch a chart with five rows. (See **Figure 17**.) Write the thesis statement in the first box of your chart.
- In the second, third, and fourth rows, write the topic that you will develop for each paragraph.

FIGURE 17 Pre-Writing Guide for Essay Questions

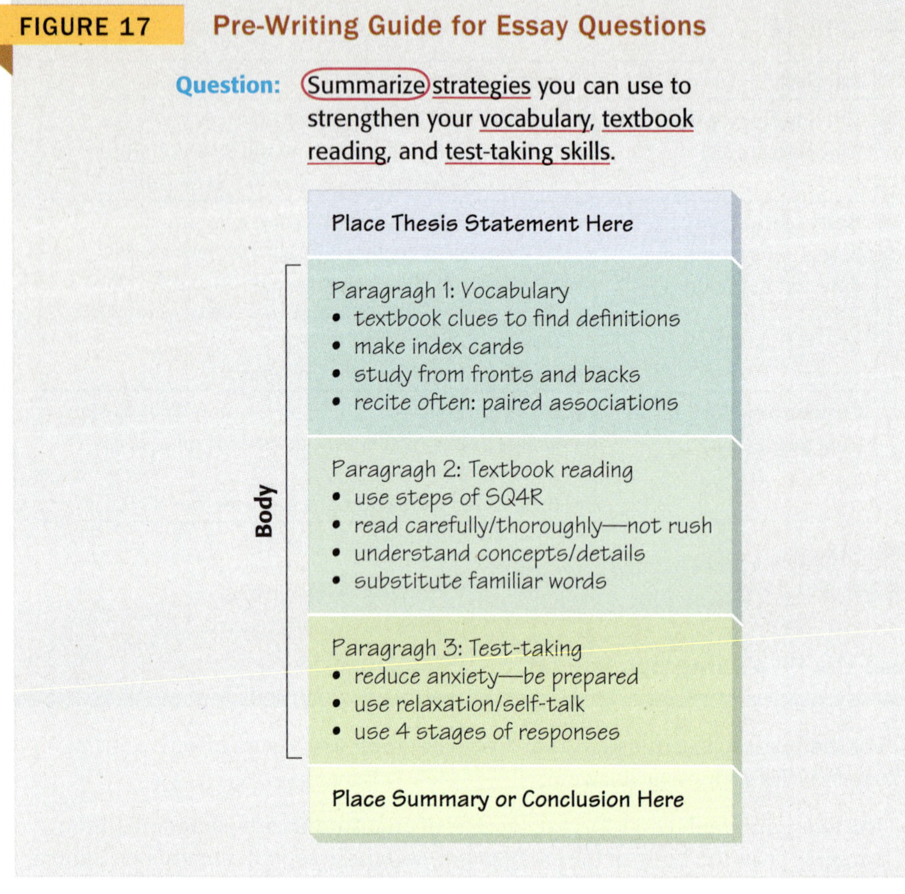

- Under each topic, which will become the main idea for the paragraph, briefly list the details you plan to use to develop the topic or main idea.
- After you write the essay, plan to summarize it in a short concluding paragraph (last row).
- If you run out of time on the test and are not able to complete your essay answer, turn in your organizational plan or notes showing the above information. You may receive partial points for your work.
- Figure 17 shows how much information you can generate and organize before you even begin writing your essay answer.

STRATEGY 51 Strengthen and Revise if You Have Time

Writing effective essays involves understanding and using effective vocabulary, writing, and spelling skills. Following are revisions you can make in your essays if you have time available during the testing period. If you do not have time to revise, familiarize yourself with the following writing tips so you can strive to implement them the next time you face an essay test.

- Replace slang or informal language with formal language or course terminology.

- Reword to avoid using the word *you*. Replace the word *you* with the word it represents, the specific noun, such as *students*.
- Replace vague pronouns such as *it* with the name of the specific item.
- Reword sentences to avoid weak "sentence starters" such as *There is ...*, *There are ...*, *Here is ...*, or *Here are ...* .
- Use sentence variety in your essay: simple, compound, complex, and compound-complex sentences. Knowing how to combine short sentences into compound, complex, or compound-complex sentences is an economical way to develop ideas. Using effective sentence variety results in an essay that is interesting to read and understand.

Learn from Your Tests

STRATEGY 52

- Writing strong essay answers becomes easier with practice.
- When you get your essay tests back, read the comments and suggestions.
- Analyze your essays and ask yourself questions: *Did I predict this question? Did I answer questions directly and in an organized way? Did I include sufficient details? How could I have strengthened my answer?*
- Adjust your studying and test-taking skills as needed to improve your performance on the next essay test.

Conclusion

This Essential Test-Taking Skills guide is designed to equip you with essential skills and strategies to improve your test-taking skills and performance. Using the fifty-two specific test-taking strategies will strengthen your ability to read, understand, interpret, and respond appropriately to a variety of test questions. Becoming an effective test-taker requires practice and attention to details. Each time you receive a graded test, take time to examine your answers and learn from your tests. Return to this guide to prepare for upcoming tests as well as refresh and refine your skills so your tests more truly reflect how well you have mastered the content of your courses.

Appendix C

Exercises, Inventories, and Checklists

EXERCISE 1.1

Learning Styles Inventory

PURPOSE: Identify your learning style preference and the strength of your modalities. Understanding your learning style preference can guide your selection of study and learning strategies to use to be more effective and successful.

DIRECTIONS: Complete the Learning Styles Inventory by reading each statement carefully. Check YES if the statement relates to you all or most of the time. Check NO if the statement seldom or never relates to you. There is no in-between option, so you must check YES or NO. Your first, quick response to a question is usually the best response to use.

	Statement	YES	NO
1.	I like to listen to and discuss information with another person.	_____	_____
2.	I could likely learn or review information effectively by hearing my own voice on a recording.	_____	_____
3.	I prefer to learn something new by reading about it.	_____	_____
4.	I often write down directions someone gives me so I do not forget them.	_____	_____
5.	I enjoy physical sports and exercise.	_____	_____
6.	I learn best when I can see new information in picture or diagram form.	_____	_____
7.	I can easily visualize or picture things in my mind.	_____	_____
8.	I learn best when someone talks or explains something to me.	_____	_____
9.	I usually write things down so that I can look back at them later.	_____	_____
10.	I pay attention to the rhythm and patterns of notes I hear in music.	_____	_____
11.	I have a good memory for the words and melodies of old songs.	_____	_____
12.	I like to participate in small-group discussions.	_____	_____
13.	I often remember the sizes, shapes, and colors of objects when they are no longer in sight.	_____	_____
14.	I often repeat out loud verbal directions that someone gives me.	_____	_____
15.	I enjoy working with my hands.	_____	_____
16.	I can remember the faces of actors, settings, and other visual details of movies I have seen.	_____	_____

(continued)

Exercise 1.1 (continued)

	YES	NO
17. I often use my hands and body movements when explaining something to someone else.	______	______
18. I prefer standing up and working on a chalkboard or flip chart to sitting down and working on paper.	______	______
19. I often seem to learn better if I can get up and move around while I study.	______	______
20. I often refer to pictures or diagrams to assemble or install something new.	______	______
21. I remember objects better when I have touched them or worked with them.	______	______
22. I learn best by watching someone else first.	______	______
23. I tend to doodle when I think about a problem or situation.	______	______
24. I speak a foreign language.	______	______
25. I am comfortable building or constructing things.	______	______
26. I can follow the plot of a story when I listen to an audio book.	______	______
27. I often repair things at home.	______	______
28. I can understand information when I hear it on a recording.	______	______
29. I am good at using machines or tools.	______	______
30. I enjoy role-playing or participating in skits.	______	______
31. I enjoy acting or doing pantomimes.	______	______
32. I can easily see patterns in designs.	______	______
33. I often know how to assemble, install, or fix something without referring to written directions.	______	______
34. I like to recite or write poetry.	______	______
35. I can usually understand people with foreign accents or dialects.	______	______
36. I can hear many different pitches or melodies in music.	______	______
37. I like to dance and create new movements or steps.	______	______
38. I enjoy participating in activities that require physical coordination.	______	______
39. I follow written directions better than oral ones.	______	______
40. I can easily recognize differences between similar sounds.	______	______
41. I like to create or use jingles or rhymes to learn things.	______	______
42. I prefer classes with hands-on experiences.	______	______
43. I can quickly tell if two geometric shapes are identical.	______	______
44. I remember best things that I have seen in print, in diagrams, or in pictures.	______	______
45. I follow oral directions better than written ones.	______	______

(continued)

Exercise 1.1 (continued)

	YES	NO
46. I could learn the names of fifteen medical instruments more easily if I could touch and examine them.	______	______
47. I remember details better when I say and repeat them aloud.	______	______
48. I can look at a shape and copy it correctly on paper.	______	______
49. I can usually read a map without difficulty.	______	______
50. I can "hear" a person's exact words and tone of voice days after he or she has spoken to me.	______	______
51. I remember directions best when someone gives me landmarks, such as specific buildings and trees.	______	______
52. I have a good eye for colors and color combinations.	______	______
53. I like to paint, draw, sculpt, or be creative with my hands.	______	______
54. I can vividly picture the details of a meaningful past experience.	______	______

SCORING YOUR PROFILE:

1. Ignore the NO answers. Work only with the questions that have a YES answer.
2. For every YES answer, look at the number of the question. Find the number in the following chart and circle that number.
3. When you finish, not all the numbers in the following boxes will be circled. Your answers will very likely not match anyone else's.
4. Count the number of circles for the Visual box and write the total on the line. Do the same for the Auditory box and Kinesthetic box.

Visual					Auditory					Kinesthetic				
3	*4*	*6*	*7*	*9*	*1*	*2*	*8*	*10*	*11*	*5*	*15*	*17*	*18*	*19*
13	*16*	*20*	*22*	*32*	*12*	*14*	*24*	*26*	*28*	*21*	*23*	*25*	*27*	*29*
39	*43*	*44*	*48*	*49*	*34*	*35*	*36*	*40*	*41*	*30*	*31*	*33*	*37*	*38*
51	*52*	*54*			*45*	*47*	*50*			*42*	*46*	*53*		
Visual Total: ______					*Auditory Total:* ______					*Kinesthetic Total:* ______				

Return to Exercise 1.1 on page 6 in your textbook to record your scores and learn the meaning of your scores.

EXERCISE 3.1

Time-Management Inventory

DIRECTIONS: Read each statement carefully. Answer YES or NO to each statement to show how you use or feel about time. This is a nongraded inventory, so answer honestly. Follow the directions at the end to score your inventory.

SENSE OF CONTROL	**YES**	**NO**
1. I feel time slips by quickly without anything important getting done.	________	________
2. I lose sense of time so do not get things done that are on my to-do list.	________	________
3. I run out of time to get assignments or tasks done on time.	________	________
4. I am aware of times I need to buckle down and plan my use of time.	________	________
5. I feel in control of time and use time to my benefit.	________	________
6. I take charge and use new strategies when I feel I am unproductive.	________	________

STRATEGIES	**YES**	**NO**
7. I waste quite a bit of time trying to figure out how to start a task.	________	________
8. I am used to chaos and confusion in the way I do things.	________	________
9. I experience stress and frustration because I do not meet deadlines.	________	________
10. I am more productive when I set aside and use time to work on a project.	________	________
11. I finish projects on time, which boosts my sense of confidence.	________	________
12. I organize priorities and dedicate sufficient time to work on priorities.	________	________

SCHEDULES	**YES**	**NO**
13. I work without a schedule because I like the flexibility.	________	________
14. I do not have sufficient time to read and review notes each week.	________	________
15. I am a spontaneous person so I study when I am in the mood.	________	________
16. I procrastinate less when I work with an organized schedule and plan.	________	________
17. I create a structure for my daily and weekly routines.	________	________
18. I am punctual and meet deadlines because I follow my plans of action.	________	________

BALANCE	**YES**	**NO**
19. I do not have time to spend with family or friends.	________	________
20. I turn assignments in late because I forget about them or don't finish them.	________	________
21. I lack a satisfactory sense of balance in my life.	________	________
22. I sufficiently plan use of my time to fulfill most obligations and deadlines.	________	________
23. I am comfortable with the amount of time I spend with family and friends.	________	________
24. I manage the demands of time by organizing time using schedules.	________	________

SCORING:

If you are using time management effectively, the first three statements in each section are *NO* statements, and the last three statements in each section are *YES* statements. Highlight all the statements in each section that do not match the above pattern (N, N, N, Y, Y, Y). What personal patterns do you see in this inventory?

EXERCISE 3.2

How You Use Time: Three-Day Time Log

DAY 1			
Time	Activity	Time	Activity
MIDNIGHT		NOON	
12:30 A.M.		12:30 P.M.	
1:00 A.M.		1:00 P.M.	
1:30 A.M.		1:30 P.M.	
2:00 A.M.		2:00 P.M.	
2:30 A.M.		2:30 P.M.	
3:00 A.M.		3:00 P.M.	
3:30 A.M.		3:30 P.M.	
4:00 A.M.		4:00 P.M.	
4:30 A.M.		4:30 P.M.	
5:00 A.M.		5:00 P.M.	
5:30 A.M.		5:30 P.M.	
6:00 A.M.		6:00 P.M.	
6:30 A.M.		6:30 P.M.	
7:00 A.M.		7:00 P.M.	
7:30 A.M.		7:30 P.M.	
8:00 A.M.		8:00 P.M.	
8:30 A.M.		8:30 P.M.	
9:00 A.M.		9:00 P.M.	
9:30 A.M.		9:30 P.M.	
10:00 A.M.		10:00 P.M.	
10:30 A.M.		10:30 P.M.	
11:00 A.M.		11:00 P.M.	
11:30 A.M.		11:30 P.M.	

DAY 2			
Time	Activity	Time	Activity
MIDNIGHT		NOON	
12:30 A.M.		12:30 P.M.	
1:00 A.M.		1:00 P.M.	
1:30 A.M.		1:30 P.M.	
2:00 A.M.		2:00 P.M.	
2:30 A.M.		2:30 P.M.	
3:00 A.M.		3:00 P.M.	
3:30 A.M.		3:30 P.M.	
4:00 A.M.		4:00 P.M.	
4:30 A.M.		4:30 P.M.	
5:00 A.M.		5:00 P.M.	
5:30 A.M.		5:30 P.M.	
6:00 A.M.		6:00 P.M.	
6:30 A.M.		6:30 P.M.	
7:00 A.M.		7:00 P.M.	
7:30 A.M.		7:30 P.M.	
8:00 A.M.		8:00 P.M.	
8:30 A.M.		8:30 P.M.	
9:00 A.M.		9:00 P.M.	
9:30 A.M.		9:30 P.M.	
10:00 A.M.		10:00 P.M.	
10:30 A.M.		10:30 P.M.	
11:00 A.M.		11:00 P.M.	
11:30 A.M.		11:30 P.M.	

EXERCISE 3.5

Part I: Weekly Time-Management Schedule

FOR THE WEEK OF			NAME				
TIME	MONDAY	TUESDAY	WEDNESDAY	THURSDAY	FRIDAY	SATURDAY	SUNDAY
12–6 A.M.							
6–7:00							
7–8:00							
8–9:00							
9–10:00							
10–11:00							
11–12 NOON							
12–1:00 P.M.							
1–2:00							
2–3:00							
3–4:00							
4–5:00							
5–6:00							
6–7:00							
7–8:00							
8–9:00							
9–10:00							
10–11:00							
11–12 A.M.							

Exercise 3.2 (continued)

DAY 3			
Time	Activity	Time	Activity
MIDNIGHT		NOON	
12:30 A.M.		12:30 P.M.	
1:00 A.M.		1:00 P.M.	
1:30 A.M.		1:30 P.M.	
2:00 A.M.		2:00 P.M.	
2:30 A.M.		2:30 P.M.	
3:00 A.M.		3:00 P.M.	
3:30 A.M.		3:30 P.M.	
4:00 A.M.		4:00 P.M.	
4:30 A.M.		4:30 P.M.	
5:00 A.M.		5:00 P.M.	
5:30 A.M.		5:30 P.M.	
6:00 A.M.		6:00 P.M.	
6:30 A.M.		6:30 P.M.	
7:00 A.M.		7:00 P.M.	
7:30 A.M.		7:30 P.M.	
8:00 A.M.		8:00 P.M.	
8:30 A.M.		8:30 P.M.	
9:00 A.M.		9:00 P.M.	
9:30 A.M.		9:30 P.M.	
10:00 A.M.		10:00 P.M.	
10:30 A.M.		10:30 P.M.	
11:00 A.M.		11:00 P.M.	
11:30 A.M.		11:30 P.M.	

THREE-DAY TIME LOG			
Activity	Day 1	Day 2	Day 3
School: Classes, labs, studying, test preparation			
School: Meetings, practices			
Work: Job			
Work: Parenting, chores, other work			
Leisure: Family			
Leisure: Friends			
Leisure: Personal time; recreation			
Naps, Sleep			
Snacks, Meals			
Other/Unaccounted for Hours			
	TOTAL HOURS:	**TOTAL HOURS:**	**TOTAL HOURS:**

Exercise 3.5 (continued)

Part II: Time-Management Self-Assessment Checklist

Name ______________________________ Date ____________________

Check only the statements that are true for your weekly time-management schedule.

STUDY BLOCKS

My schedule shows:

_____ Sufficient study blocks set aside for each class using the 2:1 ratio.

_____ Each study block labeled with the subject to be studied at that time.

_____ Study blocks spread throughout the week (spaced practice).

_____ Two or more study blocks scheduled on the weekend.

_____ No marathon studying (no more than 3 study hours in a row).

_____ The majority of study hours are during the day or early evening hours.

_____ Two or more FLEX blocks scheduled throughout the week.

_____ Study times for most difficult classes scheduled earlier in the day.

_____ Study blocks for lecture and math classes scheduled shortly after class.

FIXED ACTIVITIES

My schedule shows:

_____ Sufficient hours of sleep each night.

_____ A fairly regular sleep schedule throughout the week.

_____ Time set aside for three meals a day.

_____ My work schedule.

_____ Specific meetings or appointments that occur on a weekly basis.

BALANCING YOUR LIFE

My schedule shows:

_____ Time set aside to spend with family and friends.

_____ Time set aside for exercise, hobbies, or recreation.

_____ Time set aside for necessary errands, chores, or personal responsibilities.

_____ Time set aside to work on specific goals.

GENERAL GUIDELINES

Check only the statements that apply to you or your schedule

_____ I walked through each day in my mind and believe it is realistic.

_____ As much as is possible, I used my peak energy times during the day to study.

_____ I color-coded my schedule so different activities are easier to identify.

_____ Using a schedule will help me have a more organized week.

_____ Using a schedule will help me achieve more tasks during the week.

_____ I will strive to follow this schedule to my greatest abilities this week.

_____ I will note problem areas on the schedule and use this information to adjust next week's schedule.

_____ I will use a "star system" to track the blocks of time I follow successfully.

QUESTIONS/COMMENTS/EXPLANATIONS

EXERCISE 4.1

Goal-Setting Inventory

DIRECTIONS: Are you a skillful goal setter? For each statement, circle the response that best characterizes you.

1 = never or seldom 2 = sometimes 3 = always or almost always

	Statement			
1.	I find sufficient time to complete goals that I write.	1	2	3
2.	I use the GPS goal-setting strategy to write goals that are clear and specific.	1	2	3
3.	I start term-long assignments shortly after they are assigned.	1	2	3
4.	I am confident and not afraid to try to achieve new goals.	1	2	3
5.	The purpose or importance of my goals is clear to me.	1	2	3
6.	I take time to create short-term goals for things I need to achieve within the next week, several weeks, or the month.	1	2	3
7.	I use a checklist process to keep track of steps I complete in achieving my goals.	1	2	3
8.	I use goal setting to organize tasks, assignments, and obligations.	1	2	3
9.	I break larger goals into smaller steps or subgoals.	1	2	3
10.	I use positive self-talk, affirmations, and visualization to help me stay motivated and productive.	1	2	3
11.	I use rewards as incentives to complete goals.	1	2	3
12.	I analyze my goal-setting processes and make adjustments when necessary to improve my goal-setting skills.	1	2	3
13.	I begin working on my goals expecting to achieve the goal successfully.	1	2	3
14.	Using goal-setting strategies results in less stress for me.	1	2	3
15.	When I use goal-setting strategies, I reduce or eliminate procrastination.	1	2	3

TOTAL SCORE: __________

SCORING:

40–45 Congratulations! You are a skillful goal setter!

30–39 You are an effective goal setter who frequently benefits from setting goals.

20–29 You are on your way to becoming an effective goal setter; identify ways you can strengthen or expand your skills to become a more effective goal setter.

0–19 You have not yet learned the benefits of setting goals. Get ready for an exciting new journey! Begin using goal-setting strategies to achieve your desired outcomes and increase your performance.

EXERCISE 4.6

Social Adjustment Scale (Stress Test)

PURPOSE: Good and bad events in one's life can increase stress levels. Knowing how to manage stress reduces the chances that stress will take a negative toll on your health and emotional well-being. In 1967, Dr. Thomas H. Holmes and Dr. Richard H. Rahe developed the following "stress test" to help individuals identify their stress levels. By knowing stress levels, people can make an even greater asserted effort to use strategies to manage stress effectively.

DIRECTIONS:

1. In the following list of events, circle every experience that you have had in the *past twelve months.*
2. Total the point values next to each of the experiences you circled. Use that total to find your stress level in the scoring section that follows.

Event	Point Value
Death of a Spouse	100
Divorce	73
Marital Separation	65
Jail Term	63
Death of a Close Family Member	63
Personal Injury or Illness	53
Marriage	50
Fired at Work	47
Marital Reconciliation	45
Retirement	45
Change in Health of a Family Member	44
Pregnancy	40
Sex Difficulties	39
Gain of a New Family Member	39
Business Readjustments	39
Change in Financial State	38
Death of a Close Friend	37
Change to a Different Line of Work	36
Change in Number of Arguments with Spouse	35
Mortgage over $50,000	31
Foreclosure of Mortgage	30

Event	Point Value
Change in Responsibilities at Work	29
Son or Daughter Leaving Home	29
Trouble with In-Laws	29
Outstanding Personal Achievements	28
Partner Begins/Stops Work	28
Begin or End School	26
Change in Living Conditions	25
Revision of Personal Habits	24
Trouble with Boss	23
Change in Work Hours or Conditions	20
Change in Residence	20
Change in School	20
Change in Recreation	19
Change in Religious Activities	19
Change in Social Activities	18
Loan Less than $50,000	17
Change in Sleeping Habits	16
Change in Number of Family Gatherings	15
Change in Eating Habits	15
Vacation	13
Holidays	12
Minor Violation of Laws	11
TOTAL SCORE	

SCORING:

Low Stress Level <149

Mild Stress Level 150–200

Moderate Stress Level 200–299

Major Stress Level >300

Source: Reprinted from *Journal of Psychosomatic Research*, 11 (2), Holmes, T. H. & Rahe, R. H., "The social readjustment rating scale," pp. 213-218. © 1967 with permission from Elsevier.

EXERCISE 5.7

Working Memory Inventory

DIRECTIONS: Think back to the last time you sat down to study. Answer the following questions.

Circle **1** if you did not use the working memory strategy during the study block.

Circle **2** if you used the working memory strategy occasionally during the study block.

Circle **3** if you used the working memory strategy consistently during the study block.

1.	As I studied, I was aware of different ways I encoded the information.	1 2 3
2.	I used selective attention to focus on important stimuli and ignore the unimportant stimuli and distractions.	1 2 3
3.	I changed my approach to more active learning when I realized I was shifting into using rote memory.	1 2 3
4.	I studied without the interference of visual or auditory stimuli from a television or background music.	1 2 3
5.	To avoid information dropping out of my short-term memory, I started thinking about or working with information as soon as I read it.	1 2 3
6.	I limited the number of items I studied at one time by using the Magic 7 ± 2 Theory.	1 2 3
7.	I rehearsed or repeated the information in some form at least one time.	1 2 3
8.	I worked slowly to give my working memory time to process information.	1 2 3
9.	I broke large chunks of information in my notes or in the textbook into smaller units to study.	1 2 3
10.	I used elaborative rehearsal to study factual information and multiple repetition to study process (procedural) information.	1 2 3
11.	I paid attention to categories of information or schemas connected to the new information I was studying.	1 2 3
12.	I maintained a positive attitude toward studying and toward the subject matter and materials.	1 2 3
13.	I used visualization and recitation when I studied and rehearsed information.	1 2 3
14.	I intentionally created new retrieval cues so I could recall the information more quickly at later times.	1 2 3
15.	I avoided overloading working memory by using selectivity to identify important ideas to focus on learning.	1 2 3
16.	I used some form of self-quizzing and feedback during the study process.	1 2 3
17.	I created clear associations to work as retrieval cues for me.	1 2 3
18.	I either felt a natural interest or created an interest in studying.	1 2 3
19.	I set a learning goal when I studied so I knew what I wanted to accomplish.	1 2 3
20.	I used multisensory strategies to work with the information.	1 2 3

TOTAL SCORE: ________

YOUR SCORE:

20–35 You can make better use of your working memory. Look at all the items that received a **1**, indicating you do not use these strategies. Adjusting the way you study to include these strategies will strengthen your working memory and academic performance level.

36–50 You are making average use of your working memory, but there is room to improve. Strive to include the strategies marked with a **1** or a **2** on a more consistent basis when you study.

51–60 You are using your working memory effectively. Continue to use all of the strategies consistently when you study.

EXERCISE 6.4

Memory Principles Inventory

DIRECTIONS: Complete the following inventory by answering YES or NO to each question. Be honest with your answers so they reflect your *current* use of the principles.

SELECTIVITY	YES	NO
1. Do you spend a lot of time studying but seem to study the "wrong information" for tests?	_______	_______
2. Do you get frustrated when you read because everything seems important?	_______	_______
3. Do you tend to highlight too much when you read textbooks?	_______	_______
4. Do your notes seem excessively long and overly detailed?	_______	_______
5. Do you avoid making study tools such as flashcards because you are not sure what information to put on the study tools?	_______	_______

ASSOCIATION	YES	NO
1. Do you tend to memorize facts or ideas in isolation?	_______	_______
2. When you try to recall information you have studied, do you sometimes feel "lost" because there is no direct way to access the information in your memory?	_______	_______
3. Do you feel that you are memorizing numerous lists of information but not really understanding what they mean or how they are connected?	_______	_______
4. Do you "go blank" on tests when a question asks for information in a form or context different from the way you studied it?	_______	_______
5. Do you lack sufficient time to link difficult information to familiar words or pictures?	_______	_______

VISUALIZATION	YES	NO
1. When you finish reading, do you have difficulty remembering what the paragraphs were even about?	_______	_______
2. Do you have difficulty remembering information that appeared in a chart your instructor presented on the chalkboard or on a screen?	_______	_______
3. Do you find it difficult to recall a visual image of printed information?	_______	_______
4. When you try to recall information, do you rely mainly on words rather than pictures?	_______	_______
5. When your instructor explains a new concept by giving a detailed example or anecdote (story), do you have difficulty recalling the example or anecdote after you leave class?	_______	_______

ELABORATION	YES	NO
1. Do you learn individual facts or details without thinking about the schema in which they belong?	_______	_______
2. Do you frequently attempt to use rote memory to memorize facts, definitions, or rules?	_______	_______
3. Do you complete a math problem and immediately move on to the next problem?	_______	_______
4. Do you study information in the same order and in the same form in which it was presented?	_______	_______
5. Do you avoid creating new study tools that involve reorganizing information?	_______	_______

(continued)

Exercise 6.4 (continued)

CONCENTRATION

	YES	NO
1. Do you often experience divided attention because too many unrelated thoughts disrupt your thinking?	______	______
2. Do you have so many interruptions when you study that you are not quite sure what you have accomplished at the end of a study block?	______	______
3. Do you miss important information during a lecture because your mind tends to wander or daydream?	______	______
4. When you are reading, do you find it difficult to keep your mind focused on the information in the textbook?	______	______
5. Do you study with the television, radio, or stereo turned on?	______	______

RECITATION

	YES	NO
1. When you review for a test, do you do all or most of your review work silently?	______	______
2. Do you have difficulty defining new terminology out loud?	______	______
3. Do you have difficulty clearly explaining textbook information to another person?	______	______
4. When you rehearse information out loud, do you often feel that your explanations are "fuzzy," unclear, or incomplete?	______	______
5. Do you feel awkward or uncomfortable talking out loud to yourself?	______	______

INTENTION

	YES	NO
1. When you sit down to study, do you set a goal to complete the assignment as quickly as possible?	______	______
2. Do you always have the same purpose in mind when you sit down to study?	______	______
3. Do you lack curiosity, interest, or enthusiasm in the course content for one or more of your classes?	______	______
4. When you begin learning new information, do you find setting a specific learning goal difficult to do?	______	______
5. Do you study facts, details, or concepts in the same way that you study steps or processes for a procedure?	______	______

BIG AND LITTLE PICTURES

	YES	NO
1. Do you have problems distinguishing between main ideas and individual details in textbook passages?	______	______
2. Do you understand general concepts but oftentimes have difficulty giving details that relate to the concept?	______	______
3. Do you grasp specific details but oftentimes have difficulty connecting them together to form a larger picture or a concept?	______	______
4. Do your lecture notes capture main ideas but lack details?	______	______
5. Do your notes include running lists of details without a clear method of showing main ideas?	______	______

FEEDBACK

	YES	NO
1. Do you use tests as your main means of getting feedback about what you have learned?	______	______
2. Do you keep taking in new information without stopping to see whether or not you are trying to learn too much too fast?	______	______

Exercise 6.4 (continued)

3. When you are rehearsing, do you "keep on going" even if you sense that you have not clearly understood something? ______ ______
4. Do you tend to use self-quizzing only when you are preparing for a test? ______ ______
5. If you get feedback that you did not complete a math problem correctly, do you ignore your original work and try working the problem again? ______ ______

ORGANIZATION — YES / NO

1. Does information from lectures often seem to be one continuous stream of information without any apparent organization or structure? ______ ______
2. Do you have difficulty remembering the sequence of important events or the steps of a process? ______ ______
3. When you try to do a "memory search" to locate information in your memory, are you usually unable to find the information? ______ ______
4. Do you spend most of your time trying to learn information in the exact order in which it is presented? ______ ______
5. Do you feel unsure about rearranging, reorganizing, or regrouping information so that it is easier to learn and recall? ______ ______

TIME ON TASK — YES / NO

1. When your assignment is to read and study a specific chapter, do you spend a lot of time on the assignment but not make contact with it again for several weeks? ______ ______
2. When you are studying, do you often feel as though you are trying to study too much information too quickly? ______ ______
3. When you study, do you change to a second subject as soon as you complete the assignments for the first subject? ______ ______
4. Are some of your study blocks more than three hours long? ______ ______
5. In at least one of your courses, do you spend less time studying that subject than most other students in class do? ______ ______

ONGOING REVIEW — YES / NO

1. Once you have completed an assignment, do you put it aside until close to the time of the next test? ______ ______
2. Do you have problems remembering or recalling information that you know you learned several weeks earlier? ______ ______
3. Do you need to add more review time to your weekly study schedule? ______ ______
4. Do you study fewer than two hours per week for every one hour in class? ______ ______
5. Do you sit down to study and feel that you are all caught up and have nothing to study? ______ ______

ASSESSING YOUR CURRENT USE OF THE PRINCIPLES OF MEMORY:

1. A NO answer indicates you are already using the Principle of Memory when you study. If you gave NO answers to all the questions within one Memory Principle section, you are using the Principle of Memory consistently and effectively.
2. A YES answer indicates that you will benefit by learning to use this Principle of Memory more effectively when you study. The more YES answers you have, the greater the need to add this Principle of Memory to your learning strategies or study techniques.

EXERCISE 7.1

Academic Preparation Inventory

DIRECTIONS: After identifying a specific class and the most recent test grade you received in that class, think back to the days prior to that test. Check **YES** or **NO** for each statement.

What is the specific class you are using for this inventory? ______________________

What was the last test grade you received in this class? ______________

	YES	NO
1. I had all the reading assignments and homework assignments done on time.	______	______
2. I attended class regularly and was prepared for each class.	______	______
3. I reviewed comments and my responses on my homework assignments when they were returned.	______	______
4. I asked questions about information I did not understand.	______	______
5. I worked with a tutor, with a study partner, or in a review group to prepare for the test.	______	______
6. I participated in class discussions, asked questions, and responded to questions during class.	______	______
7. I followed my time-management schedule and used the 2:1 ratio.	______	______
8. I was an active learner and created a variety of study tools to rehearse and review information.	______	______
9. I spent time each week reviewing information that I had previously studied.	______	______
10. I knew the definitions for all the textbook terminology.	______	______
11. I used study techniques that gave me feedback; I used both positive and negative feedback constructively.	______	______
12. I read my textbook carefully and took notes on important textbook information.	______	______
13. I was able to stay fairly motivated about the class and the work.	______	______
14. I was organized, understood assignments, and had the materials necessary to study and review.	______	______
15. I created a specific plan of action to prepare for the test.	______	______
16. I avoided cramming the night before the test.	______	______
17. I felt confident that I was prepared for the test.	______	______
18. I can honestly say that I gave it my best.	______	______

All the **YES** responses for the above strategies indicate you are using those strategies effectively.

All the **NO** responses indicate strategies that you could use more effectively to achieve better test results.

EXERCISE 7.9

Test Anxiety Inventory

DIRECTIONS: Check the responses that seem to best describe you this term.

	NEVER	SOMETIMES	ALWAYS
1. I have trouble sleeping the night before a test.	_____	_____	_____
2. I can feel a lot of tension in my shoulders, arms, or face on the day of a test.	_____	_____	_____
3. My heart beats fast during a test, and I feel hot, clammy, or downright sick during a test.	_____	_____	_____
4. I am irritable, snappy, impatient, and sometimes even rude right before a test.	_____	_____	_____
5. I try to find excuses not to go to school on the day of a test.	_____	_____	_____
6. I prepare for tests by cramming the day or the night before the test.	_____	_____	_____
7. I read my textbook, but when I start to review for tests, I get worried about how much I do not remember.	_____	_____	_____
8. I procrastinate so much about studying that I am always behind in my assignments.	_____	_____	_____
9. I find myself blaming the teacher, my family, or my friends for the fact that I am not prepared for tests.	_____	_____	_____
10. I run short on time to study and do not make summary notes or review effectively.	_____	_____	_____
11. My negative voice is quick to remind me that I never do well on tests.	_____	_____	_____
12. I cannot seem to forget how disappointed I was with my last grade on a test; I really blew it.	_____	_____	_____
13. It is difficult for me to get motivated to study for tests because the results are always discouraging.	_____	_____	_____
14. I fear the consequences of failing a test because so much is riding on getting good grades.	_____	_____	_____
15. I get so nervous about tests because anything less than my personal standards deflates my self-esteem.	_____	_____	_____
16. I get stuck on one question and do not want to move on until I remember the answer.	_____	_____	_____
17. I get distracted and annoyed by the littlest things others do in class during a test.	_____	_____	_____
18. I am so anxious to get out of the classroom that I seldom check my answers or proofread.	_____	_____	_____
19. I turn in tests that are incomplete even when I have more time.	_____	_____	_____
20. Without knowing why, I panic and start changing answers right before I turn the test in.	_____	_____	_____
21. I make careless mistakes on tests. Sometimes I can't believe the answers that I marked.	_____	_____	_____
22. My mind goes blank, but as soon as I leave the classroom after taking a test, I remember the answers.	_____	_____	_____

Answers in the **NEVER** column = Not major indicators of test anxiety.

Answers in the **SOMETIMES** column = Possible indicators of text anxiety; seek ways to alter your approach.

Answers in the **ALWAYS** column = Strong indicators of test anxiety; use strategies to reduce test anxiety.

EXERCISE 8.3

Reading Process Inventory

DIRECTIONS: Reading is a complex process that involves many thinking and comprehension processes and functions. In the following inventory, circle **1, 2,** or **3** to show the processes you use or do not use when you read your college textbooks. Use the following information to select your answer 1, 2, or 3.

1 = use seldom or never 2 = use sometimes 3 = use on a regular basis

1. I am interested and eager to start new chapters and learn new information. 1 2 3
2. I use spaced practice to read textbooks so I can avoid engaging in marathon reading. 1 2 3
3. I read slowly and carefully to allow sufficient time to understand, process, and integrate new information. 1 2 3
4. I stay with a difficult paragraph until I figure out a way to understand the information. 1 2 3
5. I adjust my reading rate depending on my level of familiarity with the material and the complexity or the level of difficulty of the content. 1 2 3
6. I use thorough reading strategies, not recreational reading strategies, when I read college textbooks. 1 2 3
7. I use overview reading to skim a chapter or difficult sections of information before I begin the process of careful, thorough reading. 1 2 3
8. I verbalize, recite, visualize, and use feedback when I read my textbooks. 1 2 3
9. I immediately change my strategies when I realize I have shifted to the automatic pilot mode and am not focusing my attention on reading. 1 2 3
10. I chunk up or chunk down as needed to grasp information in meaningful ways. 1 2 3
11. I begin a new chapter by reading the headings and subheadings, the marginal notes, bold print, graphic materials, and summary materials. 1 2 3
12. On separate paper or next to the headings or in the margins of the textbook, I write questions for sections of information in a chapter. 1 2 3
13. I use a method of notetaking that is appropriate for each textbook. 1 2 3
14. I use the Read-Record-Recite Cycle when I read college textbooks. 1 2 3
15. I recite key information by explaining information out loud, in my own words, and without looking at printed text. 1 2 3
16. I can explain a specific reading process that I use for each textbook, but the process is not always the same for each textbook. 1 2 3

ANALYZING YOUR RESULTS:

- Processes marked with **1** are processes you lack that may weaken your reading skills and textbook reading success. Consider adding these strategies to your reading systems.
- Processes marked with **2** are used sometimes but not consistently. Using these processes more consistently strengthens your reading skills and comprehension.
- Processes marked with **3** are strategies that contribute to your success as an effective critical reader of your college textbooks. Continue using these processes consistently.

EXERCISE 9.1

Active Reading Inventory

DIRECTIONS: Think about the way you read your college textbooks. Answer the following questions.

Circle **1** if you do not use this strategy when you read your textbooks.

Circle **2** if you use this strategy occasionally when you read your textbooks.

Circle **3** if you use this strategy consistently when you read your textbooks.

1.	I create a plan of action before I begin reading a new textbook chapter.	1	2	3
2.	I highlight and mark main ideas and the important supporting details in every paragraph.	1	2	3
3.	I use word, punctuation, definition, word structure, and context clues to identify definitions of terminology and unfamiliar words.	1	2	3
4.	I circle vocabulary terms and highlight their definitions.	1	2	3
5.	I interact with printed materials by taking notes, copying diagrams, and creating study tools.	1	2	3
6.	I read out loud or verbalize as I read.	1	2	3
7.	I visualize information as I read.	1	2	3
8.	I recite and check my accuracy throughout the reading process.	1	2	3
9.	I make brief marginal notes next to important paragraphs.	1	2	3
10.	I use a notetaking system to capture the important information in the chapter.	1	2	3
11.	I ask questions and create study questions throughout the reading process.	1	2	3
12.	I carefully examine charts, tables, illustrations, and graphs, and attach notes or brief summaries next to the graphic materials.	1	2	3
13.	I use available resources and online materials that are available for the textbook.	1	2	3
14.	I stay with a paragraph until I understand its meaning or content.	1	2	3
15.	I use active reading strategies to avoid slipping into the automatic pilot mode.	1	2	3
16.	I adjust my reading rate based on the difficulty and complexity of the material.	1	2	3
17.	I create definition flashcards or vocabulary sheets to study terminology.	1	2	3
18.	I push myself to analyze, evaluate, and use critical thinking skills.	1	2	3
19.	I identify and label organizational patterns in paragraphs.	1	2	3
20.	I am an active reader, not a passive reader.	1	2	3

SCORE: | | | |

TOTAL SCORE: ________

YOUR SCORE:

20–35 You need to apply more effort to using active reading strategies to understand your college textbook material more thoroughly. Look at all the items that received a **1**. Strive to increase comprehension by adding these strategies to your textbook reading strategies.

36–50 You are using many active reading strategies effectively, but there is room to improve. Strive to include the strategies marked with a **1** or a **2** on a more consistent basis when you read your textbooks.

51–60 You are using active reading strategies effectively. Continue to use all of the strategies consistently when you study.

EXERCISE 9.5

Annotation Checklist

DIRECTIONS: After annotating a passage, use the following checklist to assess your work.

	NO	SOMEWHAT	YES
1. I completely highlighted only one sentence, the topic sentence, in every paragraph.	______	______	______
2. I selectively highlighted key words or phrases to show details that support the topic sentence.	______	______	______
3. I avoided highlighting excessively to the point that most of the paragraph is highlighted.	______	______	______
4. I circled all terminology that appeared in special print.	______	______	______
5. I highlighted only the key words or phrases that define the terminology.	______	______	______
6. I avoided highlighting every example; instead, I highlighted selective examples that can work as memory cues.	______	______	______
7. I numbered details in the paragraphs that appear with ordinals.	______	______	______
8. I wrote brief notes in the margins.	______	______	______
9. I used abbreviations for some of the information that I wrote in the margins.	______	______	______
10. To avoid highlighting too much, I sometimes use brackets to remind me about larger blocks of important text.	______	______	______
11. For important graphic materials, I marked them and their captions in some meaningful way.	______	______	______
12. At a glance, I can quickly pick out the important points when I review each paragraph.	______	______	______
13. I used colors effectively.	______	______	______
14. I reread my annotations by first reading out loud only the information that was highlighted or marked.	______	______	______
15. I practiced stringing ideas together by adding my own words to explain the annotated information.	______	______	______
16. I recited the annotated information without looking at the printed materials.	______	______	______

EXERCISE 9.8

Part I: Cornell Notetaking Self-Assessment Checklist

Name ____________________ Date ____________________

Topic of Notes ____________________ Assignment ____________________

RECORD STEP	**YES**	**NO**
1. Did you clearly show headings in your notes so you can see the main topics?	______	______
2. Did you underline the headings and avoid putting numbers or letters in front of the headings?	______	______
3. Did you leave a space between headings or larger groups of information so that your notes are not cluttered or crowded?	______	______
4. Did you include sufficient details so that you do not need to return to the textbook to study this information?	______	______
5. Did you use numbering for the different details under the headings?	______	______
6. Did you indent and use dashes or other symbols to show minor supporting details?	______	______
7. Did you use meaningful phrases or shortened sentences that will be clear at a later time?	______	______
8. Did you paraphrase or shorten the information so that your notes are not too lengthy?	______	______
9. Did your notes refer to important charts, diagrams, or visual materials in the chapter, or did you make reference to the textbook pages in your notes?	______	______
10. Did you write on only one side of the paper, leaving the back side blank?	______	______
11. Did you label the first page of your notes (course, chapter number, and date) and use page numbers on the other pages?	______	______
12. Did you write your notes so that they are neat and easy to read?	______	______

RECALL COLUMN (REDUCE STEP)	**YES**	**NO**
1. Did you move each heading into the recall column and underline it?	______	______
2. Did you use a two-and-one-half-inch margin on the left for the recall column?	______	______
3. Did you include study questions in the recall column for the key points in your notes?	______	______
4. Did you include enough information in the recall column to guide you when you recite your notes?	______	______
5. Did you include in the recall column some key words that you need to define or explain?	______	______
6. Did you write the questions and the key words directly across from the corresponding information in your notes column?	______	______
7. Did you avoid writing too much information or giving yourself all of the information in the recall column, thus leaving you with little to recite from memory?	______	______
8. Did you try using the recall column?	______	______
9. Did you add or delete information in the recall column after you tried using that column for reciting?	______	______

Exercise 9.8 (continued)

Part II: Cornell Notetaking Instructor Assessment Form

Name ______________________ Date ______________________

Notes for ____

Check the statements that apply to a specific set of Cornell notes.

YOUR NOTES COLUMN

_____ You clearly showed and underlined the headings.

_____ Your notes will be easier to study because you left a space between new headings or sections of information.

_____ Your notes show accurate and sufficient details.

_____ You used meaningful phrases or shortened sentences effectively so that the information is clear and understandable.

_____ You shortened information effectively and captured the important ideas.

_____ Your notes are well organized. You effectively used numbering and indentations for supporting details.

_____ You included important visual graphics from the textbook.

_____ Your notes are neat and easy to read.

_____ You used notetaking standards effectively: you wrote on one side of the paper, you included a heading on the top of the page, and you numbered pages.

YOUR RECALL COLUMN

_____ You used a 2½-inch column.

_____ You placed your headings, questions, and key words directly across from the information in your notes.

_____ Your questions and key words are effective.

_____ You may need to add more self-quizzing questions, visual cues, or hints to guide reciting and create an effective recall column.

_____ You need to use a 2½-inch recall column on the left.

_____ You need to place the headings, questions, and key words directly across from the information in your notes.

_____ You need more meaningful questions and key words in the recall column.

_____ You are giving yourself too much information in the recall column; use questions without answers so that you will have more to recite.

AREAS FOR IMPROVEMENT IN YOUR NOTES

_____ Strive to identify and underline headings.

_____ Leave a space before you begin a new heading or section of information so your notes will be less crowded or cluttered.

_____ Include more information in your notes. Your notes lack some important details.

_____ Short phrases or isolated words lose meaning over time. Use more sentences or more detailed phrases to capture important ideas.

_____ Use shortened sentences to capture the important ideas. Your notes are unnecessarily lengthy.

_____ Strive for clearer organization. Number and indent supporting details.

_____ Include graphic information in your notes.

_____ Strive for neater penmanship and readability.

_____ Write on one side of the paper. Include a heading on the first page. Number all the pages of your notes.

OTHER COMMENTS

Photocopy this form before you use it.

EXERCISE 10.2

Organizational Patterns

1. NEWSPAPERS AND LENDING LIBRARIES

Chronological? Process?

In addition to novels, newspapers and political pamphlets became increasingly available in the eighteenth century, especially in Britain and the Dutch Republic where censorship laws were relaxed or abolished. Reading newspapers had often been a collective activity in which one person read aloud to a group, but increasingly newspapers were read privately and silently, like novels, and passed along until the next day's newspaper was available. As the variety of reading material expanded, it is likely that Europeans received more information about the world and, often lost in the contents of the page in front of them, had a wider range of imaginative reading experiences than people had ever had before.

Source: Kidnet et al., *Making Europe: The Story of the West,* 2e, p. 516.

2. GLOBAL WARMING

Chronological? Process?

Many scientists believe that global warming is already producing serious climate change, for as temperatures rise, more water evaporates, causing more rainfall and bigger storms, which lead to more flooding and soil erosion. People suffer and die all along the causal chain. This was tragically evident in 2005, when Hurricanes Katrina and Rita delivered knockout punches to coastal Louisiana, Alabama, Mississippi, and Texas, killing an estimated 2,300 people and causing many billions of dollars of damage (Brym, 2009: 53-81).

Source: Bryme, Lie. *Sociology,* 3e, © p. 377-378.

3. COASTS

Comparison-Contrast? Whole-and-Parts?

Because coasts are influenced by so many factors, perhaps the most useful scheme for classifying a coast is based on the predominant events that occur there: erosion and deposition. **Erosional coasts** are new coasts in which the dominant processes are those that *remove* coastal material. **Depositional coasts** are *steady or growing* because of their rate of sediment accumulation or the action of living organisms (such as corals).

Source: Garrison. *Oceanography: An Invitation to Marine Science,* 8e, p. 12.

4. GREENHOUSE EFFECT

Definition? Examples? Cause-Effect?

Glass in a greenhouse is transparent to light but not to heat. The light is absorbed by objects inside the greenhouse, and its energy is converted into heat. The temperature inside a greenhouse rises because the heat is unable to escape. On Earth, **greenhouse gases**—water vapor, carbon dioxide, methane, chlorofluorocarbons, and others—take the place of glass. Heat that would otherwise radiate away from the planet is absorbed and trapped by these gases, causing a surface temperature to increase.

Source: Garrison. *Oceanography: An Invitation to Marine Science,* 8e, p. 533.

EXERCISE 10.5

Visual Notes Checklist

Name ______________________ Date ____________

Topic ______________ Check one: ________ Visual mapping ________ Hierarchy

ORGANIZATION

	YES	NO
1. The skeleton with level-one and level-two information is clear and easy to identify.	______	______
2. The lines connecting levels of information are clear and easy to follow.	______	______
3. The visual notes are uncluttered and easy to read.	______	______
4. Headings and supporting details are well spaced.	______	______
5. Only key words or short phrases appear on the visual notes and show use of selectivity.	______	______

VISUAL EFFECTS

	YES	NO
1. I used colors or color-coding to emphasize different information or levels of information.	______	______
2. I used borders, shapes, or pictures for some information.	______	______
3. I wrote all of the information on a horizontal plane.	______	______

STUDYING FROM VISUAL NOTES

	YES	NO
1. I have mentally imprinted the image of the skeleton.	______	______
2. I can visualize the skeleton without looking at the notes.	______	______
3. I have practiced reciting level-three and level-four information without referring to my notes.	______	______
4. I have completed at least one reflect activity with my notes.	______	______
5. I have reviewed my notes at least one additional time.	______	______

EXERCISE 11.1

Classroom Listening Factors Inventory

DIRECTIONS: Read each set of statements carefully. Check the statement that most reflects your behavior or attitude in a typical lecture class in which you are enrolled.

1. Interest Level

_____ A. I am not interested in the topic; in fact, it bores me.

_____ B. I do not have a genuine interest in the topic, but I know it is important to learn.

_____ C. I find ways to expand my interest in the topic, such as discussing it with others.

2. Seating Location

_____ A. I sit in the back of the classroom so I can see everything that goes on.

_____ B. I sit in the middle of the classroom so I can see the screen or chalkboard clearly.

_____ C. I sit in the front of the classroom so I have fewer distractions and a clearer view of visual materials.

3. Materials and Preparedness

_____ A. I often arrive to the classroom just as the lecture begins; I am seldom tardy.

_____ B. I arrive with sufficient time to select a good seat and "settle in."

_____ C. I arrive a few minutes early and prepared with sufficient paper, pens, my textbook, and class work.

4. Familiarity with the Topic

_____ A. I am curious at the beginning of each class about the topic for that day's lecture.

_____ B. I use the course syllabus to identify the topic for the day's lecture; then I survey the corresponding pages in the textbook.

_____ C. I read the textbook section or chapter for the lecture before class so I am familiar with the topic, definitions, and the kind of information I can find in the textbook.

5. Focused Attention

_____ A. I tend to "tune out" when the information is too technical or difficult to follow.

_____ B. I am aware that my concentration fades in and fades out multiple times during the lecture; I refocus as quickly as possible.

_____ C. I block out distractors so my concerted effort can be directed toward following the instructor's thinking and explanations.

6. Emotional Responses

_____ A. I immediately let an instructor know if I disagree with or dislike something he or she says during a lecture.

_____ B. I am aware during a lecture of the times when I do not agree with the instructor's information or point of view.

_____ C. I put my personal opinions aside so I can listen carefully to the information presented by an instructor before questioning or disagreeing with the information.

(continued)

Exercise 11.1 (continued)

7. Asking Questions

_____ A. I like to challenge the instructor by asking any questions as they pop into my mind.

_____ B. I jot down questions during a lecture and then ask them at an appropriate time.

_____ C. I ask open-ended clarifying questions to learn more about the topic; for example, I might ask: *What are some ways this could be used?* or *Why is it important to . . . ?*

8. Checking Understanding

_____ A. I wait until after class to look at my notes to see what I understand.

_____ B. I ask questions or show my confusion at the point during a lecture when I do not understand what the instructor is presenting.

_____ C. At an appropriate time, I rephrase or paraphrase information that I do not understand clearly; for example, I might ask: *Do you mean that . . . ? Is it correct then to say that . . . ?*

9. Levels of Information

_____ A. I know that everything the instructor presents is important to remember.

_____ B. I use verbal and nonverbal clues to identify the main points of a lecture.

_____ C. I use verbal, nonverbal, and visual clues, such as information the instructor writes on an overhead or presents on a slide, to identify important information.

SCORING YOUR INVENTORY:

How many responses did you have in each category? Write the number of responses:

A_____ B_____ C_____

RESPONSES FOR A represent ineffective listening behaviors and attitudes.

RESPONSES FOR B represent adequate listening behaviors and attitudes that you can further strengthen.

RESPONSES FOR C indicate effective active learning behaviors and attitudes to use during lectures.

EXERCISE 11.5

Lecture Notetaking Checklist

DIRECTIONS: Select any set of lecture notes you have for any one of your courses. Rank the quality of each of the following items in your notes, with **3** representing the highest quality.

1.	The notetaking system I used was effective for the lecture.	1 2 3
2.	The headings or main ideas are clear in my notes.	1 2 3
3.	I paraphrased the instructor's words.	1 2 3
4.	I used shortened sentences but did not lose the meaning.	1 2 3
5.	I used abbreviations and/or symbols in my notes.	1 2 3
6.	I used a combination of printing and cursive writing.	1 2 3
7.	I left a gap or shifted to paragraph form when I started falling behind taking notes.	1 2 3
8.	My notes include definitions for important terminology.	1 2 3
9.	My notes include supporting details: dates, names, facts, or statistics.	1 2 3
10.	My notes summarize examples without including every detail.	1 2 3
11.	I numbered individual details so they are easy to identify.	1 2 3
12.	I used the instructor's verbal, visual, and nonverbal clues to help identify important information for my notes.	1 2 3
13.	My notes include explanations for details or for steps in a process.	1 2 3
14.	My notes either include visual materials or references to textbook pages that have those visual materials.	1 2 3
15.	My notes are well-organized and have sufficient details so I will be able to use them for studying and review.	1 2 3

TOTAL SCORE: ________

SCORING YOUR RESPONSES: Total all the circled numbers for your final score.

15–20 Strive to use more effective strategies; your notes may lack sufficient information to be effective as a study tool to review lecture content.

21–40 Continue developing your notetaking skills for the areas ranked 1 and 2; your notes include adequate information for studying, but they could be stronger.

41–45 Continue using your notetaking skills; you have quality notes that you can use to study and review.

Exercise 11.5 (continued)

DIRECTIONS TO THE INSTRUCTOR:

In the ______________________________ course, students are developing their lecture notetaking skills. One of your students, ______________________________, chose to use your lecture class to practice notetaking skills. Your feedback on the student's notes would be greatly appreciated. Please take a few minutes to review the student's notes and answer the following questions. Students are asked to turn in this questionnaire with their practice notes.

Instructor's Name ____

Class ____

1. Do the notes appear to include the important information presented in the lecture?

________Yes ________No ________Somewhat

Comments:

2. Do the notes also show information that was presented on the overhead projector, blackboard, PowerPoint slides, or other form of visual presentation?

________Yes ________No ________Somewhat

Comments:

3. In what way could this student improve his or her notes for your lecture?

Appendix D
Excerpts

Understanding Stress and Stressors

EXCERPT 1

HOW DO PYSCHOLOGICAL STRESSORS AFFECT PHYSICAL HEALTH?

You have probably heard that death and taxes are the only two things guaranteed in life. If there is a third, it surely must be stress. Stress is woven into the fabric of life. No matter how wealthy, powerful, attractive, or happy you might be, stress happens.

It comes in many forms: a difficult exam, an automobile accident, standing in a long line, reading about frightening world events, or just having a day when everything goes wrong. Some stress experiences, such as waiting to be with that special person, can be stimulating, motivating, and even desirable, but when circumstances begin to exceed our ability to cope with them, the result can be stress that creates physical, psychological, and behavioral problems. Stress in the workplace, for example, costs U.S. businesses more than $150 billion each year as a result of employee absenteeism, reduced productivity, and health care costs (Chandola, Brunner, & Marmot, 2006; Sauter et al., 1999; Schwartz, 2004; Spector, 2002).

Stress is the negative emotional and physiological process that occurs as individuals try to adjust to or deal with stressors. ***Stressors***, in turn, are environmental circumstances (such as exams or accidents) that disrupt or threaten to disrupt people's daily functioning and cause people to make adjustments. ***Stress reactions*** are the physical, psychological, and behavioral responses (such as nervousness, nausea, or fatigue) that occur in the face of stressors (Taylor, 2002).

Stress The process of adjusting to circumstances that disrupt or threaten to disrupt a person's daily functioning.

Stressors Events or situations to which people must adjust.

Stress reactions Physical and psychological responses to stressors.

Some of us are more strongly affected by stressors than others, and we may be more strongly affected on some occasions than on others. Why? As described in more detail later, several *mediating factors* influence the relationship between people and their environments. These mediating factors include (1) the extent to which we can *predict* and *control* our stressors; (2) how we *interpret* the threat involved, (3) the *social support* we get; and (4) our *skills* for coping with stress. Mediating factors can either minimize or magnify a stressor's impact. In other words, as shown in **Figure 10.1**, stress is not a specific event but a transaction between people and their environments. It is a *process* in which the nature and intensity of our responses depend on what stressors occur and how they are affected by factors such as the way we think about them and how much confidence we have in our coping skills and resources.

FIGURE 10.1 The Process of Stress

Stressful events, stress reactions, and stress mediators are all important components of the stress process. Notice that the process involves many two-way relationships. For example, if a person has effective coping skills, stress responses will be less severe. Having milder stress responses can act as a "reward" that strengthens those skills. Further, as coping skills (such as refusing unreasonable demands) improve, certain stressors (such as a boss's unreasonable demands) may become less frequent.

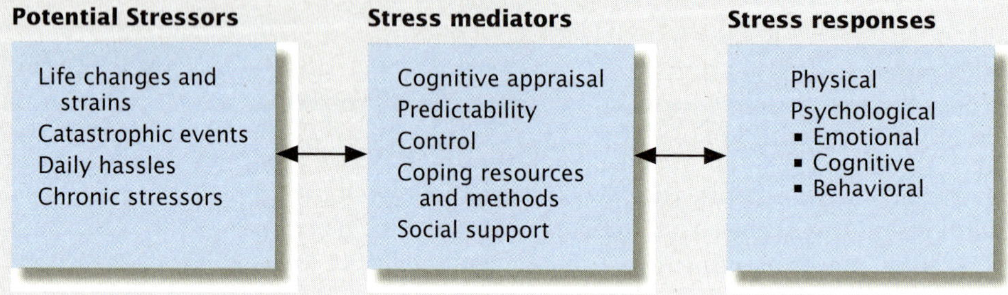

Practice Visualization

EXCERPT 2

Sometimes, when we imagine giving a speech, we see the worst-case scenario. We see ourselves trembling, forgetting what we planned to say, dropping our notes, tripping on the way to the podium, and so on. Although a speech rarely goes this badly, these negative images stay in our minds. They increase our anxiety and often set up what is called a self-fulfilling prophecy: If you see yourself doing poorly in your mind before your speech, you set yourself up to do so in the speech. There are two solutions to this negative dynamic: visualization and affirmations.

Visualization. Visualization is a process in which you construct a mental image of yourself giving a successful speech. Research on the benefits of visualization before giving a speech suggests that one session of visualization (about fifteen minutes) has a significant positive effect on communication apprehension. The techniques of visualization are used by a wide range of people—athletes, performers, executives—and can range from elaborate to quite simple processes. For public speakers, the most effective process works as follows:

Find a quiet, comfortable place where you can sit in a relaxed position for approximately fifteen minutes. Close your eyes and breathe slowly and deeply through your nose, feeling relaxation flow through your body. In great detail, visualize the morning of the day you are to give your speech.

You get up filled with confidence and energy, and you choose the perfect clothing for your speech. You drive, walk, or ride to campus filled with this same positive, confident energy. As you enter the classroom, you see yourself relaxed, interacting with your classmates, full of confidence because you have thoroughly prepared for your speech. Your classmates are friendly and cordial in their greetings and conversations with you. You are *absolutely* sure of your material and your ability to present that material in the way you would like.

Next, visualize yourself beginning your speech. You see yourself approaching the place in your classroom from which you will speak. You are sure of yourself, eager to begin, and positive in your abilities as a speaker. You know you are organized and ready to use all your visual aids with ease. Now you see yourself presenting your speech. Your introduction is wonderful. Your transitions are smooth and interesting. Your main points are articulated brilliantly. Your evidence is presented elegantly. Your organization is perfect. Take as much time as you can in visualizing this part of your process. Be as specific and positive as you can.

Visualize the end of the speech: It could not have gone better. You are relaxed and confident, the audience is eager to ask questions, and you respond with the same talent as you gave your speech. As you return to your seat, you are filled with energy and appreciation for the job well done. You are ready for the next events of your day, and you accomplish them with success and confidence.

Now take a deep breath and return to the present. Breathe in, hold it, and release it. Do this several times as you return to the present. Take as much time as you need to make this transition.

Research on visualization for public speakers suggests that the more detail we are able to give to our visualizations (what shoes we wear, exactly how we feel as we see ourselves, imagining the specifics of our speech), the more effective the technique is in reducing apprehension. Visualization has a significant effect on reducing the nervousness we feel because it systematically replaces negative images with positive ones.

From Griffin. *Invitation to Public Speaking*, 3e. © 2009 Cengage Learning.

EXCERPT 3 Adopting a Healthy Lifestyle

A basic look at your lifestyle patterns begins by looking specifically at your lifestyle choices in the areas of nutrition, exercise, and sleep. These three areas tend to influence your level of stress, the ways you respond to a variety of stressors, and the degree to which you achieve your goals. Adopting a healthy lifestyle for many is a lifelong goal and not something you can check off as having completely achieved. The following sections provide you with healthy lifestyle choices to use for the areas of nutrition, sleep, and exercise.

NUTRITION

You are what you eat. Unfortunately, people experiencing stress frequently turn to fast foods and snacks that are high in fat and sugar, which produce an energy surge as blood sugar in the body increases and then is followed by a quick drop in energy as the blood sugar decreases. Foods high in sugar may lead to diabetes, obesity, heart disease, and other health issues. Foods high in fat contribute to health problems such as heart problems, high cholesterol, and increased blood pressure. Using the following nutritional guidelines can help you begin making healthier lifestyle choices:

- **Complex carbohydrates:** Instead of eating foods loaded with sugar, choose foods that break sugars down more slowly and release energy over a more sustained period of time. Complex carbohydrates, such as those found in grains, cereals, rice, pasta, bread, and potatoes, protect blood levels from the roller coaster effect of highs and lows.
- **Fruit and vegetables:** Consume three to four helpings of fruits and vegetables each day. In addition to providing you with essential vitamins and minerals, these foods increase your brain's production of serotonin, a brain chemical that stabilizes mood swings and promotes a sense of happiness. Multivitamins can supplement your dietary needs for vitamins and minerals, but they are not a substitute for good eating.
- **Items to avoid:** Limit your use of nicotine, caffeine, and alcohol; avoid nonprescription drugs. People often use more of these products when under stress, but they are not effective ways to cope with stress, and their health consequences may lead to more serious problems.

EXERCISE

Physical activity reduces the physiological effects of stress. Plan twenty to thirty minutes a day, a minimum of three times a week, for exercise—at a gym, running, or through a physical education course, a yoga class, an intramural sport, or a community exercise program. In addition to reducing your stress level and giving yourself a mental break from thinking about a stressor, the benefits of regular exercise are many:

- **Mental break:** Exercising not only reduces your stress level, but it provides you with a mental break by shifting your attention away from the stressor.
- **Oxygen to the brain:** Exercise gets oxygen moving more smoothly to your brain. Your concentration level increases, and information enters and moves through your memory system more efficiently.
- **Healthy heart:** Exercise improves your cardiovascular system, thus reducing your risk of more serious health conditions that may result from prolonged stress.
- **Stronger body:** Exercise strengthens your body, making it more resistant to the physical and emotional effects of stress. A healthy body becomes better equipped to handle stress, resist illnesses, and feel less fatigue.

SLEEP

Stress can disrupt your regular sleep patterns, and sleep deprivation can cause stress, creating a vicious cycle of fatigue of the body and diminished cognitive functioning. Under stress, some people sleep too little, while others sleep too much. People who sleep too little may experience symptoms of *insomnia*, the inability to fall asleep. People who sleep too much may be using excessive sleep to avoid feeling overwhelmed or helpless, to escape from the world, and to avoid dealing with their sources of stress. The following guidelines can help you obtain a healthy lifestyle that includes adequate sleep:

- **Eight hours of sound sleep:** On your weekly time-management schedule, plan to get eight hours of sound sleep per night.
- **Sleep pattern:** Strive to achieve a regular, predictable pattern of sleep throughout the week. Sleeping eight hours during the week and then five hours per night on the weekends, or sleeping six hours during the week and ten hours during the weekend creates the need for your body to keep adjusting to an irregular schedule. You will find that your days become more productive, your body more resilient, and your mind sharper on a more consistent basis when you have an established sleep pattern.
- **Relaxation strategies:** When faced with a night of tossing and turning, the inability to fall asleep has the tendency to create more stress and anxiety as you are fully aware of your need for sleep but are not able to fall asleep. When restless or stressed, shift your focus away from the stressor by relaxing in a prone position, engaging yourself in a relaxation technique, listening to soft music, visualizing pleasant scenes or memories, or practicing progressive relaxation techniques.
- **Professional advice:** If your inability to fall asleep and get a good night's sleep, or your inability to limit your nightly sleep to eight hours, persists for more than one month, underlying medical conditions, medications, or more deep-seated issues may be affecting your sleep patterns. Consult a counselor or a physician to discuss your sleep disorder.

EXCERPT 4 Semantic Networks

Of course, not all information fits neatly into conceptual hierarchies or schemas. Much knowledge seems to be organized into less systematic frameworks, called semantic networks (Collins & Loftus, 1975). A ***semantic network*** **consists of nodes representing concepts, joined together by pathways that link related concepts.** A small semantic network is shown in **Figure 7.13**. The ovals are the nodes, and the words inside the ovals are the interlinked concepts. The lines connecting the nodes are the pathways. The length of each pathway represents the degree of association between two concepts. Shorter pathways imply stronger associations.

Semantic networks have proven useful in explaining why thinking about one word (such as *butter*) can make a closely related word (such as *bread*) easier to remember (Meyer & Schvaneveldt, 1976). According to Collins and Loftus (1975), when people think about a word, their thoughts naturally go to related words. These theorists call this process *spreading activation* within a semantic network. They assume that activation spreads out along the pathways of the semantic network surrounding the word. They also theorize that the strength of this activation decreases as it travels outward, much as ripples decrease in size as they radiate outward from a rock tossed into a pond. Consider again the semantic network shown in **Figure 7.13**. If subjects see the word *red,* words that are closely linked to it (such as *orange*) should be easier to recall than words that have longer links (such as *sunrises*).

From Weiten. *Psychology,* 9e. © 2011 Cengage Learning.

FIGURE 7.13 A semantic network.

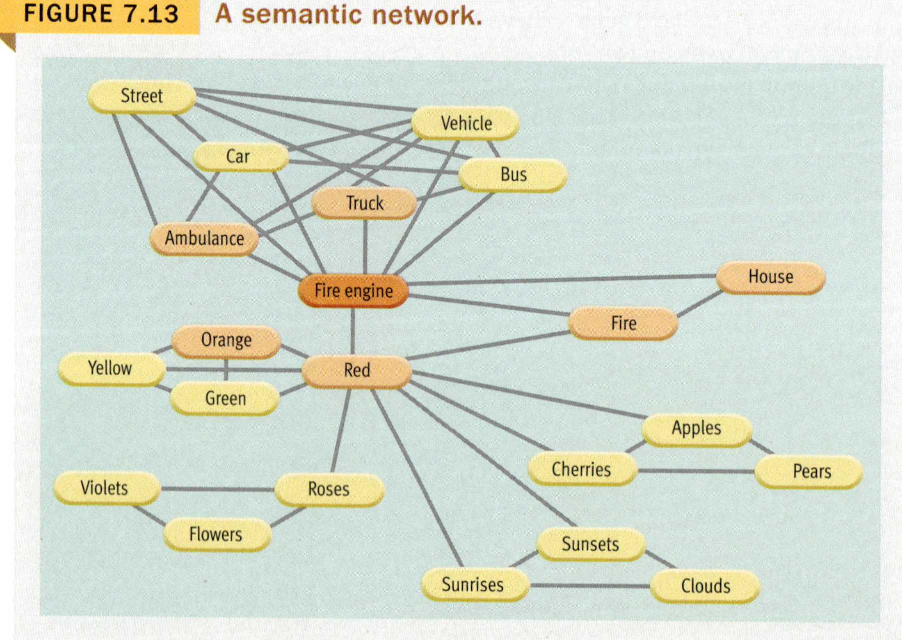

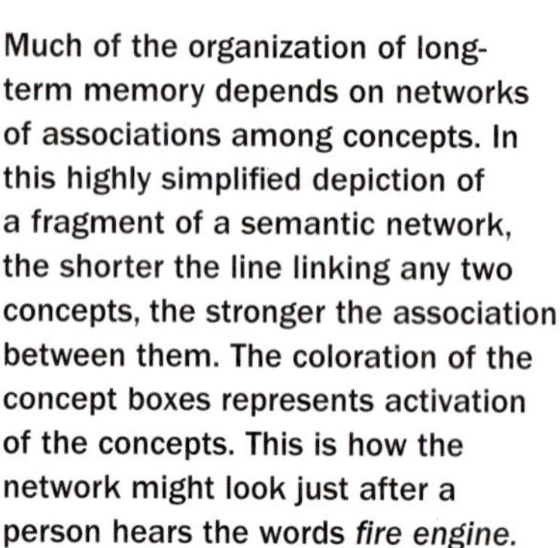

Much of the organization of long-term memory depends on networks of associations among concepts. In this highly simplified depiction of a fragment of a semantic network, the shorter the line linking any two concepts, the stronger the association between them. The coloration of the concept boxes represents activation of the concepts. This is how the network might look just after a person hears the words *fire engine*.

Source: Adapted from Collins, A. M., & Loftus, E. F. (1975). A spreading activation theory of semantic processing. *Psychological Review, 82,* 407–428. Copyright © 1975 by the American Psychological Association.

Building Blocks of Medical Language

EXCERPT 5

Medical terms are composed of several parts, referred to as "elements." Each element has its own meaning and location in the term. Like building blocks, they can be combined to create thousands of different words. Learning the meaning of commonly used word elements and applying this knowledge to decipher medical terms is much more efficient than trying to memorize each new word as it is encountered.

The three principle elements that make up medical terms are roots, prefixes, and suffixes.

ROOTS AND COMBINING FORMS

The **root** is the part of the medical term that gives the main meaning. It usually, but not always, refers to the structure and function of the body. All medical terms have at least one root. The following are examples of roots:

- *gastr*– stomach
- *enter*– small intestine
- *cardi*– heart

Combining forms consist of roots plus a vowel, usually the letter "o," separated from the root with a slash mark:

- gastr/o
- enter/o
- cardi/o

SUFFIXES

Suffixes are word elements that are attached to the end of the roots and combining forms to add to or change their meaning. All medical terms have a suffix. Some common meanings of suffixes include:

- Pathological (disease) conditions
- Diagnostic procedures
- Surgical procedures
- Pertaining to
- Produced by
- Resembling

Recall that the combining form is used when the suffix begins with a consonant, as in the following example:

- cardi/o + megaly = cardiomegaly
- heart + enlarged = enlarged heart

Notice that the slash mark is dropped when the suffix is attached to the combining form.

When the suffix begins with a vowel, it is attached to the root word, as in the following example:

- gastr + itis = gastritis
- stomach + inflammation = inflammation of the stomach

Each suffix can be added to many roots. Knowing that -*itis* means "inflammation" enables the learner to know that the following words all indicate an inflammation of the body part indicated in the root:

1. Appendicitis: Inflammation of the appendix
2. Arthritis: Inflammation of the joint
3. Gastritis: Inflammation of the stomach

Another common suffix is *-ectomy*, which means "surgical removal." Like *-itis*, it can be combined with many root words. In each case, it means removal of the part indicated by the root word:

1. Appendectomy: Removal of the appendix
2. Gastrectomy: Removal of all or part of the stomach
3. Lumpectomy: Removal of a lump

When suffixes are listed in medical dictionaries and word lists, they are positioned alphabetically with other entries, preceded by a dash, and identified as a word element. Dictionary entries typically include the language of origin, as in the following sample dictionary entries:

- *-megaly*: word element (Gr.) enlargement
- *-itis*: word element (Gr.) inflammation
- *-ectomy*: word element (Gr.) surgical removal

PREFIXES

Prefixes are word elements that are attached to the beginning of roots and combining forms to add to or change their meaning. Many, but not all, medical terms have a prefix. Some common meanings of prefixes include the following:

- Location
- Position
- Direction
- Time
- Number
- Negation, absence of
- Color

Just as with suffixes, the same prefixes can be attached to many root words, resulting in thousands of variations. Knowing that the prefix *hyper-* means "abnormally increased" or "excessive" gives a clue to the meaning of the hundreds of words that contain this element, including the following examples:

1. Hyperacid: Abnormally or excessively acidic
2. Hyperactive: Exhibiting abnormally increased activity
3. Hypertension: Persistently high blood pressure

In the same way, knowing that *poly-* means "many" or "much" helps decipher the following examples:

1. Polyatomic: Made up of many atoms
2. Polyglandular: Pertaining to or affecting many glands
3. Polyphobia: Irrational fear of many things

When prefixes are listed in medical dictionaries and word lists, they are located alphabetically, followed by a dash, and identified as a word element, as in the following sample dictionary entries:

- *epi-* word element (Gr.) over
- *hyper-* word element (Gr.) abnormally increased; excessive
- *poly-* word element (Gr.) many; much

DECIPHERING MEDICAL TERMS

Learning the meanings of commonly used word elements and understanding how they combine enable the health care worker to decipher thousands of medical terms. When confronted with a new term, start at the far right, with the suffix. Think of each word as a combination of building blocks, fitted together to create a precise meaning. Work from right to left, identifying and defining each element, as in the following examples:

Example #1: cardiology

1. Starting from the right, find element *-logy*
2. Determine meaning: study of
3. Moving left, find element *cardio*
4. Determine meaning: heart
5. Combine elements: study of the heart

Example #2: polyarthritis

1. Starting from the right, find element *-itis*
2. Determine meaning: inflammation
3. Moving left, find element *arthr*
4. Determine meaning: joint
5. Moving left, find element *poly*
6. Determine meaning: many, much
7. Combine elements: inflammation of many joints

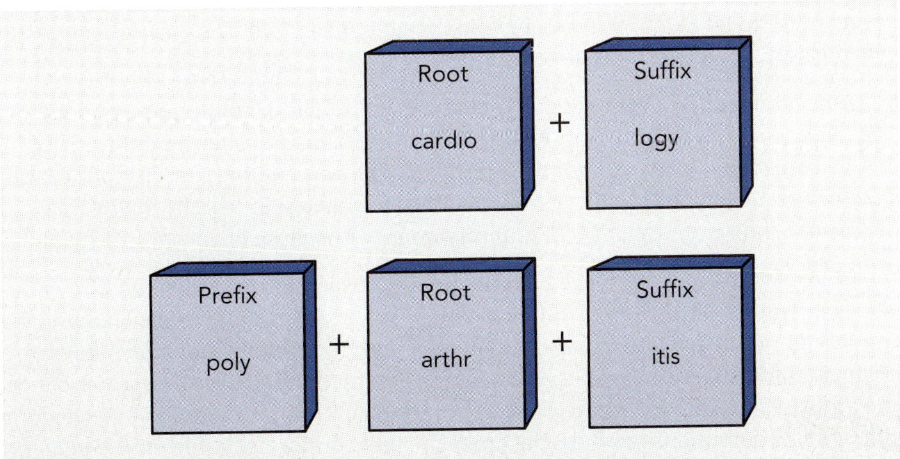

From Mitchell, Haroun. *Introduction to Health Care*, 2e © 2007 Cengage Learning.

EXCERPT 6 Professional Leadership

Leadership is an important concept in health occupations. **Leadership** is the skill or ability to encourage people to work together and do their best to achieve common goals. A **leader** is frequently defined as an individual who leads or guides others, or who is in charge or in command of others. A myth exists that leaders are born. In fact, leaders develop by their own efforts. Leaders combine visions of excellence with the ability to inspire others. They promote positive changes that benefit their professions and the people they serve. Anyone can learn to be a leader by making an effort to understand the principles of leadership. In a group, every member who makes a contribution to an idea can be considered a leader. The leadership in the group passes from person to person as each individual contributes to the achievement of the group's goals.

Leaders can often be classified into broad categories. Some of the categories include: religious, political, club or organizational, business, community, expertise in a particular area, and even informal or peer group. Leaders in these categories often develop based on their involvement with the particular category. An individual who joins a club or organization may become a leader when the group elects the individual to an office or position of leadership within the group.

Leaders are frequently classified as one of three types based on how they perform their leadership skills. The three main types of leader are *democratic, laissez-faire,* and *autocratic.*

- **Democratic leader:** encourages the participation of all individuals in decisions that have to be made or problems that have to be solved. This leader listens to the opinions of others, and then bases decisions on what is best for the group as a whole. By guiding the individuals to a solution, the leader allows the group to take responsibility for the decision.
- **Laissez-faire leader:** more of an informal type of leader. This leader believes in noninterference in the affairs of others. A laissez-faire leader will strive for only minimal rules or regulations, and allow the individuals in a group to function in an independent manner with little or no direction. This leader almost has a "hands-off" policy, and usually avoids making decisions until forced by circumstances to do so. The term *laissez-faire* comes from a French idiom meaning "to let alone" and can be translated to mean "allow to act"; therefore, it is an appropriate term to use for this type of leader.
- **Autocratic leader** often called a "dictator." This individual maintains total rule, makes all of the decisions, and has difficulty delegating or sharing duties. This type of leader seldom asks for the opinions of others, emphasizes discipline, and expects others to follow directions at all times. Individuals usually follow this type of leader because of a fear of punishment or because of an extreme loyalty.

All types of leadership have advantages and disadvantages. In some rare situations, an autocratic leader may be beneficial. However, the democratic leader is the model frequently presented as most effective for group interactions. By allowing a group to share in deciding what, when, and how something is to be done, members of the group will usually do what has to be done because they want to do it. Respecting the rights and opinions of others becomes the most important guide for the leader.

From Simmers, et. al. *Introduction to Health Science Technology,* 2e © 2009 Cengage Learning.

The Scientific Method

EXCERPT 7

The **scientific method** of inquiry is based on three main concepts: observation, experimentation, and the development of theories or natural laws (**Table 1-2**). The first step in the scientific method is the actual observation and recording of facts. Much of the work of a scientist involves **observation** and the collection of data. This helps scientists to gain as much information as they can about the natural phenomena they are studying and then record that information in an organized way. Observation also involves conducting experiments. **Experiments** are controlled observations that help to answer questions about what scientists are trying to discover. The next step in the scientific method is the formulation of a **theory** that might explain how or why the natural phenomenon that is being studied is occurring. This is also called a **hypothesis**, which is an explanation that is supported by a set of facts. The final step in the scientific process is the formulation of a natural law that explains the phenomenon that is being studied. The formulation of a natural or a physical law helps to explain how certain aspects of the natural world operate and, more importantly, how they can be used to make predictions. Scientists often use observations they have made in the past to make inferences about what might occur in the future. An **inference** is a prediction or conclusion that is made about a future event based on previous scientific observations. The scientific method is a formal and organized procedure that scientists around the world use to make accurate investigations of the natural world.

TABLE 1-2 The scientific method is a formal procedure that scientists use to answer questions

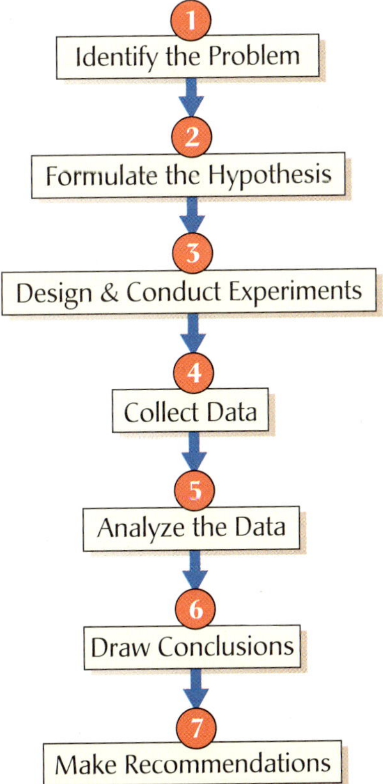

From Butz. *Science of Earth Systems*, 2e © 2004 Cengage Learning.

EXCERPT 8 How to Listen Critically

When you listen to a speech critically, you mentally check it for accuracy, comparing what the speaker says with what you personally know and what your own research tells you. You also listen to assess the strengths and weaknesses of the reasoning and supporting materials presented in a speech. Note that listening critically is different from listening to judge or find fault with a message. Rather, **critical listeners** listen for the accuracy of a speech's content and the implications of a **speaker's message**. Critical listeners benefit by remaining open to new ideas, but they also listen carefully to how speakers develop those ideas into arguments. Additionally, they consider the impact of a speaker's ideas and how they may affect immediate audiences as well as larger communities.

To help you listen to speeches critically, ask yourself the questions in Table 3.1 and then follow the suggested guidelines. Asking these questions will help you assess a speaker's claims and arguments before you make decisions about their value or strength.

When we listen critically, we allow for dialogue because we avoid making quick decisions about good and bad, right and wrong. Listening critically encourages us to ask questions about ideas so we are better able to respond to claims and explore issues with others.

TABLE 3.1 Guidelines for Critical Listening

Question	Guideline
• How fully has the speaker developed an idea? Is something left out, exaggerated, or understated? Does the speaker use sound reasoning? Are claims based on fact or opinion?	• Speakers must develop all major arguments fully rather than present them without explanation and development. Speakers should not exaggerate arguments or understate their importance. Major ideas should be supported by evidence in the form of examples, statistics, testimony, and the like.
• What sources does the speaker rely on? Are they credible? How are they related to the speaker's topic? Will the sources benefit if facts are presented in a certain way? For example, is the tobacco industry arguing that smoking isn't harmful?	• Speakers must use credible sources that are as unbiased as possible. Speakers must cite sources for all new information. Sources should be cited carefully and with enough detail so the audience knows why the source is acceptable.
• Are the claims the speaker makes realistic? What are the implications of those claims? Who is affected by them? In what way? Has the speaker acknowledged these effects, or are they left unstated? Are there other aspects of the issue the speaker should address?	• Speakers must make realistic and logical claims and acknowledge different perspectives. They must also acknowledge those affected by their arguments and acknowledge the effects of their proposed solutions. When speakers take a position, they must not present their position as absolute or the only one possible.
• How does this speech fit with what I know to be true? What is new to me? Can I accept this new information? Why or why not?	• When speakers make claims that go against your personal experience, see if you can discover why. Sometimes, the answer lies in cultural differences or in a speaker's research. Try to be open to different views of the world while at the same time assessing the speaker's evidence and reasoning objectively. Before you reject a speaker's claims, engage the speaker in a civil discussion to find out why your perspective differs.
• What is at stake for the speaker? How invested is the speaker in the topic and the arguments being made? How will the speaker be affected if the audience disagrees?	• All speakers are invested in some way in their topics and arguments. However, some arguments benefit a speaker more than anyone else. Identify the speaker's motives so you can better understand why she or he is making particular claims.

Index